"Scripture commands us to pay careful attention not only to our actions but also to our hearts. Yet, as many Christians know, the fight against indwelling sin can be one of the most challenging and exhausting aspects of the Christian life. In this book, Jeremy Pierre shows us how to deal with our hearts according to the truths of the gospel. This book, firmly committed to the sufficiency and authority of Scripture, is a needed resource for the church."

**R. Albert Mohler, Jr.,** President of the Southern Baptist Theological Seminary

"In *The Dynamic Heart in Daily Life*, Jeremy Pierre wonderfully describes how a heart with dynamic faith will so value things that God finds valuable that God becomes the 'control desire' in human experience, emotion, and choice. This insight provides not simply an understanding of human motivation but a profoundly helpful tool for transformative Christian counseling."

**Bryan Chapell,** Pastor, Grace Presbyterian Church; author of *Holiness by Grace* and *Christ-Centered Preaching*

"I am delighted to see this book in print. Jeremy Pierre has ministered to me as a friend and colleague much more than he realizes. Now, through this book, many others can see why he is so appreciated by his students, seminary associates, and fellow church members. In these pages pastors, counselors, caretakers, and just about anyone who works with people will find help to better understand the heart and experience of the person in front of them, and thereby be more fully equipped to minister Christ to that person."

**Donald S. Whitney,** Professor of Biblical Spirituality, The Southern Baptist Theological Seminary; author of *Spiritual Disciplines for the Christian Life* and *Praying the Bible*

"There is nothing more important in counseling and Christian growth than understanding what God's Word says about the heart. That is why I am excited and thankful for Jeremy Pierre's new book. He thoroughly unpacks what Scripture says about the heart and then brings to light how we can practically fulfill this instruction in our counseling and in our everyday life. I highly recommend it and look forward to using this volume in many aspects of local church ministry."

**Steve Viars,** Senior Pastor, Faith Church, Lafayette, Indiana

"Thoughts. Emotions. Choices. All three are important aspects of human experience. Overlook one or more aspects, and ministry to struggling people will be truncated at its best and dangerous at its worst. In this well-organized resource, Jeremy Pierre paints a three-dimensional picture of our hearts in relation to God, self, others, and the circumstances of life. In so doing he gives pastors, counselors, and other leaders a helpful, Christ-centered framework for wise and balanced ministry."

**Michael R. Emlet,** Faculty and Counselor, Christian Counseling and Educational Foundation (CCEF); author of *CrossTalk: Where Life and Scripture Meet*

"Christians are privileged today to have access to many books that are true and helpful. But every now and then a book comes along that is truly brilliant. *The Dynamic Heart* is such a book. Dr. Pierre expertly weds a theology of the soul and an explanation of the practice of personal care to create one of the most important books ever written in the biblical counseling movement. Every student and practitioner of counseling needs to become familiar with the concepts in this book."

**Heath Lambert,** Associate Pastor, First Baptist Church Jacksonville, Florida; Executive Director, Association of Certified Biblical Counselors

"In this illuminating work, Pierre shines a light on our hearts so that we have a more profound understanding of both others and ourselves. Still, this book is not fundamentally about human beings but about human beings in relationship with God. As a master teacher, Pierre helps us think through what it means practically for God to be the Lord of our hearts and the Lord of our lives. What a delight to read a book that is written so clearly, and the illustrations and anecdotes bring home wonderfully the message of the book. At the same time, Pierre is faithful biblically and theologically. Counselors, pastors, and, yes, all Christians will want to read this book."

**Thomas R. Schreiner,** James Buchanan Harrison Professor of New Testament Interpretation and Associate Dean, The Southern Baptist Theological Seminary, Louisville, Kentucky

"Jeremy Pierre's masterful piece, *The Dynamic Heart in Daily Life*, offers a theologically robust, intellectually rich, and conceptually accessible model of human psychology that is thoroughly biblical in nature. This book offers both counselor and counselee a comprehensive assessment of the inner dynamics at play upon the human experience while providing, thoughtful, practical wisdom in applying scriptural truth to that aspect of our humanity known most deeply by God alone—the heart. A genuinely enlightening read."

**Jeremy Lelek,** President, Association of Biblical Counselors

"Dysfunction occurs when a heart's worship design is directed away from God and toward self," says Pierre. This book is packed with biblical wisdom, keen observations, pastoral sensitivity and understanding, and practical applications into very complex issues in order to help the counselor and counselee move from the fallen dynamics of the heart to the joyful experience of the redeemed soul. Definitely, it is the best I have seen in this field.

**Miguel Núñez,** Senior Pastor International Baptist Church of Santo Domingo; President, Wisdom & Integrity Ministries

What a load of wisdom—biblical, theological, psychological, and relational—is contained within this book! It may be the most comprehensive treatment of the human heart written by a Christian counselor in our day. Evident throughout is the guidance of a thoughtful, godly, caring, and open-hearted Christian, guided himself by deep biblical convictions. It will be widely recognized as an outstanding contribution to biblical counseling literature.

**Eric L. Johnson,** Lawrence and Charlotte Hoover Professor of Pastoral Care, The Southern Baptist Theological Seminary

"If we understand other people accurately we will be nearly overwhelmed by the complexity of their lives—Dr. Pierre wants us to get close to the brink as a way to walk humbly with those we help. But then, like an experienced pastor-teacher, he takes us into sound doctrine and actually equips us to know and help with wisdom and love."

**Edward T. Welch,** CCEF faculty; psychologist; best-selling author

"Jeremy Pierre understands that in order to shepherd the flock, the pastor must also be a doctor of souls. In this book he provides biblical knowledge, shows how to make a proper diagnosis, and sharpens our skills in prescribing the remedy Scripture provides. It is a must-read for all involved in pastoral care. I recommend it with unreserved enthusiasm."

**Alistair Begg,** Senior Minister, Parkside Church, Chagrin Falls, Ohio

"We've all had this thought many times, no doubt: How profoundly helpful it would be to understand better why people (including you) do, and say, and act, and feel, the way we do. Even better, how liberating it would be to see what can be done to help people (including you) change and grow in human wholeness and Christlikeness. Jeremy Pierre's *The Dynamic Heart in Daily Life* provides such perspective, and I can guarantee every reader that they will benefit greatly in self-understanding from reading this profound, biblical, sane, and insightful book. One will find here a theology of the heart, a theology of human experience, and a theology of counseling that is revolutionary. For your own heart's sake, and for the benefit of others you have the privilege to help in their growth, I strongly encourage a careful reading of this excellent primer on the human heart."

**Bruce A. Ware,** T. Rupert and Lucille Coleman Professor of Christian Theology, The Southern Baptist Theological Seminary

"This book explores the deepest recesses of the human heart. Why do we love what we do? Why do we choose what we do? Why can't we seem to change? From other guides, such an exploration could be depressing and scary or abstract and irrelevant. This book is different. Drawing from a deep grasp of the gospel and years of experience with people, Jeremy Pierre presents a wise, hopeful, joyful map for change. Read this, and march on toward renewal."

**Russell Moore,** President, Ethics & Religious Liberty Commission of the Southern Baptist Convention

# THE
# DYNAMIC HEART
# IN DAILY LIFE

. . . .

## CONNECTING CHRIST
## TO HUMAN EXPERIENCE

. . . .

JEREMY PIERRE

New
Growth
Press

newgrowthpress.com

New Growth Press, Greensboro, NC 27404
Copyright © 2016 by Jeremy Pierre

Unless otherwise indicated, Scripture quotations are taken from *The Holy Bible, English Standard Version.* Copyright © 2000; 2001 by Crossway Bibles, a division of Good News Publishers. Used by permission. All rights reserved.

Scripture quotations marked (NKJV) are taken from the New King James Version®. Copyright © 1982 by Thomas Nelson. Used by permission. All rights reserved.

Cover Design: Faceout Books, faceoutstudio.com
Typesetting and eBook: Lisa Parnell, lparnell.com

ISBN 978-1-942572-67-1 (Print)
ISBN 978-1-942572-58-9 (eBook)

Library of Congress Cataloging-in-Publication Data
    Names: Pierre, Jeremy, 1979– author.
    Title: The dynamic heart in daily life : connecting Christ to human experience / Jeremy Pierre.
    Description: Greensboro, NC : New Growth Press, 2016.
    Identifiers: LCCN 2016025520 | ISBN 9781942572671 (pbk.)
    Subjects: LCSH: Change (Psychology)—Religious aspects—Christianity. | Christianity—Psychology. | Experience (Religion) | Pastoral counseling.
    Classification: LCC BR110 .P54 2016 | DDC 253.5/2—dc23
    LC record available at https://lccn.loc.gov/2016025520

Printed in India

27 26 25 24 23 22 21 20          7 8 9 10 11

## Dedication

*To my mom,*
a model of self-reflection

*To my dad,*
a model of moving past such business

*To my Sarah,*
whose basic sensibility grounds the earth

*To my kids,*
whose sheer momentum stirs the sky

# CONTENTS

. . . .

# ACKNOWLEDGMENTS

This book is the product of a semi-capable man surrounded by people much better than he.

New Growth Press took a chance on a unique premise, and I am grateful. Barbara Juliani asked me tough questions in the proposal process, and I knew this was the place to be. Beth Hart's editorial perspective freshened and improved what is here. I pray this book will be worthy of New Growth's history of faithful publication led by Mark and Karen Teears.

I am grateful to the institution that trained me and now employs me, the Southern Baptist Theological Seminary. I have given it my money, and it has given some of it back. But business aside, the best place to write a book like this is the culture set by Dr. Albert Mohler for a sweeping theological vision of all of life. I am also grateful to my provost, Dr. Randy Stinson, and my dean, Dr. Adam Greenway, for their support.

Clifton Baptist Church, the cheerful people of Frankfort Avenue, have loved my wife and me since the first year of our marriage. The gospel is strong there for sinners like us. I am grateful to the men who have pastored me over the years, Tom Schreiner, Shawn Wright, Bruce Ware, and John Kimbell, as well as other faithful men who have pastored alongside me.

Certain colleagues have been key to the development of this book and deserve my thanks. Robert Cheong consistently challenged me to see things from other people's eyes. Eric Johnson taught me that an unexpected benefit of intellectual sparring can be friendship. Jim Orrick and Stuart Scott were particularly generous with their wisdom to a junior faculty member in their respective fields.

Certain friends also need special thanks. Matt and Jeannie Hall have always treated the victories and defeats of the Pierre family as their own, and we love them for it. Brian Payne would deliver biblical encouragement to me in the unmistakable idiom of rural Alabama like some prophet of the South, and my soul would receive it as such. BJ Walters was so relentlessly positive I found myself both encouraged and annoyed. Scott Moodie's cynicism was purifying. Oren Martin would insert the perfect measure of sarcasm into the darkest of situations.

I also want to thank the folks I've been privileged to work with in various ways. To my staffers whose excellent work allowed me the margin (and peace of mind) to write: Kari McCulloch, Maegan Clark, and Allie Klein, as well as Tom Scott, Grant Castleberry, Garrett Milner, and Tyler Clark. Also to my Ph.D. students who saw early drafts of this material yet still managed to show me respect.

I am the middle kid of a big family, and that family even now frames my existence. What I observed about the swirling dynamics of very different people living under one roof is reflected in these pages. I have already dedicated this book to my mom and dad, but I also want to acknowledge that Ron and Barb Pierre's love for the Bible compelled me to love it myself. That same love resides deep within my in-laws, Rick and Beth Leisure, who are also parents to me. My brothers Chris and Daniel are extensions of my soul—or I an extension of theirs—in everything important and not-so-important. My sister Lisa is contagious joy. My sister Wendy, a rare sort of kindness. My oldest brother, Jonathan, inheritor of a little brother's admiration.

My wife, Sarah, is the anchor and the light of my soul, mixed metaphor notwithstanding. She grounds me in turbulence and brightens me in darkness. She provided my dearest stewardship: Allie, Ronnie, Marlie, Frankie, and Betsie, whom I threaten to refer to in public as "the fruit of my loins" if they do not obey. They are my favorite little images of God, and I will spend my life showing them the way to find him.

That way—the only way—is Jesus. Who can speak of the Savior without failing? One bright day when we finally see him, we will come closer to succeeding. Until then, he settles for our spotty praise. And not just settles for it, but sanctifies it as precious to him. No doubt, Jesus is a friend of sinners. And being his friend—can we dare hope it's true?—is what we were made for.

· · · ·

# Introduction

How should I praise thee, Lord! How should my rhymes
Gladly engrave thy love in steel,
If what my soul doth feel sometimes,
My soul might ever feel!

Although there were some forty heav'ns, or more,
Sometimes I peer above them all;
Sometimes I hardly reach a score,
Sometimes to hell I fall.

— *George Herbert, "The Temper"*[1]


Our favorite poets, musicians, and storytellers resonate with us because they capture our experience so beautifully. The poet Herbert describes here what even a knuckleheaded thirteen-year-old boy can recognize on his own: human experience is consistent only in its inconsistency. If only we could freeze our hearts in a perpetual state of warmth and joy, like permanent, unyielding steel. But our hearts are not steel. They are living things, and therefore changing things. Sometimes we fly so high we scrape the top of heaven. Sometimes we barely make it off the ground. No doubt, people are dynamic creatures.

The ability to capture the experience of another person not only makes for a good poet, but also a good friend—not to mention counselor, pastor, or parent. Anyone involved in personal ministry of any kind knows how hard daily life can be to understand. That is what this book is about—understanding the experience of others in an attempt to help them. The goal of understanding is not merely to empathize, but also to help others see how their experience is best understood in light of what God says about it. If all goes well, you may understand your own experience better, too.

But this is no easy task. Philosophers and theologians have, for ages, explored the simple question of why people do what they do, with scientists perhaps crowding them out a bit in recent decades. Even with such a chorus of expertise, our own experience is an obscurity to us. What is a person doing by living, breathing, experiencing this world? We can feel something so strongly at one time, only to find that feeling gone a moment later. We know what it is to give full mental assent to the truth of something, but act as if it did not matter. We can recognize that we should not desire a certain object, but go on wanting it anyway. We can simultaneously disapprove of our actions, yet continue to carry them out. Our interpretation of a situation can change with a simple word from someone else, then shift back again when we are alone. We are a mystery to ourselves.

But we are not a mystery to God. These pages are dedicated to showing how God designed people with dynamic hearts to experience the world fully only when connected to Christ. Human experience is custom-made to relate to an unseen God. Many people think of a relationship with God as some flat "religious mode" that even the particularly pious can only inconsistently maintain. But Scripture presents faith as the springtime that brings color to the whole landscape of human experience. God designed people to relate to him dynamically, just as he relates to them dynamically. The gospel of Jesus Christ tells us about a dynamic interchange between God and people, whereby Christ gives his righteousness to them— not just as legal declaration, but as actual transformative power over their thoughts, desires, and choices. A thinking, wanting, choosing God that made his people to do the same shares his heart with them through his gospel.

Faith is the means by which the gospel is received; thus, faith is at the center of heart transformation. God designed people from the very beginning to base their entire experience on what he says about them and their world. People ought to interpret the world as God interprets it, value the objects he values, commit to what he says is worthy of commitment. But because sin has corrupted people's hearts, they are unable to believe God's words on their own. Only the Holy Spirit can give the gift of faith and thus the power to change, and he does so through Scripture as the Word of God. Faith is how God restores his design for the human heart so that people can commune with him and reflect his character. This is true both for initial conversion as well as ongoing union with Christ. By faith, people receive Christ's righteousness and progressively manifest it in the dynamic functions of their hearts. Where a heart once dynamically responded in fleshly ways, by faith it dynamically responds in righteous ways. Consequently, the Bible is central to the change process as faith comes through hearing, and hearing through the Word of Christ (Rom. 10:17). Though faith is a gift of God, it is also an active human response of trust in what God has revealed about himself. Thus, the aim of ministry is faith in Christ granted by the Spirit through the Word.

This book explores a faith-centered understanding of people accompanied by a Word-centered methodology for helping people. I believe that the regular stuff of human experience—the thoughts, values, and commitments that motivate human behavior—are where faith in Christ expresses itself in human experience. If people are born as thinking, wanting, choosing beings, then they need to be reborn as thinking, wanting, and choosing beings. In other words, faith allows people to think differently as they receive the knowledge of God from his Word, to want differently as they begin to value what God loves, and to choose differently as they commit themselves to what he says is worthy. This subtle, progressive change displays itself in the way people experience all of life, including the way they relate to God, to themselves, to other people, and to the circumstances that surround them.

## Dynamic Heart Change

So how should we think about the simple declaration of Jesus that people function in a relatively straightforward way, "the good person out of the good treasure of his heart produces good, and the evil person out of his evil treasure produces evil, for out of the abundance of the heart his mouth speaks" (Luke 6:45)? Figs come from fig bushes. Brambles come from bramble bushes. Seems simple.

Imagine flying high above the Midwestern countryside. Anyone seeing the rolling fields squared off by roads and hedges would recognize it as farmland—simple farmland. However, to understand the way the land drains out, the appropriate crops to plant, or the land's likely yield, a person would have to inspect more closely than a flyover. Similarly, people's lives may look simple without a closer look. People in crisis might appear to be simply in need of trusting God more, but a closer look reveals they experience feelings they cannot explain, have intrusive thoughts they never had before, or find themselves perplexed by an unpredictable ebb and flow of motivation.

People do not have to be in crisis to feel the complexity. I often see it in my own daily life. I cannot quite explain why I feel a certain way or say a certain thing. I often cannot describe what draws me toward certain people or makes me annoyed with others. Why am I convinced the ship has sunk one moment, and then believe it unsinkable the next? Even on eternal matters—perhaps especially on eternal matters—how can I be so compelled by the majesty of God in one moment, and so cold and earthly in the next?

God designed the human heart to be both varied and varying, and he delights in his craftsmanship. By varied, I mean that human hearts function with a complex spectrum of thoughts, feelings, and choices that flow seamlessly together. By varying, I mean that this spectrum bends, adapts, expands, contracts, vacillates, turns—always dynamically responding to everything around it. Healthy change directs those dynamic responses to reflect the righteousness of God.

My goal is to give a theological vision of how faith in Christ restores the dynamic human heart and a practical vision of how to help people join in on the process. The coming chapters lay out a detailed theology of human experience. By a theology of human experience, I mean that theology, as revealed in Scripture, supplies the categories for people to understand their own experience. Theology is the standard by which people should measure their experience, not human experience the standard by which people measure theology. Because faith comes through hearing, and hearing through the Word of Christ (Rom. 10:17), the authority lies with Scripture, not with personal perception. People are often only partially aware of the beliefs and values residing within them, and they will tend to read these beliefs and values into Scripture. People must become more willing to listen to God's voice for what it actually is rather than what they want it to be. As Scripture is thus received in the heart, God's revelation shapes people's thoughts, feelings, and choices.

A theology of human experience also requires an understanding of human experience that is as broad as the Bible's. Personal ministry, in general, and counseling, in particular, should be directed to the full breadth of how the heart functions. For example, the dynamic heart does more than think; therefore, change takes more than knowing the right information. Accurate knowledge of God and his world is vital to heart change; however, having accurate beliefs is inadequate for changing a human heart. When people begin to shift their thinking, their experiential dilemma involves powerful emotions. The experience of fear greatly influences thinking processes. Sometimes, fear is so strong that the very capacity for thought is undermined. The effect of desires and emotions on the way people think is important to consider in ministry.

Similarly, people's feelings are connected to their thoughts and their choices. The heart has reasons for its desires and feelings, even when they seem powerful, mysterious, and overwhelming. People suffering under emotional strain can find comfort that they have a certain level of control over feelings that seem completely out of control. This control is not necessarily direct or immediate; even the weakest negative emotion that plagues people cannot simply be extinguished. While due attention must be given to the physiological aspect of emotion, a balanced view of the dynamic heart gives hope that people can exert some level of influence over their emotions, even if that influence is gradual.

Finally, the dynamic heart does more than just choose; therefore, change is more than making the right decisions. Thoughts and feelings influence people's choices. Without the knowledge of Christ and a love for him, people will not obey him with a whole heart. If either understanding or desire is ignored, then appeals to change people's actions will only amount to temporary or shallow behavioral change. Even the most elementary understanding of Scripture shows the danger of addressing outward behavior apart from inward motivation. Doing so implies that people have the power to change themselves by their own determination. Appeals to change actions alone do not carry the weight of the heart in producing a healthy inner life.

## The Journey to Understanding the Dynamic Heart

I will develop three main sections of thought. The first addresses how people respond to life dynamically. God made the dynamic functions of the heart to reflect the beautiful complexity of his own personhood. People are his image bearers, and their relationship to the world is directly connected to their relationship to him. How the heart actively responds to God determines how it responds to everything else.

The second section addresses what people dynamically respond to. The human heart does not operate in a vacuum, but is always responding to something. Considering the situational factors of personal experience is vital for understanding how a person is responding to life. The four main categories of daily experience include God, self, others, and circumstances. Human experience involves responding to an unseen God who upholds all things by his power. It also involves self-perception, harboring an opinion of self shaped by certain ideals and desires. People are also always responding to other people, dynamically shaping them and being shaped by them. Finally, human experience involves response to circumstances, the events and situations of life in a world bigger than the individual.

The third and final section lays out a methodology for counseling and, by extension, any interpersonal ministry of the Word. This section provides an understanding of people that can adequately address complex problems by showing how faith in Christ is the central means by which the heart is restored.

## Section 1

# The Beauty of Human Experience:

## How the Heart Responds Dynamically

Human experience should be celebrated for the beauty of its complexity. Caring for human beings is a lot harder than caring for pets or garden plants precisely because of this complexity. But that complexity is the reflection of a complex God. Humans share a beauty with him that nothing in creation can match.

The main goal of this book is to equip counselors, pastors, caretakers, or anyone else interested in helping people with a framework to understand human experience theologically—that is, as God designed it. Only by understanding how God designed people will you understand the person in front of you. Knowing people's experience is a necessary part of helping them, and so is knowing how that experience connects to Christ. Maybe you will better understand your own experience along the way, too.

Caring for people requires understanding the delicate interplay between the internal responses of people's hearts and the external factors of their situation. In other words, people are designed with a dynamic response system that interacts with the various components of their situation. If counselors do not carefully consider the interchange between the two, they will not be able to adequately address what needs to change.

This is the first of two sections that will construct a theology of human experience. It will address how God designed the heart to respond dynamically. The following five chapters address how the human heart responds dynamically. The purpose of these chapters is to equip counselors and caregivers to understand the experience of the folks in their care.

# CHAPTER 1

· · · ·

# THE DYNAMIC HEART

*Head and heart have battled long enough.*
*It's time they got their acts together, literally.*

— *Andrew Tallon*[1]

Human experience is so vast and mysterious, so dull and routine. Human thoughts can skim the edges of eternal realms a few seconds before entertaining the urge for a Shamrock Shake from McDonalds. People deeply love others and yet are bored to death while talking to them. Individuals demonstrate epic resolve in tragedy but have difficulty getting up to exercise on Monday mornings. How can anyone describe such an incredible, regular thing? Poets and songwriters try to capture the sum of human experience, but at best they capture one small aspect of humanity. Likewise, philosophers and scientists observe in part. At best, they trace the corners of human experience, catching glimpses of its form. People know what they experience, but defining it can be like grasping vapor. Yet, even though vapor cannot be held, its essential properties and how it behaves can be understood.

So it is with human experience. No one can program human experience to follow an entirely predictable pattern, but everyone can certainly understand its general operating principles. In fact, it is vital to do so. When people recognize the contours of their experience, they can seek help for themselves and offer help to others in need. Gladly for us, the human experience is a shared experience.

God designed people theomorphically—meaning, the functions of the human heart are reflective of divine internal functions.[2] Every human being on the green earth is made to image the same God, and therefore they share the same framework for inner experience. They operate according to the same design in different contexts and with different influencing factors. This chapter explores people's theomorphic design because understanding the breadth of human design helps people understand themselves and helps them offer adequately complex counsel to others. No one should treat people as merely rational beings in need of instruction, nor as merely emotional beings in need of healing, nor as merely decision-makers who need the right motivation. The truth is broader than each of these.

This is the first of five chapters addressing how the human heart responds dynamically. The purpose of these chapters is to equip counselors and caregivers to understand the experience of the folks in their care. The primary point of this chapter is: Human experience is three-dimensional. The human heart responds cognitively, through rational processes based on knowledge and beliefs. It also responds affectively, through a framework of desires and emotions. It also responds volitionally, through a series of choices reflecting the willful commitments of the heart. These three aspects of the heart's response are all a part of how people were designed to worship God.

## Surface Issues and Deeper Counsel

A man sits in a counseling room, recounting a recent fight he had with his wife. He is an unhappy man generally, but he had exploded on her with an anger that surprised them both. The words that poured from him in that wild-eyed frenzy can only be described as wicked. In the ferocity of the moment, he stormed out of the room kicking things as he went. He even put a hole in one of the doors.

The evening ended in his leaving the apartment and sitting at the bar for a few hours. As he relates all this to his counselor, he stares at his shoes.

The counselor has a significant choice to make before he opens his mouth and sets the trajectory of care. He could set a trajectory arching low along the surface of the situation, pointing out what is obvious in an attempt to bring clarity and quick action. The husband's anger, expressed in a relationally harmful and sinful manner, caused this conflict. His explosion could fairly be labeled a fit of anger, to use the apostle Paul's words, which is a work of the flesh (Gal. 5:20). Tracing the theme of anger in Scripture would give plenty of material to discuss why anger can be displeasing to God (Eph. 4:26–32; Col. 3:8; James 1:19). Obviously, the husband must repent of this sin and replace his anger with kindness, gentleness, and self-control—seems pretty straightforward.

But the obvious thing to say is not always the best. Pointing out this man's behavior as sin and calling him to change is not wrong. Helping him see those inner urges as alarming is not wrong either. In fact, these very things must occur. But how a counselor does this can be flat and one-dimensional. It can ignore the complex dynamics of both the relationship and the man's heart. A wise counselor will proceed in ways that square with the husband's experience, that resonate with heart dynamics of which he may or may not be aware.

The trajectory the counselor sets must aim deep, breaking the surface of this husband's anger, plunging deep into the why, not satisfied with hovering around the what. Why did he finally burst, and over that particular thing? How does the husband's anger relate to his general emotive stance toward life? How does his anger fit into the husband's relational dynamics? What awoke within him that sinister urge to harm? This husband did not have a generic anger inside him that happened to overflow. There is no generic anger. There is only a heart believing certain things, wanting certain things, choosing certain things—and anger is just his impassioned method of getting them.

The husband is looking at his shoes because he knows something alarming is going on inside him, and he needs a three-dimensional picture of it. As his self-awareness about his anger grows, he will see what he is believing about his world, seeking from those around him, and devoted to attaining. The husband will see what he needs to see in order to change. He will need more than self-awareness to change, but he cannot have less.

In order to answer the *why* question in people's life and behavior, they need to have a framework for understanding *how* humans experience the world. A biblical framework of human experience comes from a much more complex use of Scripture than simply trying to look up human experience or human psychology in the concordance and finding nothing, so reverting to looking up more antique ways of saying something similar: heart, soul, spirit, mind, will, and who could forget the all-important psychological term *intestines.*[3] Now, these terms are vital to our understanding of how Scripture describes human experience, but the question we are asking is not, *What is the heart?* so much as, *How is the heart described as functioning?* Specifically, *How is the heart described as functioning to dynamically reflect its Creator?*

What people are doing as they experience life is reflecting the spiritual personhood of God as physical beings. Humans are theomorphic—formed as beings whose every thought, desire, and choice is designed to show the physical world the personhood of God. This personhood is characterized by both simplicity and complexity. It is one entity, but this one entity is three-dimensional.

## Simple and Complex

Perhaps because psychological categories starting back with Freud are so deeply ingrained in Western culture, it is common to think of people as made up of various components. The id, the ego, and the superego have fallen on hard times as the dominant categories. Nonetheless, different psychological theories, especially those considered intrapsychic, continue to represent people as having various, often opposing, forces operating within them. At a popular level, often people say, "It's not a spiritual problem; it's a psychological problem," or "His problems are emotional, not spiritual."

Such statements properly recognize that human experience is complex and multifaceted, but they betray a dismissal of people's simplicity. Humans are unified in their personhood because God is unified in his personhood. People experience the world as spiritual beings made to reflect God. Spirituality, thus, is not a separate function, but expresses itself in the full breadth of psychological function.

Scripture uses different anthropological terms—heart, soul, spirit, mind, and more—to describe a simple, singular human experience. The authors of Scripture use these different terms to describe human functioning in largely the same way, which implies that they refer to the same internal reality.[4] The terms for soul, spirit, and mind describe the same types of function as the term for heart. In other words, they all do the same thing, indicating the various biblical terms for human experience do not refer to multiple spiritual organs that do different things.

The biblical authors understand human experience as flowing from one, unified heart. I primarily use the term heart throughout this book. The Greek on which it is based, *kardia*, has the widest semantic range, meaning "the focus of his being and activity as a spiritual personality" and relates to "the unity and totality of the inner life represented and expressed in the variety of intellectual and spiritual functions."[5]

Why is the simplicity of the heart so important to establish? Because people are unified beings, their inner experience is not fragmented into multiple, often disconnected, often conflicting forces. People's problems are not either spiritual or psychological, mental or emotional, moral or social. People are moral agents who conduct themselves from a singular response system for which they are responsible before their Creator. Because this is true, all human problems are spiritual problems. Invasive thoughts, haphazard emotions, disjointed personalities, unwelcome impulses—they all are problems of a unified response system designed by God.

I will discuss later how these experiences have physiological elements that are often beyond a person's immediate control. So when I say all human problems are spiritual problems, I am not saying they are merely spiritual. People have bodies as well—bodies that function not as vehicles for an independent soul that drives it, but more like the canvas and paint embodying the ideas of an artist. People are embodied souls, and their physical makeup is the necessary physical correlate to their spiritual heart.

Spiritual problems are not a category alongside mental, emotional, or behavioral problems. Yes, these categories allow for helpful distinctions in how the heart is expressing itself, but all human responses are by nature spiritual. Whatever the complexity of social, biological, or developmental factors, all those things are different contexts and influences on a spiritual heart operating before God. People are simple, in that they are wholly spiritual persons.

But they are also complex. Though Scripture speaks of the heart as a unified object, it describes it three-dimensionally. The heart is alive and dynamic, functioning in a multifaceted way, similar to how one physical object has to be understood according to three axes of measurement: height, width, and breadth. In order for an object to be three-dimensional, it must be measurable along these three axes. Similarly, the human heart responds cognitively, through rational processes based on knowledge and beliefs. It also responds affectively, through a framework of desires and emotions. It also responds volitionally, through a series of choices reflecting the willful commitments of the heart. Thinking, feeling, and choosing are complex, dynamic heart responses.

Thinking, feeling, and choosing are different perspectives on the same, singular function. These three functions are necessarily interrelated. Thoughts can lead to feelings that can lead to choices; choices can also lead to thoughts that can lead to feelings; just as feelings can lead to choices that can lead to new thoughts. The following diagram illustrates how the heart's function can begin at any perspective and then move in any direction, even as they interrelate and overlap.

## The Dynamic Heart: Functions

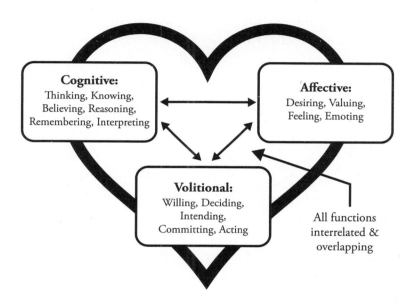

People cannot fully separate thought, feeling, and choice in their responses. Imagine a dad who loses an infant daughter. His most prominent experience at first may be sheer anguish. The deep sorrow reveals how the dad valued his daughter and the aching desire to have her back. His affections are at work. The dad is also interpreting the situation according to what he believes about the world, and those beliefs may very well be strained by the weight of emotion he feels. He once believed the world to be a generally happy place, but this new experience shapes his prior reasoning. His thought process works in relationship with his emotions. His cognition is at work. But there is also another important element to his experience. The dad will also find it difficult to maintain resolve, to choose life in a new reality without his daughter. The emotional weight and the shifting beliefs will influence the way he makes decisions and choices in this new reality. The volition is at work. All three dimensions of his experience are important to acknowledge in his grief, since each has a powerful influence on the others.

People are thinking beings, desiring beings, and choosing beings simultaneously. Scholars have described this simultaneous, multifaceted functioning in various ways, calling cognition, affection, and volition as a triune "modes of intentionality," "domains of experience," or "ways of being."[6] Perhaps it would be helpful to think of these different modes of heart movement as similar to the different modes of the earth's movement as a rotating, tilting, and orbiting planet. All of these terms describe the movement of the earth, but each from a different set of concerns. The earth's rotation explains days; the earth's tilting and orbiting explain seasons and years. They are directly related in the final product of what a person in a particular location on earth will experience as day or night, season of the year, and visual display of the sky above. Just as scientists can explore the earth's singular position from these different perspectives, so the heart's functions can be examined more closely individually.

### Cognition—The Thinking Heart

A vital aspect of human experience is cognition—the ability to think, to acquire knowledge, to process information, to believe certain propositions as true, and to interpret new information based on those beliefs. People are, in large part, what they know and understand. The Old Testament refers to these processes as occurring in the heart,[7] and the New Testament follows suit.

In the Synoptic Gospels, Jesus acknowledges internal reasons, perceptions, and understandings as occurring within the heart. When the scribes came to accuse Jesus of blaspheming, Matthew describes that "Jesus, knowing their thoughts, said, 'Why do you think evil in your hearts?'" (Matt. 9:4; par. Mark 2:8; Luke 5:22).

Similarly, when the disciples argued about who was the greatest, Luke said, "But Jesus, knowing the reasoning of their hearts, took a child and put him by his side" (Luke 9:47). Jesus, again, draws a direct link between perception, understanding, and the heart when he confronted the grumbling crowds, saying, "Do you not yet perceive or understand? Are your hearts hardened?" (Mark 8:17).

The apostle Paul often refers to the cognitive functions of the heart in his epistles as well. Similar to the gospel narrators, Paul attributes the internal dialogue of human reasoning to the heart, saying, "Do not say in your heart, 'Who will ascend into heaven?'" (Rom. 10:6). He attributes human imagination to the heart, "What no eye has seen, nor ear heard, nor the heart of man imagined, what God has prepared for those who love him" (1 Cor. 2:9; par. Isa. 64:4). The heart contains knowledge, "For God, who said, 'Let light shine out of darkness,' has shone in our hearts to give the light of the knowledge of the glory of God in the face of Jesus Christ" (2 Cor. 4:6). The heart may also lack knowledge, "They are darkened in their understanding, alienated from the life of God because of the ignorance that is in them, due to their hardness of heart" (Eph. 4:18).

The biblical writers present people as thinking creatures. They reason and understand. They possess knowledge. They remember past situations, interpret them in the present, and project estimations of their future based on their own structures of plausibility. What people believe about the world determines how they interpret new information they receive as they live in it. The thoughts of people's hearts are of monumental importance to the trajectory of their lives.

### Affection—The Feeling Heart

According to Scripture, the human experience also involves affection. Strong desires and emotions motivate people. People value certain things and act accordingly. These desires and values work themselves out in a complex spectrum of emotion—from sadness to happiness, anger to disappointment, relief to panic. People are, in large part, what they desire, value, and feel.

The Old Testament attributes feelings and emotions to the heart.[8] The New Testament follows suit here as well: desire and passion reside in the heart, and the heart generates emotions. The gospel writers, particularly John, refer to the heart in this way. The heart is the place where desires operate (Matt. 5:28), and the heart is indeed dedicated to what people desire and value, as Jesus reminded his disciples, "For where your treasure is, there your heart will be also" (Matt. 6:21; par. Luke 12:34). The heart feels intense emotion, "Did not our hearts burn within us while he talked to us on the road?" (Luke 24:32). The heart can experience distress and fear, "Let not your hearts be troubled, neither let them be afraid" (John 14:1, 27). The heart also experiences sadness and joy, "sorrow has filled your heart" (John 16:6), but "your hearts will rejoice" (John 16:22). Luke mentions many emotional responses and attributes them to the heart, saying, "my heart was glad" (Acts 2:26; Acts 46) and "they were cut to the heart, and they gnashed at him with their teeth" (Acts 7:54 NKJV). The heart experiences satisfaction (Acts 14:17), and sorrow at departing from loved ones breaks the heart (Acts 21:13).

Paul frequently attributes feelings to the heart. He describes the heart as containing lust and desire (Rom. 1:24). Paul also references his own heart as experiencing pain and sorrow over those who are not saved (Rom. 9:2) and desiring for them to be so (Rom. 10:1). His heart is tearfully anguished over concern for the well-being of others (2 Cor. 2:4; 3:2; 6:11). Affection for others is expressed as their being in the heart (2 Cor. 7:3; 8:16; Phil. 1:7; 1 Thess. 2:17). Feelings of peace are experienced in the heart (Phil. 4:7; Col. 3:15–16).

The biblical writers describe people as beings who desire and emote. These desires are a significant facet of human existence, motivating them to action and adding color to the experience of life. People long for certain things, and deeply feel their loss as well as their gain. They have value systems by which they judge the world, and their emotions are the gauge of the value they place on certain objects. When people want something, they pursue it. People's affections are a glorious part of who they are. The desires of people's hearts are also of monumental importance to the trajectory of their lives.

### Volition—The Intentional Heart

Human experience also involves intentions and choices. People actively make choices all day long. These countless decisions flow from the more hidden dedications of the heart. Whether strongly conscious or less conscious, the heart's intentions drive a person's actions. People are, in large part, what they choose to be.

The Old Testament also refers to the heart as the place of intentions and choices,[9] and once again the New Testament keeps in step. In the Gospels, the writers often mention the heart as that place where the will functions. Intentions are attributed to the heart, "But I say to you that everyone who looks at a woman with lustful intent has already committed adultery with her in his heart" (Matt. 5:28). People's true dedications and choices reside in the heart rather than on the lips, "This people honors me with their lips, but their heart is far from me" (Matt. 15:8; Mark 7:6; par. Isa. 29:13). Likewise, Jesus says, "What comes out of the mouth proceeds from the heart" (Matt. 15:18). The heart is cited as where people make a decision either out of consent or compulsion, "So also my heavenly Father will do to every one of you, if you do not forgive your brother from your heart" (Matt. 18:35). Similarly, the means by which Satan controls the will of Judas Iscariot is by putting an intention in his heart (John 13:2).

Luke refers to the heart in this way frequently in the book of Acts. Satan again provokes willful action by means of the heart, "Ananias, why has Satan filled your heart to lie to the Holy Spirit and to keep back for yourself part of the proceeds of the land?" (Acts 5:3). Luke uses even more specifically volitional language in the following verse, "Why is it that you have contrived this deed in your heart?" (Acts 5:4). Clearly, decisions for future action are made in the heart, as many more passages in Acts indicate, "it came into his heart to visit his brothers" (Acts 7:23). Loyalties of the will take place in the heart, "Our fathers refused to obey him, but thrust him aside, and in their hearts they turned to Egypt" (Acts 7:39). Turning from God is also referred to as "the intent of the heart" (Acts 8:22).

Paul also refers to the intentional functions of the heart frequently. The heart can be willful against God, "But because of your hard and impenitent heart you are storing up wrath for yourself on the day of wrath when God's righteous judgment will be revealed" (Rom. 2:5). Paul says that "the purposes of the heart" are reasons for being condemned or commended (1 Cor. 4:5). He also attributes the act of making a decision to the heart, "But whoever is firmly established in his heart . . ." (1 Cor. 7:37). A Christian slave must obey his master willingly, that is, "with a sincere heart" (Eph. 6:5; par. Col. 3:22).

The biblical writers understand people to be moral agents capable of intent, decision, and choice. People intend certain purposes in their actions. They make decisions based upon the loyalties of their hearts. They resolve to accomplish certain things. They dedicate their efforts to certain ideals. People have active wills that direct their conduct. The intentions of people's hearts are also of monumental importance to the trajectory of their lives.

## The Integrated, Worshipping Heart

Why is the thinking, feeling, and intentional heart so important to God? Why did he design human hearts so intricately? The answer is simple. God designed the heart's functions for worship: he wants people to respond to him with the complex beauty that reflects his own. Dynamic hearts worship God in daily life—in the way they think, the things they want, the choices they make. When people use those aspects of their heart in a way that reflects God's character, they are worshipping. Cognitively, when people believe the testimony of God's Word, they worship him. Affectively, when people value what God values, they worship him. Volitionally, when people submit their choices to God's will, they worship him.

People were made to worship God with all their heart—the full breadth of their internal experience and external conduct. God wants people to reflect his own complex beauty as they respond to him and to his world. God created people as responders, and they answer back to God according to the purpose of their existence.[10] Jesus said that the entire Law and Prophets rests on this, "to love the Lord your God with all your heart and with all your soul and with all your mind. This is the great and first commandment" (Matt. 22:34–40; ref. Deut. 6:4–6). God based the old covenant law upon this command, and Jesus fulfilled this law in the new covenant. God planned for this whole-hearted, dynamic love between himself and humans from the beginning, and he remains committed to his plan until the end.

God designed people's hearts for a singular purpose: worship. As the heart's thinking, feeling, and choosing serve this singular purpose, these functions are interrelated; they are different perspectives of the heart's singular function. Human beings experience the world in a multifaceted way, and those facets are integrated, which means they necessarily influence one another. As John Frame explains, "To speak of human 'faculties' is to speak of diverse perspectives in terms of which we can look at the various acts and experiences of the human mind. None of the faculties, so understood, exists or acts apart from the others, each is dependent on the others, and each includes the others."[11] God precisely designed people and delights in his design, calling people very good (Gen. 1:31). He gave people dynamic hearts to love him in the way we conduct ourselves on this green earth.

## The Dynamic Heart in Daily Life

The world would be a living nightmare if any one of these aspects of human response were missing. Imagine how dangerous the world would be if people's feelings did not accompany thoughtful reflection or if people's knowledge did not coordinate with their choices. People make countless decisions on a given day—and both knowledge and feelings are necessary moral guides to those choices.

Imagine if all the decisions people made throughout their day were void of emotional investment. How would they interact with their family? What would they say to a coworker who tells them about a cancer diagnosis? How would they respond to the homeless they pass on the street? Imagine these scenarios as a cold comprehension of facts. Emotion-less responses are incomplete responses.

Emotion is a vital aspect of sane human response. Neuroscientist Antonio Damasio studied patients who suffered damage to a specific part of the brain that largely controls emotionality. Rather than being more sound in their reasoning, people who experienced this damage made terrible decisions about moral situations that others instinctively knew to be clear. Those affective instincts—gut feelings—are necessary to good decisions. Damasio concludes, "The fragile instruments of rationality need special assistance" in the form of human emotive capacities.[12] People's emotional stance toward a situation allows them to preselect their options, making an actual real-life choice possible in a world of infinite potential responses.

Consider another scenario. On a given Sunday morning, people may have a wide variety of options open before them—a bike ride around town, breakfast at their favorite diner, enjoying a good novel on their back porch, going to church—all of which could be logically deduced according to the various beliefs they have. But vital to the process is people's emotional inclinations and volitional commitments about each option. The embarrassment people feel if the neighbor you had invited to church saw them skipping church, the guilt of not going, the joy they experience hearing the Word preached, the commitment they feel to their Sunday school class—these emotions influence the decision no less than rational arguments for going to church.[13]

What if, on the other hand, people were to remove cognition, so that all of their daily decisions were simply the result of their feelings? The world would be full of grown-up babies, acting out of their immediate desires, unprocessed by an accurate knowledge of the world around them. People would be slaves of passion, pursuing immediate pleasure and avoiding pain. Sounds like a college fraternity.

Thinking is a necessary companion to feeling, since all emotions are based on perceived value. In order to feel, people have to have some understanding. For example, I cannot feel delight in my higher monthly yields or fear at losses unless I have some concept of how stock investments work. I cannot feel disgust at a politician's veiled racist statement without some knowledge of the history of racial tensions in America. God honors both the thinking and the feeling aspects of human responses. Matthew Elliot explains, "If emotions are merely physiological impulses, they can be ignored, controlled, or trivialized, while, if they have as their essential element thinking and judgment, they are an essential part of almost everything we think and do."[14]

People's thinking capacities allow them to possess knowledge and discern truth. Emotions require beliefs. It is difficult to imagine a scenario in which an adult could feel emotion void of any knowledge, apart from some neurological dysfunction (which is a definite possibility in a fallen world). When people are sad, they feel sad about something. The same is true when they are angry, happy, relieved, or fearful. There is cognitive content to their emotion, and these influence the choices they make.

## The Dynamic Heart and Human Problems

Returning to the angry husband illustration, Scripture has a lot to say to him as he looks down at his shoes. But to make Scripture land well, this man needs to move his gaze from his shoes to his heart. God has revealed what human beings are and how they function, a reliable guide for this husband to understand his experience. Good counsel understands then explains people's experiences in ways that ring true to them yet also casts a new light of understanding in accordance with the Bible. A wise counselor will not give one-dimensional instruction, but three-dimensional insight.

What if, instead of saying the obvious thing to this angry husband, a counselor asked the kind of questions that constructed a three-dimensional model of his experience? A counselor could help this husband consider how that fight revealed certain thought patterns and belief structures. In other words, his angry explosion displayed what he believes about the world. What beliefs were most active in his thoughts, not just at the time of the explosion, but also from day to day? Remember, he was unhappy long before he was angry. His unhappiness flows from a certain understanding of his life, of his wife, of his situation, and of God. It may help the man to explore where certain beliefs may have started, from past experiences or relationships.

But exploring the husband's beliefs is not sufficient. A counselor must also help him understand his emotions and desires. Anger was the presenting emotion, but anger is never alone. The general sense of dissatisfaction and unhappiness that blanketed his life is just as important, if not more so. Emotions are the expressions of desires. What does he wish were true of his life? By what values is he measuring his wife or himself? The furious kicking and screaming was not arbitrary, but flowed from a burning desire for something that he viewed his wife as hindering him from getting. The goal is to help the husband understand what desires are being expressed in his feelings, what particular objects he is valuing so deeply he is willing to go to war for them. Doing this will allow the counselor to eventually cast a positive vision for what the feelings were designed to do: to value God higher than all else and to hold every other desire in service to it. This is part of worship. When this is not occurring, feelings are not functioning properly.

In addition to the husband's thinking and feeling, his intentions also need to be addressed. At some point, he chose to erupt at his wife. Whether he was cognizant of the moment or not, the husband voluntarily entered into his behavior. But that choice was not merely an anomaly. He will need to consider the pattern of choices that characterize his conduct, especially toward his wife. Had the husband been choosing not to express his thoughts or feelings to his wife, and his resolve finally melted in the heat of his anger? But the personal choices involved in his anger are wider than the way he relates to his wife. He made that choice out of a deeper structure of commitments. What do the husband's general pursuits indicate about those structures? How does he choose to use his time or his money? Does he actively follow after God in the way he conducts himself, or does he see God's intrusion in his life as burdensome? Worshipping God means to obey willingly. The way the husband treats his wife is not just about his intentions toward her, but his loyalty to the God who designed him.

In counseling and in other forms of personal ministry, the trajectory of care must delve deep into the dynamic heart instead of skim along the surface of the presenting issue. Counselors, pastors, and lay leaders can say more than the obvious thing. They can seek to understand others' experiences so that they may help them understand it for themselves. A theology of human experience allows counselors to do this because God designed the heart to respond like he does in thought, desire, and intention.

Counseling should be directed to the breadth of the heart's functions—thinking, feeling, choosing. Emphasizing one aspect without due attention to the others will lead to a lopsided view of people and a lopsided methodology in handling them. A goal of the counselor should be to work toward the unification of these functions so that change is whole-hearted and not compartmentalized. Often troubles come from people's inability to square, for instance, their feelings with what they know to be true and to what they claim to be committed. If unification of the heart is a methodological principle for counselors, then they will perceive that the problem lies not just in an errant or inordinate desire in itself, but in that desire's failure to line up with the other functions of the heart.

The unification of the heart is the unification of faith; the heart's functions work in step with one another as faith in Christ has greater influence over their mutual operation. A divided heart moves toward becoming an undivided one. This leads to greater peace and consistency in a person's experience. This consistency is certainly not invariable, as we will consider in the next chapter.

# CHAPTER 2

· · · ·

# THE DYNAMIC EXPRESSION
# OF THE HEART

The point is that, for the most part,
we make our way in the world by means of
under-the-radar intuition and attunement—that we live
not so much by what we know but instead by know-*how*.

— *James K. A. Smith*[1]

Theological competence is ultimately a matter
of *being able to make judgments* that display the mind of Christ.

— *Kevin Vanhoozer*[2]

The tricky thing about human beings is that they are not readily aware of what is going on inside them. Some people are more self-aware than others, but in general, people are not actively conscious of everything they experience in a given moment. This is why they find themselves acting in ways that seem automatic to them. How many times have you heard someone say, "I don't know what I was thinking"; or, "I can't help how I feel"; or, "It was a knee-jerk reaction"? What people are most aware of in the moment is how they understand the situation now, how they feel about it now, and what they do about it now.

Why might a country boy on a visit to the city instinctively feel fear when he sees a hooded figure walking toward him on the street, when a person from the city may not think twice about it? Why might a lone hipster drinking fair trade coffee feel mild disgust as he watches a middle-aged mom loading groceries and children into her minivan? Why does a teenager look down at an incoming call from her mom and feel instantly annoyed? None of these folks consciously chose their response in the moment. All of these responses seem to arise naturally from within a person without their distinct intention in the moment. They are intuitive.

But that does not mean they are accidental. No, these intuitive responses are the active emanations of a dynamic heart. A country boy feels fear as the hooded figure approaches not necessarily because cities are more dangerous, but because he has certain presuppositions about city life, perhaps engrained in him through movies or TV news. The hipster dismissing the overburdened mom may be operating out of a value system that pits children against the finer things of life. The teenager annoyed with her mom's call is showing what she believes about her mom as well as what she wants from her. The seemingly automatic responses that characterize people's daily experience flow from the dynamic functions of the heart. As people grow in self-awareness, they begin to understand how their beliefs, desires, and commitments result in their knee-jerk responses to life.

This is the second of five chapters addressing how the human heart responds dynamically. The primary point of this chapter is: The dynamic functions of the heart express themselves intuitively—that is, as seemingly automatic responses to the situation at hand. People are often not aware of the deeper beliefs, desires, and commitments that shape the way they respond in the moment. Helping people involves tracing what their responses to life reveal about the deeper contours of their hearts.

## Intuitive Responses

As I explored in the last chapter, people function with an active heart. In this chapter, I want to zoom into these functions and explore how they work out in a person's experience—how they create a trajectory in a person's life. God designed people to live out of the deeper structures of their thoughts, feelings, and choices. By trajectory, I mean this: Each of the heart's functions—cognition, affection, and volition—has a deep, established structure that expresses itself in surface, interactive ways. It is like the solid and liquid state of water—the characteristics of the liquid are the flowing expression of the characteristics of the solid state from which it came. Frozen sewer water is not all that offensive until some source of heat causes it to thaw—it is in the liquid state that the undesirable characteristics become evident. Similarly, frozen spring water is not all that helpful to a thirsty man until some source of heat thaws it. Have you ever been at the zoo on a hot day, only to find your water bottles had remained frozen in the cooler? You are at the mercy of the vendor selling the overpriced liquid version because you do not have immediate access to the thirst-quenching qualities of the frozen water. While people may not immediately understand their own immediate responses, a bit of self-reflection will help them see the beliefs, desires, and commitments frozen deep below the surface.

How does each aspect of the heart's function specifically express itself in this intuitive design? Beliefs express themselves as interpretations, desires as feelings, and commitments as choices. To give a bit more detail: For cognition, the way people interpret a situation reveals their established belief structures. For affection, the way people feel about a situation expresses deeply held desires. For volition, the choices people make in life reveal the deeper commitments of the heart. These are the three dimensions of one intuitive response in the moment.

Perhaps it would be helpful to expound on the illustration of the frozen and liquid state of water. Out of the heart flows all responses—even the seemingly automatic ones. With each aspect of its function, the heart operates like an icy mountain cap thawing under warming conditions into a lively river. The warming conditions are the situations to which the heart responds. The solid ice is the beliefs, desires, and commitments of the heart. The flowing river represents the active responses of each function: the interpretations, feelings, and choices that instinctively flow out into the situation. The characteristics of the liquid are the flowing expression of the same characteristics of the solid state, so the immediate response is simply the expression of the established character of the heart. Frozen mountain peaks only water the valley below when it thaws.

But people are always paying closest attention to the streaming river, often not realizing that if the water that flows into the valley is problematic, they should pay attention to the icy peaks. People might not always be aware of their deeply held beliefs, their established desires, or their grounded commitments. People are usually more aware of the surface expression of their hearts than the deeper commitments. They are more aware of the way they are interpreting an immediate experience than the beliefs that have led them to do so. They are more aware of the feelings they have in a certain moment than of the desires that directed those feelings. They are more aware of the choices they end up taking than the commitments they expose with those choices. However, people can grow in awareness and understanding of their deeper commitments. The melting ice always reveals itself to those who dwell in the valley. Likewise, people's behavior reveals their dynamic heart.

Helping people seek God, therefore, means helping them cultivate greater self-understanding. Biblical self-reflection does not result in self-indulgence, but in self-discernment. When people learn more about themselves, they can then weigh their responses before the Word of God. The Word of God helps us discern between healthy, God-honoring responses and harmful, God-denying responses.

The apostle Paul recognized the intuitive way we respond in his prayer for the Philippian believers, that "your love may abound more and more, with knowledge and all discernment, so that you may approve what is excellent" (Phil. 1:9–10). Paul's thought has movement to it—knowledge results in the ability to see a situation more clearly (that is, closer to God's perspective). The knowledge of God found in the Word is received by the believers of Philippi, then expressed as discernment in the living situations they found themselves. They would need a baseline of knowledge of who God is and how he sees the world to rightly interpret what is pleasing to him in the milieu of opportunities, dilemmas, and situations of their context. Scripture does not index every type of specific situation Christians will encounter—not for the believer of first-century Philippi, not for the believer of twenty-first-century America, not for the believer of twenty-third-century China.

Situations do not come preprocessed as to what faithfulness looks like. Believers constantly face complex and shifting situations: Should a newly converted Christian wife still attend weekly services when her Muslim husband has threatened to kill her in a cultural context where he could do it? When is a man's struggle with pornography disqualifying from ministry? As Christians face these situations, God intends Scripture to deposit truths within people that then flow outwardly in response to the situations around them. In other words, "*doctrine provides direction for seeing, judging, feeling, and acting in ways that display spiritual fitness.*"[3]

Recent studies on intuition illustrate the importance of self-reflection. The concept of intuition has been studied widely, in everything from neuroscience to political theory. Social psychologist Jonathan Haidt describes intuitions as "the dozens or hundreds of rapid, effortless moral judgments and decisions that we all make every day."[4] These decisions have both cognitive and emotive elements as they process information. Haidt says if people attribute their decisions exclusively to reasoning—the cognitive processing of facts apart from any emotional disposition toward those facts—they would miss the main driving force behind why people do what they do. No one makes decisions merely from cold logic.

They make decisions intuitively, which involves a person's emotive inclination toward something. Most people do not buy the latest Mercedes-Benz merely because they have logically deduced that it is superior to other makes. They buy it because they want it for various reasons—social status, cutting edge design, differentiation from neighbors, brand loyalty—and the cognitive reasoning acts as supplement and support. People make choices not because they have made a cognitive calculation, but because they sense that it is the right thing to do.

Haidt is touching on something a theology of human experience understands in a more satisfying way: all of those intuitive impulses are spiritual in nature. An intuition—people's immediate sense of a situation—is simply the unrehearsed expression of an active heart. Intuitions are spontaneous, "arising from internal impulses or causes; without effort or premeditation; self-acting," to quote *Webster's*. People's intuitions—the seemingly automatic sense they have for what is good and bad, right and wrong, safe or unsafe, attractive or unattractive—are the reflexive responses that arise out of the deeper structures of their beliefs, values, and commitments.

A theology of human experience describes intuition as God's design that gives people the ability to respond immediately to present situations as a reflexive expression of established beliefs, values, and commitments. This means that the reliability of people's intuitions is directly related to the reliability of their beliefs, values, and commitments. Imagine if people had to labor consciously through all of the orbits of knowledge related to a simple decision like where to go out to eat—information about their budget, various restaurants' reputations or menu items, the meals they have recently eaten, traffic patterns in different parts of town. Instead, people intuitively factor in the considerations most important to them, and they find themselves thinking, "White Castle" (an unfortunate example, perhaps, since choosing that restaurant is a sure sign of human dysfunction). The same intuitions operate when people are asked an unexpected question or come across an unanticipated situation. In fact, the heart's functions are always operating intuitively, whether they are aware of these operations or not.

## A Biblical Scale of Awareness

Some have tried to capture the complexity of people's intuitive function by making a division between the conscious and the subconscious aspects of their experience, beginning most famously with Freud. Psychodynamic approaches have gotten far more sophisticated since Freud, but the basic division between a conscious and a subconscious has been largely maintained. The main problem with such a division is that it makes the subconscious something generally inaccessible to a person without sophisticated methods of psychotherapy to bypass the defenses of the conscious mind. But using language like "conscious" and "subconscious" as labels implies too wide of a separation. The psychotherapeutic methods of making the connection between the two usually do not display the kind of direct discourse that Scripture uses in addressing people, even in their complexity.

Scripture presents a multifaceted view of human beings that does not fall into this same error of division. The biblical writers maintain two important points in tension: On the one hand, people are indeed estranged from the deepest level of self-knowledge. On the other, people are directly responsible for responding rightly to God, which includes those aspects of their experience of which they are not immediately aware. Consider both points.

Regarding the first point, the language of Scripture makes reference to a depth of experience not immediately perceptible to a person. David acknowledges this in a few places. After expounding on the goodness of God's law, David makes a contrast between the comprehensive wisdom of God and his own lack of purity within, "Who can discern his errors? Declare me innocent from hidden faults. Keep back your servant also from presumptuous sins; let them not have dominion over me! Then I shall be blameless, and innocent of great transgression" (Ps. 19:12–13). The psalm contrasts God, who has no inner error and can discern all things, with David, who is full of error and unable to discern it. A similar line of reason is in Psalm 139:23–24, "Search me, O God, and know my heart! Try me and know my thoughts! And see if there be any grievous way in me, and lead me in the way everlasting!" David recognizes that he does not have the powers of discernment that God does, even regarding his own experience.

Other texts indicate this same human incapacity. The New Testament uses similar language that addresses the possibility of self-deception. The most explicit texts deal specifically with sin's tendency to blind people to an accurate self-knowledge. Jesus spoke of the inability of people to discern everything inside them, particularly the depth of their sin, when he pointed out the religious leaders' tendency to point out the speck in a brother's eye but fail to be aware of the log in their own (Matt. 7:3). The apostle John used this logic, "If we say we have no sin, we deceive ourselves, and the truth is not in us" (1 John 1:8). The reflexive "we deceive ourselves" is displayed in people thinking of themselves as without sin. This is not necessarily people's belief that they are sinless; rather, it is any self-belief that does not say the same thing as God does about how sinful they are. Therefore, John contrasts the concept of saying we have no sin with the next verse, confessing our sin to God (1:9). The core of confession agrees with God's assessment of sinfulness. No one walks around literally saying, "I have no sin." But everyone walks around unaware of the depths of their sin and in need of God's Word to reveal it to them so that they can agree with him about it.

The writer of Hebrews describes this dynamic as well, "Take care, brothers, lest there be in any of you an evil, unbelieving heart, leading you to fall away from the living God. But exhort one another every day, as long as it is called 'today,' that none of you may be hardened by the deceitfulness of sin" (Heb. 3:12–13). An evil, unbelieving heart is synonymous with being hardened by the deceitfulness of sin. It is a reflexive concept—the heart is hardened by the self-deceptive mechanism of sin, which would lead a person to fall away from the living God. The solution is for others to exhort one another—and to do so regularly, daily even. The specific focus of that exhortation is warning signs of the kind of unbelief that lead Israel to grumble and disobey (Heb. 3:14–19). This passage indicates the necessity of others to bring about self-awareness regarding the deeper issues of the heart.

This first point is simply that Scripture gives indication that people are incapable of being immediately aware of everything going on inside them, but gives no reason to believe that there is a distinct division between the conscious and the subconscious. This is why I am more comfortable with language of intuition, because it shows that there is a trajectory to human functioning—sort of a cognitive, affective, and volitional preprocessing that drives human processing in a given situation. If this is correct, then instead of conscious and subconscious, the language of less conscious and more conscious more accurately aligns with Scripture. Intuition is nothing different than people's deeply held beliefs, desires, and commitments driving their active response to everything around them. In other words, a biblical view of people recognizes that they may be less conscious of certain activities of the heart, but they are no less responsible for them. Human intuitions are the result of what they trust, what they love, to what they are committed.

The second point to hold in tension with the first is that people are responsible for the whole trajectory of their responses. Intuitions are not just automatic responses that are mysteriously forced on a person, but rather part of their moral activity. The Bible teaches that the things within people never just happen. As moral agents, people are active participants. That goes for the aspects of their experience of which they are more aware and those of which they are less aware. What many have come to call intuitions are merely the extemporaneous expressions of the dynamic heart. The following illustrations explore how beliefs, intentions, and feelings express themselves intuitively in people's lives.

## Cognition: Beliefs and Understanding

All experiences are interpreted experiences. People cannot help but try to make sense out of the things that happen to them. And sometimes the way they make sense out of something differs from the way someone else makes sense of it. I have a hard time, for instance, understanding how optimistic people think. To me, the world is always on the verge of nuclear war. To them, love will find a way. So when we read the same news article about unrest in the Middle East, I interpret it as the next step toward seeing my son drafted into the Army. They interpret it as an unfortunate but relatively inconsequential incident in the grand scheme of things. I do not get reasonable people.

This illustrates the complexity of the cognitive aspect of the heart's function. Sure, the difference between an optimistic and pessimistic interpretation of life is closely related to personal disposition, but even those dispositions are expressions of belief. People's core beliefs lead them to interpret their experiences in certain ways. A person's theories of meaning are shaped by the beliefs that most characterize him. Christian philosopher Nicholas Wolterstorff explains, "In weighing a theory one always brings along the whole complex of one's beliefs. One does not strip away all but those beliefs functioning as data relative to the theory being weighed. On the contrary, one remains cloaked in belief—aware of some strands, unaware of most."[5] Wolterstorff is discussing the formal process of weighing a carefully-constructed theory, but I would argue that people go through this same process in the countless casual interpretations they make throughout their day. They interpret a situation based not only on beliefs directly related to the situation, but on a whole framework of beliefs, many of which they are less aware.

From the early years of a person's life, human beings construct beliefs about their world, assembled into a complex (and often inconsistent) web of ideas. People have many different spheres of beliefs about many different things, and all of these understandings are more or less important to the way people organize their experience of the world. Some are relatively easy to change, such as beliefs about the best laundry detergent, favorite clothing brand, or which team will win the World Series. Some beliefs are more difficult to change, like what people believe about their hometown, their understanding of their identity, or their beliefs about God. Some spheres of belief have little to do with others—beliefs about the planetary system and beliefs about the best burger in town.

The more central beliefs people hold can be called control beliefs.[6] Control beliefs are the core convictions that carry most influence over all other beliefs—organizing them and making sense of their relationship to one another. Whatever beliefs are most active over time in people's minds will become central. This core structure of belief is the lens through which people perceive their world. People are not blank slates in their understanding of the events of life, but they interpret events through an established matrix of belief. People's experience of life events are predetermined by the structures of their heart.

Helping people understand their own experience of life requires drawing attention to the fact that their perceptions of the various situations of their lives are not objectively accurate, but rather a reflection of preestablished beliefs they hold, which may or may not be accurate.

Here is an example. Say I am trying to improve my diet and my wife pours me a glass of orange juice. This bare fact will be interpreted by me in some way. If I believe that orange juice is good for me (because of advertising or classes in nutrition), then I will understand her action as a considerate way of helping me get out the door in the morning while sticking to my goal of healthy eating. *Good call on the OJ—vitamins and energy for the day.* This interpretation depends on other beliefs as well, like the conviction that I need to take care of my body or that my wife is supposed to help me be responsible with my health.

But if I instead believe that orange juice is bad for me (because of an article I saw linked on Twitter), then I interpret my wife pouring me a glass as an act of war. All of the accompanying beliefs about my duty to take care of my body and my wife's responsibility to help me result in a negative interpretation of her action. *I might as well eat a Snickers with all the sugar in that 12-ounce glass.* My relationship with orange juice (not to mention my wife) will be different according to my beliefs.

## Cognitive Heart Response                    Situation

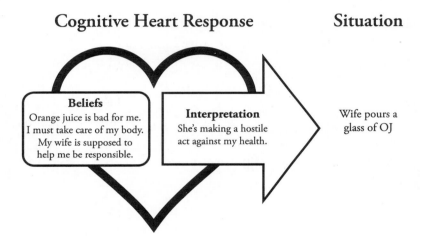

**Beliefs**
Orange juice is bad for me.
I must take care of my body.
My wife is supposed to
help me be responsible.

**Interpretation**
She's making a hostile
act against my health.

Wife pours a
glass of OJ

People's interpretation of the events and relationships in their lives is very important. How do they talk about what happened to them? What offends them or causes them discouragement? What angle do they tend to take in describing the particular problem they face? The way people interpret their experience is a direct route to what they believe about the world. Whatever waters of interpretation flow down to the surface can be traced upward to their frozen core of established belief. Once beliefs have been exposed, they can be weighed against God's Word. For Christians, those control beliefs ought to be those most directly taken from Scripture as God's special revelation, so that those beliefs he says are most important determine the shape of their thinking.[7]

Nonetheless, control beliefs are not merely cognitive propositions. If the heart is indeed interrelated and dynamic, then incorporated in those control beliefs are values and commitments. In other words, control beliefs should also be thought of as control values and control commitments as well.[8]

## Affection: Desires and Feelings

People feel their wants. Why do people experience fear when the doctor tells them that the biopsy revealed cancer? Their fear reveals a desire for bodily health. Why do people experience relief—an entirely different emotion—when the doctor tells them that the report was clear? The same desire for bodily health reveals itself in relief. Emotions are the surface expression of deeper desires and values. When I want something, I feel certain emotions regarding it. When I do not want something, I feel a different set of emotions regarding it. The beautiful spectrum of human feelings displays people's disposition, their evaluation of certain objects in their lives.

Emotions, then, serve as the gauge of desire. Negative emotions generally display either the perceived loss of a desired object or the perceived reception of an undesirable one. People become sad when they sense a close friendship is fading, and they become anxious when they gain a new rival. People feel frustrated when they do not get through their task list, even more so when their boss gives them an additional project they think should have gone to another department.

In the same way, positive emotions generally display either the perceived reception of a desired object or the perceived loss of an undesirable one. People feel happy when they finally get to that three-day weekend or when a meeting they have dreaded is unexpectedly canceled. People feel relief when they get a good report from their doctor precisely because they have gained a desired object—bodily health—and have lost an undesirable object—a particular illness.

People have tried to classify emotions in many different ways. It is difficult even to find words that capture the complex range of emotional experience—anger, anguish, annoyance, anxiety, confidence, despair, disappointment, discouragement, disgust, embarrassment, envy, excitement, fear, grief, guilt, happiness, hatred, hope, horror, indifference, interest, pity, regret, shame, shock, sorrow, surprise, wonder. Different classifications, though, generally recognize a distinction between positive and negative emotions. Anger, fear, and disgust are categorical examples of negative emotion, while happiness, satisfaction, and wonder are examples of positive.

What's the difference between negative and positive emotion? Typically, the distinction is simply what people sense as pleasant or unpleasant in the experience of it. Indeed this is true, but it fails to get to the deeper explanation of the distinction between the two: Different emotions are valuations. Emotions gauge how desirable or undesirable people find the particular situations or objects to which they respond. Negative emotions show negative evaluations, and positive the opposite.

Just as people have controlling beliefs, they also have control desires. There are many spheres of desires, some more important and some less, some related to one another and others less so. A person may desire a glass of cold water or a mug of hot chocolate, two beverages with opposite qualities. But perhaps the common control desire that links the two is physical relief—from either the hot summer sun or the cold winter wind. Regardless, depending on the circumstance, people would feel happy upon receiving the drink (and maybe a little guilty as well in the case of the hot chocolate). The things people get most actively worked up about emotionally, whether positive or negative, are generally the things they most want. These desires can then be evaluated in light of Scripture, so that they can be ordered rightly by faith.

Consider an example. Most people can only imagine what it would feel like to lose a child in a car wreck. The sheer intensity of emotion is difficult to capture in words, but perhaps what would first come to mind would be sorrow and despair. Perhaps less obvious would be other feelings, like fear or guilt. Whatever the particular cocktail of emotion, it would be intense, immediate, and longstanding. Why?

For the same reason I have been seeking to establish: because the emotions are direct gauges of what people value. The deeper people value something, the deeper the emotional response attached to its loss. So, the sorrow of grieving parents shows a desire for the child but also for the values that child represented to them: relational intimacy, the potentiality of a young life, the security that comes from an intact family. And, whether grieving parents are aware of it or not, perhaps one of their deepest unrecognized values is for a world where little children do not die. Their deep hatred of death is displayed in the deep sorrow they experience.

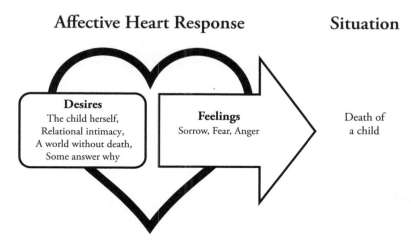

**Affective Heart Response**          **Situation**

**Desires**
The child herself,
Relational intimacy,
A world without death,
Some answer why

**Feelings**
Sorrow, Fear, Anger

Death of
a child

The agony is an indication of the love. This example shows, by the way, that negative feelings are not necessarily inaccurate or wrong. If a parent lost a child in such a tragic way, and they felt none of these feelings, their friends and family would be concerned that they do not have an accurate grasp of the situation's reality. Negative feelings can be the appropriate assessment of negative situations, as in the case of this example.

But negative feelings can also be an inappropriate assessment of situations that are not negative. A man feels threatened when he sees the sale price of his brother's new home in the newspaper. The same goes for the positive. That same man feels a quiet satisfaction when his brother admits he cannot make the mortgage payment.

When helping hurting people, a counselor listens for emotive words and observes emotive behavior. Listening for feelings helps gauge the desires of the heart. Once those desires become more evident, they will eventually display their priority as well—which ones are control desires that seem to be most important in determining the others? Those are what the counselor is after. So far, I have discussed control beliefs and control desires, but the third way to think of intuitive response is control commitments.

## Volition: Commitments and Choices

"I didn't intend to hurt you," a guy says to his now-ex girlfriend as she cries into her hands. Of course he did not intend to hurt her. He just dumped her, that is all. His words, of course, do little to comfort her, and much to frustrate her. What he is claiming is that his intentions were not for her harm, and maybe that is true. But people's intentions and choices are more complex than that; they are heart functions that people choose. The poor girl understands what the boy does not: his choices revealed deeper intentions.

A choice is the outflow of complex structures of commitment. Choices in daily life reveal those established structures of commitment. This trajectory operates in every situation, whether people are conscious of them or not. Why would a mom choose to peruse Twitter for a half hour rather than help her children with their homework? She knows she ought to help the kids, but she does not want to move. She chooses to stay on the couch. She may not consciously intend to neglect her children, but in these moments, her actions show a greater loyalty to her own ease of mind than to the good of her children. Yet, this same mom will at other times arise to comfort a child scared by the dark. She could have ignored the child and he would have eventually fallen asleep, but her decision in that moment showed a greater loyalty to the good of her child than to her own comfort.

Commitment is the heart devoting itself to something it deems worthy. These commitments are like the solid state of water, and the choices that result are the liquid state. People committed to the environment will make environmentally friendly choices in what car to purchase, what products to buy, or how much to water their lawn. Prisoners of war committed to their country will choose to endure brutal treatment rather than give up its secrets. As people understand their decisions, they will unearth the deeper commitments that drive those choices.

Human commitments form a sort of web or interrelation. Some are strong and some weak, some deeper and some shallower, some permanent and some temporary. Just as people have control beliefs and control desires, so they have control commitments that influence and organize lesser commitments. People are simultaneously committed to their family identity, their alma mater, their sports teams, their churches, their careers, their cultural heritage, their political stances, and more. These do not all hold the same level of importance or permanence. A person's commitment to the Alabama Crimson Tide should have far less influence over daily decisions than one's commitment to serving the church or community. Unfortunately, I have never met an Alabama fan who has demonstrated this. I joke, of course. But the point remains: commitments overlap, interpenetrate, cooperate, and conflict with one another. They are an untidy web, and the strongest prevail over the weakest.

An example illustrates control commitments. A friend of mine once told me a story about his father that emerged only after his father's unexpected death in a military exercise. Not long after the funeral, a friend from his dad's squadron approached his mother with a photo in hand. The image was a candid shot of the squadron, partying at an event in which many of the young pilots had received their call signs. In the background of the photo a figure is slumped over, his head lowered into his hand, squarely covering his eyes. The figure looks like a mourner in the middle of a group of revelers. And that is exactly what he was.

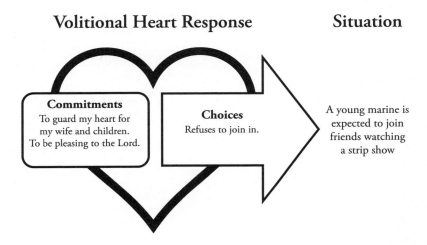

The figure was his dad. He was covering his eyes because, unbeknownst to him, the entertainment for the event were strippers. In response, his dad positioned himself in the back corner, turned away from the action. The friend reported, "Everyone respected him for it, but no one had the guts to follow him." In the midst of the social pressure and separation from his wife, what made this man choose not to participate in something so seemingly normal and expected?

This man's commitments to his wife and to the God he loved were greater than his commitment to his squadron and their expectations. His intentions were so shaped around biblical ideals that they withstood those lesser rival commitments. Had he chosen to participate instead of cover his eyes, this man would have shown that, at least in his motivation for that evening, his commitment to social inclusion or to his own immediate pleasures were greater than his commitment to preserving his affections for his wife in obedience to his God.

## Multifaceted Intuitive Response

Cognitive, affective, and volitional aspects of intuitive response can be explored separately to establish how beliefs lead to certain understandings, desires lead to certain feelings, and commitments lead to certain choices. Nonetheless, each of these responses constitutes a single trajectory. The frozen mountain top flows down in a single braided river.

As an example of how all three aspects comprise a single response, remember the angry husband from the previous chapter, the one who yelled at his wife. It is not enough to condemn his actions and feelings; a counselor has to help him understand his experience. A counselor observes the husband's intuitive responses and seeks to uncover the beliefs, desires, and commitments that lead to those responses. After enough observation, the priority of those things will become clear enough to guess at what is a control belief, desire, and commitment and what are derived ones.

The husband is staring at his shoes ashamed of why he responded the way he did and not even sure why. He does not consider himself an angry person. He thinks he only gets mad occasionally. The fury of that fight—the yelling, the kicking, the storming out—seemed so unreasonable to him afterward. By the time he had come home from the bar, he felt embarrassed and contrite and asked his wife to forgive him. But when he called the apartment people the next day and made up a story about the hole in the door needing repair, he could no longer deny something was wrong. He could clearly see his behavior as unacceptable in the cool light of the next morning, but would that guarantee him from acting that way in the heat of another contested evening? The husband could no longer convince himself that it would.

The husband is sensing that his responses flow from something deep within, something he does not always have clear awareness of in the moment. The counselor is observing those intuitive responses and seeking to uncover what beliefs, desires, and commitments those responses indicate have taken control of the heart. So, the counselor asks about the situation that provoked these intuitive responses and receives a few more details.

The evening had not begun well. Normally, the man and his wife got home from work about the same time. But this evening, his wife had been home early and was sitting in front of the computer. As soon as he had walked in the door, she had asked sharply, "Why is our checking account balance so low?" His answer had not been very inspiring—a couple things he had picked up here and there, a few album downloads, eating out for lunch a few times last week. "Come here and look at this!" she had demanded in response, "We have less than twenty dollars. We're in our late thirties and we both make enough not to always be in this situation. We can't get our act together enough to even think about a down payment on a house." After that, the man had exploded. Out of his mouth had come insults, accusations, and guilt-trips. He had raved, had kicked things, and had ended up at a bar. It was all a seamless, instinctive response to the situation at hand.

The counselor can help the husband understand what his intuitive response reveals about the shape of his heart only after getting more detail about what the man said in the heat of the moment, how he felt in the middle of it, the choices he made in light of it. In addition, the counselor would have to explore the history of their relationship, how the man thinks about money, his career, his wife, his spending habits, and many other related issues. Having done this, the counselor would then be able to make knowledgeable estimations of what might be going on in the heart that is expressing itself in such ugly ways in the moment.

The husband's response was three-dimensional. It was a powerful expression of his active beliefs, desires, and commitments in the way he interpreted his wife's statements, felt about what they implied, and chose to respond in the moment. His wife's initial question was about the state of their finances, and her follow-up statements were about their status in life as well as the dreams they shared. As the counselor explores how the man perceived her statements, it becomes clear he interpreted them as both accusations and assertions of her superiority. This was accompanied by his becoming angry—angrier than he later thought was reasonable. This led to his flash responses in the moment of using words to oppose, expressing his disapproval physically, and removing himself from the situation that frustrated him. This was the braided river of his response, but what about the solid structures from which it flowed?

The counselor begins to make connections for this man between his immediate response and the existing beliefs, desires, and commitments that characterize him not only in this situation, but in his life generally. He points out that the man's interpretation of his wife's statements as being accusatory and superior flow from certain beliefs he has about her (*She is a critical person who thinks she's superior to me because she earns more money*), about himself (*I've tried to be more disciplined with my spending, but how could I ever get out of this cycle when I never get the raises I deserve?*), and about many other things (*I spend my money on the little pleasures that make me able to deal with all the junk of life*). Those active beliefs lead him to interpret her statements without charity.

His feelings reveal his desires, so his anger is an indication of his wanting something badly. If the counselor were to ask him what he wanted in the moment, he would probably respond with something immediate to the situation—*I want her to get off my back*. But these surface wants represent deeper values. Getting off his back represents something more profound that he wants from her: respect. Or more specifically, his version of respect. For him, that respect is an affirmation of who he is and the choices he makes. It is to be unquestioned and undoubted. That is what he wants from her.

And when he does not get it, he attempts a number of tactics driven by his anger to get it. The choices he goes on to make show his commitment to himself, including his beliefs and desires in the situation. First he defends himself to preserve this respect he so deeply values. When that does not work, he accuses her in order to retain respect by contrast. When that does not work, he guilts her so she will offer some paltry version of respect as a consolation. And when that does not work, he throws a classic tantrum as one final expression of his displeasure at not being given his desires. His control commitment is to some conception he has of himself and his life, which is at odds with other commitments of the home.

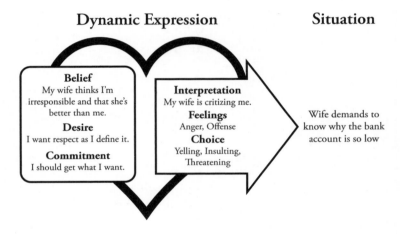

**Dynamic Expression**　　　　**Situation**

**Belief**
My wife thinks I'm irresponsible and that she's better than me.
**Desire**
I want respect as I define it.
**Commitment**
I should get what I want.

**Interpretation**
My wife is critizing me.
**Feelings**
Anger, Offense
**Choice**
Yelling, Insulting, Threatening

Wife demands to know why the bank account is so low

Counselors accomplish quite a feat if they help others come closer to acknowledging the control beliefs, desires, and commitments that lead to specific responses in the key moments of life. But simply uncovering these dynamics will not solve anything. It is a necessary, but not sufficient task in a larger process. Those control beliefs, desires, and commitments need to be weighed against what they ought to be—what God designed them to be.

The only access people have to the "oughts" of their control beliefs is God's Word, as I will show. For now, let me give a hint of how a counselor, having unearthed the intuitive dynamic going on in the husband's responses, can seek to reshape the solid structures from which the responses flowed.

The control beliefs, desires, and commitments for this husband need to be addressed with theological care. Some of his motivating beliefs may be accurate. Suppose, for instance, that his wife really is critical and accusatory. In this case, the problem with his control beliefs is not that they are false, but that they are prioritized above other beliefs than God would in the control slot. Other beliefs may be outright wrong, like his assumptions that he is entitled to a certain degree of pleasure as payment for his pain. This man needs better control beliefs, ones that flow from God's perspective of his life, such as: The labors of life indeed bring reward (Prov. 13:4), but those rewards will not bring the satisfaction people think it will (Eccl. 2:17). Even if someone else is critical of you, the response is a generous-hearted love that is not self-defensive (1 Cor. 13:4–7). Accountability is not condemnation (James 5:19–20), so someone can address a concern without it being a rejection.

The same can be said with the priority of desire. This man's control desire is for respect—specifically, his version of respect. Respect is indeed something people owe one another (Rom. 12:10) and wives ought to show to their husbands (1 Pet. 3:2), but the problem is that people tend to do two things with a genuine desire for a created good: First, they value it above what God says is of greater value. Second, they warp it into some personalized version of the genuine object. In other words, this man wants his own version of respect, and he wants it in a way not controlled by greater, Godward desires. For him, respect means affirmation of his choices; it is not to be challenged in his perspective of what life ought to be. God's version of respect is not that. God's version of a wife's respect in this situation is a willingness to help the husband lead well, which requires accountability and input from the wife. God wants this man to value other things more than this hollow version of respect, such as: A husband displays the beauty of the gospel as he treats his wife with the same care he gives his own body, laying down his personal concerns to serve her (Eph. 5:25–32). The joy found from resting in God is greater than the joy found in the little pleasure he keeps spending his money on (Ps. 16:11).

His control commitment should be clear by now. His choices in the moment reveal that he is more committed to himself—specifically his own beliefs and desires outlined above—than he is to his wife and, more importantly, to his God. His commitment to his own conception of life controls him more than what God designed people to be committed to, such as: He was created to worship God, and that worship occurs as he displays God's character in his love for others (Matt. 22:37–40). A husband is committed to his wife's good over his own and thus is marked by gentleness in his treatment of her (Col. 3:19). Growing in holiness is a greater goal than maintaining an illusion of personal respectability (Phil. 3:12). These commitments ought to control all others.

If intuitions and its control beliefs, commitments, and desires are part of human active agency, why bother mentioning them? Why not just talk about people acting and speaking out of the overflow of their hearts? As seen in the previous illustration, uncovering all these dynamics is no simple task. What makes it difficult is not merely people's intuitive design, but also the fact that this intuitive design has been corrupted by sin. To truly understand the task of helping others understand their own experience and see their need for Christ to change that experience, they need to understand the main hindrance to their dynamic hearts. The following chapter explores that thorny topic.

# CHAPTER 3

. . . .

# THE DYNAMIC HEART CORRUPTED

What sort of monster then is man?
What a novelty, what a portent, what a chaos,
what a mass of contradictions, what a prodigy!
Judge of all things,
a ridiculous earthworm who is the repository of truth,
a sink of uncertainty and error;
the glory and the scum of the world.

— *Blaise Pascal*[1]


Folks know a bad story when they read one. They can usually tell a movie is going to be bad within five minutes. A novel or a film can be bad for many different reasons, but the most devastating reason—the reason folks just cannot get into it—is when a story fails to capture the delicate beauty of human experience. Characters are flat and one-dimensional. The plot is driven by some predictable formula of outside events, not by breathing people who want things and take action to get them. The setting is artificial, not alive with the countless details that influence what a character expects from his world. People do not like such stories because they do not do justice to life.

Human experience is, in fact, the ultimate drama. Think of it. The angels of God shouted for joy at creation's dawn, but fell silent when God made his final innovation—a spiritual being with an earthen body. Such a thing had never been seen. God blended the eternal and the material into man's very being—like God and the angels, but also like cows and dirt. Adam and Eve were like God because they had been designed to represent him on earth. They were like the earth because they had to walk around on dust, from which they were made. They were the physical representation of an invisible God in this place of clay and water. Adam and Eve functioned spiritually like God—they possessed knowledge, had desires, made choices—using neurons and nerves, blood and bones. Angels were in awe.

But there is more to this drama. Like all good stories, the human drama is one of opposing forces—good versus evil. At this point, my grad school literature professors would be rolling their eyes. They would recognize the simple fact that people experience inner conflict with opposing value systems warring against one another. Remember Hamlet's morose consideration of suicide—an internal conflict between the aching desire for relief and the terror of what dreams may come. Think of the young David Copperfield wrestling with the insecurities of an abusive home, which followed him into the complexities of his adult world. These great stories explore the reality of inner turmoil.

People dislike stories without any real conflict and resolution because such stories do not speak to the reality of their experience. Human beings live their lives under a constant anxiety, a quiet threat that haunts their peace of mind. They want things deeply, but either cannot have them or are not satisfied when they do. They think carefully about their world, yet never seem to arrive at reliable conclusions. They choose who they wish to be, yet in the very choosing they remain divided. The human experience is fragmented, dysfunctional, incomplete. Inner conflict is recognized by every culture.

But in describing this conflict between one set of motivations and another, terms like good and evil assign moral superiority to one over the other. In a culture so heavily influenced by postmodernism, my literature professors are not the only ones to shy away from such labels; neighbors and friends do the same. The same impulses weave their way through our collective perspective of life: Who says that one person's internal experience relates in any way to another's? Who says that something someone else feels inside is right or wrong? People's experiences belong to them alone, right?

A theology of human experience answers objections like these. God created people with the capacity to hear from him and respond to him dynamically, and out of this loving relationship between God and people, God intends for people to enjoy each other and his green earth. But as in any good story, something went wrong. This chapter considers what goes wrong when the heart's dynamic functions are used for other purposes than worshipping God. This is the drama of good versus evil that wages in the human heart.

This is the third of five chapters addressing how the human heart responds dynamically. The primary point of this chapter is: Sin corrupts the dynamic functions of the heart. Cognitive thoughts, affective desires, and volitional choices are all moral by nature, since God designed them to be the means by which the heart worships him. Dysfunction occurs when a heart's worship design is directed away from God and toward self. Sin, much more than external action, hijacks the dynamic heart's beautiful design.

## Dynamic Corruption

Human corruption began on an ordinary day. Historic events often do not seem that historic to the people living them. In a garden long ago, the two majestic beings God had created used their capacities for purposes other than reflecting the goodness of their Creator. Adam and Eve commandeered their design to worship themselves instead of their God. Their children and grandchildren have been doing the same ever since. The corruption flows from something central to historic Christianity's understanding of humankind—sin.

The story of Genesis 3 is a tale charged with insight into the human experience as God wants people to understand it. The reason

Adam and Eve ate the fruit was far deeper than physical hunger, and the fruit left stains far deeper than a discolored chin. The outward action occurred as the result of an internal drama. Adam and Eve were living their lives as the dynamic image of God, and Satan crafted his strategy appropriately. The narrative gives insight into how the functions of Eve's heart—the ones God had designed her to use to worship him alone—were hijacked for other purposes, resulting in the original sin event.

Satan first called into question Eve's knowledge of God's words, asking her to repeat her understanding of what God had said (Gen. 3:1). Eve then repeats the content of God's previous command, showing that she accurately grasped the knowledge and also understood its implications for her conduct (3:2–3). But the serpent denied the truth of God's claim and called into question his motive for giving such false information, replacing it with a truth claim of his own: an enticing offer of even greater knowledge (vv. 4–5). He was tempting Eve with the mastery that comes from knowledge of all things, something only her Creator has.[2] The cognitive wheels in Eve's mind were turning. She was shifting her perspective on which body of knowledge was reliable. And her shifting beliefs led to a new perspective.

Presumably, she had seen the fruit many times previously, but a new desire now accompanied her vision of it. The narrator describes, "So when the woman saw that the tree was good for food, and that is was a delight to the eyes, and that the tree was to be desired to make one wise . . ." (v. 6a). This language is emotionally charged.[3] The woman had never before perceived the fruit as good—she placed a new value on the same visual information. It was delightful, desirable in light of this new knowledge from the serpent. Her shifting beliefs were accompanied by shifting desires. This desire was a further step away from God's intention for her. This value she placed on the promise of the fruit was greater than the value she placed on the promise of God's words.

These strong new desires led to a discrete choice. The connection between her desires and her willful choice is grammatically clear by a clause of result, "When the woman saw . . . she took" (Gen. 3:6). She shifted her commitment from doing God's will to doing her own. Her will was crucial, God's irrelevant. Autonomy had displaced submission.[4] This is the simple language of commitment and intent. She made her commitment, and it culminated in her action. In this way, the dynamic loop in her dynamic heart was closed. Eve had fallen into sin, and it had taken place across the breadth of her heart's function. When her thoughts were led astray and her desires manipulated, she chose to take the fruit, an intentional act of disobedience.

She further demonstrates her new loyalties by pressing Adam to the same decision, "and she also gave some to her husband who was with her" (v. 6b). Adam's sin is recorded with bewildering brevity "and he ate" (v. 6c). The narrative does not walk through Adam's motivation as closely as it does Eve's. Though he was not deceived in the same way Eve was (1 Tim. 2:14), Calvin surmises, "Adam would never have dared oppose God's authority unless he had disbelieved in God's Word."[5] Thus Adam went through a similar experience.

The effects of the sin were dynamic. Adam's report to God captures perfectly the corruption of their thinking, feelings, and choices, "I heard the sound of you in the garden, and I was afraid, because I was naked, and I hid myself" (Gen. 3:10). The sound of God's approach had once given them joy in the cool of the day, but now it filled them with a new emotion called fear. This fear came from the newfound knowledge of their nakedness, an understanding of what God had forbidden them. So they withdrew from God, a choice to turn away from him to seek safety elsewhere.

## Dynamic Unfaithfulness

Because human experience is three-dimensional, so is sin's corruption of it. Sin's corruption is dynamic, spreading to the full breadth of the heart's function. Often, sin is characterized as a failure to do what God commands—an act of rebellion, a deed of transgression. Certainly, Scripture represents sin this way—involving distinct, outward actions. But the Bible casts a vision far wider and deeper of sin's activity in people. Sin taints the content of people's thought life, the objects of their desire, the direction of their choices—the heart functions. People are aware of these out-workings to various degrees—some more, some less. Regardless, sin is constantly active in people's hearts.

The Bible constructs a complex view of sin with many shades of meaning. In all of Scripture's various descriptions of sin, people's failure to keep God's design for them is a common thread that runs through them all. God designed people to worship him with the full breadth of their hearts, and sin is worshipping anything other than God—unfaithfulness.

What is the cause, the starting point of sin? Sin begins with failure to believe God, to trust his words as true and good. Satan approached Eve to undermine her trust in God's words. The serpent first spoke to Eve, "Did God actually *say*, 'You shall not eat of any tree in the garden'?" (Gen. 3:1, emphasis mine). Bonhoeffer calls this the godless question by which "man is expected to be judge of God's word instead of simply hearing and doing it."[6] Satan knew that to undermine faith in God's words was to undermine faith in him.

The collapse of Adam and Eve's trust in God occurred in the dynamic functions of their heart. When Adam and Eve stopped trusting the words of God, their hearts no longer functioned for the purpose they were designed to function: to worship God in thought, desire, and choice. They failed to bring him glory in the way they understood their world, in the things they valued, and in the willful pursuits of their hearts. "Unfaithfulness, then," says Calvin, "was the root of the Fall. But thereafter ambition and pride, together with ungratefulness, arose."[7] And because of Adam's refusal to trust God, death touched the entirety of his soul. The same would be true of every human being since (Rom. 5:12–14).

Sin does not cognitively accept God's testimony as true, nor does it affectively value who he is, nor does it volitionally submit to his will. In human experience, this rejection is sometimes expressed as open, fist-shaking declaration and sometimes as subtle currents of the human heart trying to chart their courses around God.

Scripture consistently displays sin as dynamic. Cain did not merely murder Abel, but Cain allowed his internal desire to provoke jealousy-enraged action, resulting in a fearful engagement with God that drove him east of Eden (Gen. 4:1–16). Aaron did not merely craft a golden calf, but he allowed his fear of the people and his faltering belief in an unseen God to provoke him to it (Exod. 32:21–24). Saul did not merely kill everyone in his path in an attempt to end David's life, he did so out of a pattern of burning jealousy for his own glory over God's (1 Sam. 22:13–23; 24:9–22). The same types of dynamic descriptions occur throughout the Bible. People do not sin one-dimensionally, but three-dimensionally. Their sin was as dynamic as their internal design.

Of all the New Testament writers, the apostle Paul gives the most material for describing the dynamic outworking of sin. His description of the thinking, feeling, and choosing dynamic outworking of sin in Romans 1 is devastating. He describes those who, "by their unrighteousness suppress the truth" (Rom. 1:18). Those who do not believe actually possess a sure and sound knowledge of God, "for what can be known about God is plain to them, because God has shown it to them" (v. 19). Though people know God, they do not relate to him properly in submission and thankfulness, but become "futile in their thinking" (v. 21). Though they claim wisdom, they become fools (v. 22). All people are designed to cognitively receive a partial, but accurate, knowledge of God through what they see, but they volitionally reject this knowledge not only as untrue, but also as undesirable. Their foolish hearts are "darkened" (v. 21), which meant that God allows people to operate according to "the lusts of their hearts" (Rom. 1:24), their own "dishonorable passions" (v. 26), and their own "debased mind" (v. 28). People do not see this truth as valuable, but instead desire things that God calls evil and disordered. Failing to believe God, the essence of sin, expresses itself in how the human heart thinks, feels, and chooses.[8] Paul summarizes this whole dynamic, saying, "Therefore God gave them up in the lusts of their hearts to impurity [feeling], to the dishonoring of their bodies among themselves, because they exchanged the truth about God for a lie [thinking] and worshiped and served the creature rather than the Creator [choosing]" (vv. 24–25).

No aspect of human functioning escapes the influence of sin in Paul's description of unrighteousness. He regularly addresses the cognitive aspect of darkened understanding and deficient knowledge (Rom. 1:21–23; 10:3; 1 Cor. 8:1–2; 2 Cor. 3:14; 4:4; Eph. 4:17–18; Col. 1:21; 1 Tim. 6:5). He also frequently comments on the affective aspect of fleshly passion and corrupted desires (Rom. 6:12; 7:5; Gal. 5:24; Eph. 2:3; Phil. 3:19; Col. 2:19; 3:5; 1 Thess. 4:5; Titus 3:3). He also consistently speaks of the volitional aspect of willful disobedience and lack of submission (Rom. 2:5–8; 8:7–8; 1 Cor. 2:14; Eph. 2:1–2; 1 Tim. 1:9; Titus 1:16).

The writer of Hebrews displays the daily functioning of unbelief even more explicitly. He lays out the relationship between faith in God's Word and the intricacies of the human heart,

> For who were those who heard and yet rebelled? Was it not all those who left Egypt led by Moses? And with whom was he provoked for forty years? Was it not with those who sinned, whose bodies fell in the wilderness? And to whom did he swear that they would not enter his rest, but to those who were disobedient? So we see that they were unable to enter because of unbelief. (Heb. 3:16–19)

Notice the overlapping terms for sin: they "rebelled," they "provoked," they "sinned," they "were disobedient." All of these are summarized as "unbelief." This generation sinned because they failed to believe God's promise to deliver them safely into Canaan, and God condemned them because they were "faithless" (Num. 14:33). This faithlessness expressed itself dynamically in whose testimony they accepted as true about their chances of taking the land

(Num. 13:31–33), the grief and fear they felt as they looked across the river (14:1–3), and in the decision they made not to cross but to find their own leader to take them elsewhere (11:4). Their reason, their desires, and their intentions were the means by which they expressed their faithlessness.

The biblical writers were never simplistic about sin. Sin is not just doing something, but a comprehensive corruption of being. Out of that corrupt nature flow all kinds of sinful dynamics. As John Frame describes, "The Fall was not essentially a derangement of faculties within man. It was rebellion of the whole person—intellect as much as emotions, perception, and will—against God. My problem is not something within me; it is me."[9]

## Dynamic Sin in Daily Life

Yell at a kid, cheat on a test, or make someone feel stupid. Tell a crude joke or complain about a coworker privately to friends. These are the little actions people think of as the sins of daily life. They happen all the time. Because sin is so commonplace, people might feel like sin is not a big deal. But sin is a big deal. The greatness of human design means its corruption has devastating and far-reaching effects. In other words, sin is a big deal because people are a big deal.

Any movie fan alive in the 1980s knows what happened in *Superman III*, when synthetic Kryptonite corrupted the Man of Steel. His amazing powers were not used to bring order, but to ignite chaos—from straightening the Leaning Tower of Pisa to ripping apart oil tankers to polluting the blue oceans. No one would have cared about Clark Kent's corruption if his capacities were not so formidable. Likewise, because God designed people so wonderfully, human corruption brings devastating consequences to individual lives and to God's green earth. Whereas God originally gave people great power to spread his love and care throughout the world, because of sin they instead use this power to spread harm and suffering. Cornelius Plantinga masterfully observes, "Sin corrupts

powerful human capacities—thought, emotion, speech, and act—
so that they become centers of attack on others or of defection or
neglect. . . . Sin outstrips other human troubles by perverting special
human excellencies."[10]

Sin has far-reaching effects in all of God's green earth, especially
the human heart. Scripture shows that sin contaminates every aspect
of human experience—the deep functions of the heart as well as
their expression. The entire trajectory of function is polluted—not
just beliefs, but also understanding; not just desires, but also feelings; not just commitments, but also choices. People are corrupt in
the things they are most aware of, as well as in the things of which
they are less aware.

Returning to the metaphor of the thawing mountain ice, sin
is like pollution captured in solid form. The ice caps are not clean
and white, but streaked with a foul green. Yes, there is much goodness in those mountains; common grace exerts a preserving effect on
people created in the image of God. But sin's corruption is thorough;
the waste of a thousand pollutants are suspended amidst the frozen
water crystals. When warming conditions arise, the suspended pollution becomes active. That is how it works when people encounter
the countless situations of daily experience. Their understanding of a
situation, their feelings toward it, their choices in it will reveal what
is unhealthy in their beliefs, desires, and commitments.

Sin corrupts the thoughts and beliefs of the heart. What this
means in people's daily experience is that they believe many things
that are untrue—about God, themselves, other people, and life.
People believe that God is less glorious than he is, less relevant to
their experience, less demanding of their worship, less worthy of
their trust. People believe things about themselves that are dis-
torted by pride and self-importance. People believe simultaneously
that others are meant to serve them and that they must somehow
gain their approval at all costs. People idiosyncratically believe
that the world works a certain way and dismiss evidence to the
contrary.

Not only do people believe things that are untrue, they also misuse and misprioritize beliefs that are true. For instance, a widow might believe that her children do not pay enough attention to her. This may be an accurate belief. But she may give this belief such priority that she does not adequately dwell on other true beliefs—that her life is more than her years on earth, that she can serve others well in her present circumstances, or that the Lord is near those who are forgotten by their families. In her case, the problem is not that she believes something untrue but that she may prioritize this as a control belief.

Sin also corrupts the desires of the heart, resulting in feelings that do not align with God's values. People were made to find joy in what delights him, be disgusted by what disgusts him, be saddened by what grieves him, be angered by what angers him, and fear what he identifies as threatening. In other words, people's desires—and the emotions expressed by them—were designed to imitate God's. But sin's corruption hinders human emotions, and so people's hearts are inclined to find joy in what he hates, to be disgusted by what he says is good, to be fearful of what he says brings life. The things people value fall short of what they were designed to supremely value, and their emotions reflect this.

Consider when bosses get mad at criticism. Anger at a critical word shows their desire for employees to affirm their capability as leaders, or, to put it negatively, not to exacerbate their own insecurities about their performance as the boss. But does this desire follow the priority of desire in God's heart? Does it show that the boss's value system matches God's? Wanting affirmation is not in and of itself an evil desire, but sin twists it into a self-serving demand, and their emotional experience is shaped by it.

Sin further corrupts the commitments of the heart. People's wills are bound tight with sin, constraining their ability to choose good out of a commitment to God's glory. Their deepest loyalties are bound to self—which is another way of saying that pride pollutes everything, bending the various commitments of the heart toward the construction of an idolatrous self-image. Both superficial commit-ments (such as a person's dedication to Manchester United football) and more deeply held commitments (such as a person's career goals) are hijacked by pride and used to construct a self-image independent of God. These hijacked commitments push people to make deci-sions that dishonor God, perhaps by investing way too much time and money in following the team or by treating the needs of others as less important than this month's sales target. In people's natural state, the countless daily choices they make are bound by sin. Until overridden by higher commitments through faith in Christ, these decisions will not glorify God, build up the self, or benefit others in an ultimate sense.

Please notice my wording above. I said that all human beliefs, desires, and commitments are affected by sin's corruption, which is not the same as saying they are entirely sinful. Sin's comprehensive corruption of the heart means that the natural state of the human heart perverts each one by using them for purposes other than the worship of God. Only when God is the central object of belief, of desire, and of commitment will all other beliefs, desires, and com-mitments fall into line.

## Dynamic Idolatry

Sometimes the word "idolatry" is used so often that it can become a catch-all label for anything going wrong in a person's heart. I have witnessed counselors and pastors handle people as if every sin were always a conscious, discrete choice. These ministry leaders spend a lot of time pressing others to admit to these choices, often resulting in discouraged or infuriated people, who have not been understood or approached with wisdom. The problem is not that these minis-try leaders spoke about sin, nor is it that they used the metaphor of idolatry. The problem is that they thought of idolatry as a dis-crete, conscious choice rather than a whole-hearted inclination that expresses itself dynamically.

Idolatry occurs when the heart's dynamic functions are used to worship self instead of God by means of believing some created object will fulfill the ultimate desires of the heart and seeking it in place of God. The consequence of idolatry is that the heart takes on the blunted characteristics of what it worships.

## 1. Idolatry is dynamic self-worship.

The Canaanite fertility gods that Israel worshipped were just carved objects. Why were the Israelites so powerfully drawn toward these pieces of wood? Was it the intrinsic beauty of the image, the stellar quality of its craftsmanship? No, it was deeper than this. The Israelites believed that commitment to this god through various prescribed rituals would give them their heart's desires—fertility, safety, abundance. All these promises came without having to deal with a much-harder-to-please God who exists outside the Israelites' imagination and gives clear evidence that he could not be contained, cowed, or manipulated into giving them what they wanted. In that sense, they were worshipping themselves over and against their Creator.

Like all sin, the sin of idolatry is fundamentally a failure to believe that God is God. But the human heart is incapable of simple unbelief, in the sense that belief is absent from personal experience. There is always a replacement. People have to believe something, and that something functions as the authority by which they understand reality. In the original sin event, Adam and Eve placed God and his words with the serpent and his testimony. Upon closer consideration of where the final authority rested in Adam and Eve's hearts, Adam was repurposing the dynamic functions of his heart, transferring worship from God to himself. G. K. Beale summarizes the Genesis 3 account succinctly, "Adam was deciding for himself that God's word was wrong. This is precisely the point where Adam placed himself in God's place—this is worship of the self."[11] The heart was designed to worship, and if it is not being utilized to worship God, it will worship something else.

Applying the concept of idolatry-as-self-worship requires nuance and patience. Counselors, pastors, and church leaders should not merely rebuke an alcoholic for worshipping alcohol. At the same time, the metaphor of idolatry is powerful and accurate when describing alcoholism. Idolatry is not simple, but dynamic. Alcoholics are not bowing down before a bottle. Alcohol is merely a means for them—an object that promises something deeper. Every alcoholic is an individual, with individual beliefs, values, and commitments that are being expressed in the pursuit of alcohol. Some folks value inebriation as an escape from the complexities of life—whether they happen to be a high-functioning success in their career or a ne'er-do-well living off of other people. Perhaps alcohol is the secret lubricant of life for the people around them—drunkenness is part of the cultural fabric as a centerpiece for taking leisure, as medicine for disappointment, as the main recourse for pain. Everyone is looking to alcohol as a means of getting some perceived good without having to deal with God. When this pursuit is repeated, it becomes habitual, which means that the body shapes itself in the direction of the pursuit, reinforcing itself in an increasingly impenetrable cycle of addiction.

This whole-person pursuit becomes so automated that the motivating beliefs, desires, and commitments of a person fade into lesser and lesser consciousness. People become less free in the discrete choice to get drunk on any given occasion. But they are no less responsible because of it, since the entire trajectory of pursuit is the activity of a moral agent. In this way, idolatry is dynamic, not simple. The body and the soul are calloused and bent toward some specific object of pursuit in people's repeated attempt to rule their life on their own terms, and not God's.

This is true of the nakedly apparent forms of addiction, like alcohol and drugs, which involve certain chemical dependencies that are physically observable. But this process of habituation occurs in all sorts of pursuits, whether they would graduate to the level of addiction or not. The habits people form in their self-worship make them less aware of the beliefs, values, and commitments that lead them in the direction of a particular idol. Just like alcoholics are often unaware of why they desire alcohol so much, so are people obsessed with checking social media or eating late at night or playing video games for hours a day. The idol has become a fixation, and people become less aware of what they think the idol is doing for them.

## 2. The heart's functions take on the idol's characteristics.

In his masterful theology of idolatry, *We Become What We Worship*, G. K. Beale moves the conversation about idolatry beyond its definition to its "deleterious effects" on human beings. The primary effect he observes is that the human heart is dulled, stupefied, made lifeless, and made dumb in its spiritual capacities. The idol-worshipper, "rather than experiencing an expected life-giving blessing, has received a curse by becoming as spiritually inanimate, empty, and rebellious or shameful as the idol is depicted to be."[12] When people worship idols, their eyes and ears (as figurative of spiritual perception) simply do not work accurately as Psalm 94:7–11 and Psalm 115:4–8 show. The idols, that promise to sharpen and enliven the soul, actually blunt and kill it.

Idolatrous pursuits eventually become their own punishment. Idolatry removes the spiritual faculties from the God they were designed to imitate, and so they instead imitate pseudo-gods who have no power to grant life. Thus, people created to be like God "take on the nature of the things to which they commit themselves."[13] If people idolize sports figures, their lives take on the values and beliefs that motivate them. The same is true with a favorite band, writer, political figure, or head of industry. People look for figures that capture an ideal they are looking for, and their hearts are shaped to function like those figures.

Of course, idolatry is a two-directional interplay. People search for idols that promise the things they want, but their wants are also shaped by those idols. Before people know it, their spiritual capacities do not rise much further than the music they listen to, shows they follow, and conversations they have. And the worst part is, people barely perceive their character being mal-formed, their capacities being deadened. One of the ways people keep themselves from facing the harsh reality that they are being controlled by idols is by idol-hopping. People are embarrassed by too much dedication to one thing—no one wants to admit being dominated, since the point of idol worship is self-determination, after all. They, therefore, resist one life-dominating idol by replacing it with another with a similar promise. What sports promise people in their teenage years, their careers promise in their thirties. What one relationship promises, another relationship tries to provide when the first one fails. What one fixation promises and fails to deliver, the next fixation will gladly swear it can fulfill. People can dispose of a particular idol easily if another idol is standing by with a promise to deliver the same motivating value, all the while muting and deadening the human heart.

Human hearts, however, were designed to exude the dynamic colors of righteousness, not the muted grays of corruption. God made people to image his glory, but people have exchanged this glory for a lesser one. This exchange is the central tragedy of the universe. Fortunately, God designed another exchange. The dynamic heart is not doomed to cold, stony existence. There is a promise of restoration as Jesus, who perfectly embodied the dynamic human heart, exchanged his perfection for human's sin. God, thus, interrupts the deadening cycle of idolatry. It is the center of the Christian message. It is the center of hope for the restoration of humanity. It is the gospel.

# CHAPTER 4

. . . .

# THE DYNAMIC HEART REDEEMED

My God, what is a heart?
That thou should'st it so eye, and woo,
Pouring upon it all thy art,
As if that thou hadst nothing else to do?

— *George Herbert, "Mattins"*[1]

Scripture is timely, adapted to the varied conditions
and experiences of real people, because God is a timely Redeemer.

— *David Powlison*[2]

Life on the Mississippi can be deceptively beautiful. The glint of the setting sun on the rippling water, the smoothed ancient logs drifting slowly southward, the meandering currents playfully jabbering. The inexperienced eyes of the steamboat passengers see only beauty and romance. Meandering down the Mississippi is pure pleasure and joy. But, as Mark Twain powerfully points out, the steamboat pilot has been disillusioned of these beauties. He knows what is under the water. That "faint dimple on the river," so nice to look at for the passengers, was a "string of shouting exclamation points" to the riverboat captain, warning of a rock that could tear a vessel. Furthermore, "The sun means that we are going to have wind tomorrow; and the floating log means that the river is rising, small thanks to it: that slanting mark on the water refers to a bluff reef which is going to kill somebody's steamboat one of these nights."[3] In a world of lurking dangers and hidden corruption, the more people know about something the less they can enjoy its beauty.

This seems especially true when it comes to people. Consider the heart's dynamic corruption: people's fragmented thoughts, misguided values, and egocentric decisions. Like a steamboat pilot, the more knowledgeable people become of others and themselves, the more they know what dangers lurk under the surface of human behavior. Because the steamboat pilots knew more about the inner workings of the Mississippi than their passengers, they saw a world of lurking dangers and hidden corruption the passengers did not. The steamboat pilots' awareness of these dangers, however, also allowed them to focus upon how to overcome the potential harm. Likewise, as people look into their hearts, they learn more of sin's corruption, the lurking danger of harmful thoughts, feelings, and choices. And as they do so, they are better prepared to see their need for help.

The Bible fully acknowledges the lurking dangers in every human heart with its dynamic corruption, and yet, its pages contain a view of human beings higher than the most romantic sentiments of any other piece of literature. Human glory is not just found in what people were originally created to be—the image of a dynamic God, spiritually functioning like him in the physical world. This glory is displayed even more powerfully in what they are now redeemed to be—the image of his Son, Jesus Christ. Jesus accomplished what Adam failed to do—to love the Lord his God with his whole heart. Jesus perfectly reflected the dynamic heart of God in his own human heart. He obeyed God in every aspect of his experience, and so made it possible for human experience to be restored. Through Jesus, human experience is not just restored to its original glory in the garden. It is swept up into something even greater. Unlike the passengers enjoying the meandering Mississippi, unable to truly appreciate both the beauty and the danger of what they see, people can take an honest look at both the beauty and the danger within themselves and maintain undaunted hope.

This is the fourth of five chapters addressing how the human heart responds dynamically. The primary point of this chapter is: Faith in Christ is the means by which the dynamic heart is restored to do what it was designed for: to worship God in thought, desire, and choice. Faith is how a heart receives the righteousness of Jesus Christ and that righteousness retakes control of the dynamic design, restoring the beauty of its ability to worship God.

## Jesus's Dynamic Faith

The tragedy in the garden was not the end of humanity's story. Adam and Eve's failure to trust God indeed stains human experience and taints the dynamic functions of every human heart since. But just as every good story needs conflict, so every good story needs redemption. The antidote to sin is a fresh human experience, and the hero who brings that new human experience is Jesus. Adam failed to keep his relationship with God, and his descendants followed suit, failing to relate to God in faith. But Jesus, though tempted in a garden just like Adam, refused to listen to any voice but God's. He submitted his heart—the full breadth of its functions—to God by faith. Where Adam failed in the garden of Eden, Jesus succeeded in the garden of Gethsemane. All that human experience had been designed to do, Jesus did that night under those trees. Jesus's long walk of obedience culminated in the greatest display of faith in all of redemptive history.

This biblical narrative on the garden of Gethsemane gives readers a rare gaze into Jesus relating dynamically to his unseen Father. Jesus's thoughts, feelings, and choices align with his Father's, creating a way for all people to become sons of God. Jesus had taken Peter, James, and John up to Gethsemane with the intention of departing from them to commune with the Father, "and began to be greatly distressed and troubled" (Mark 14:33; Matt. 26:36). He then reported to the disciples "My soul is very sorrowful, even to death" (Mark 14:34; Matt. 26:38), and he withdrew to pray. Jesus's prayer time was highly emotional, for he "fell on his face" (Matt. 26:39; Mark 14:25) and was "in agony" so that he prayed with such earnestness that "his sweat became like great drops of blood falling down to the ground" (Luke 22:44).[4] The source of his great woe was the suffering and shame he was to experience on the cross, an event that Jesus knew to be the will of his Father. So distressing was the prospect to him that Jesus returned three times (Matt. 26:44) with the same request, "Abba, Father, all things are possible for you. Remove this cup from me.[5] Yet not what I will, but what you will" (Mark 14:36; Matt. 26:39; Luke 22:42).[6]

The faith that Jesus displays in the garden expresses the dynamic functions of his heart. Most evident in these narratives is Jesus's emotional struggle. His great desire was to be spared from the shame of being forsaken by God.[7] So great was this desire that Jesus repeated his prayer multiple times, fell to his face, and sweat drops like blood. Yet within the emotional turmoil, Jesus's request was based upon an understanding of who God is ("all things are possible for you") as well as a relational trust in him ("Abba, Father"). And in a remarkable, intentional effort, Jesus chooses to submit his will to God's. This is faith.[8] Thus, in the words of Hebrews, "for the joy that was set before him, he endured the cross, despising the shame" (Heb. 12:2). Jesus's desire to obey his Father and enjoy the reward of his efforts in redeeming his people was greater than his desire to be spared, and he directed his will accordingly.[9] Even in his agony on the cross, having cried out, "My God, my God, why have you forsaken me?" (Matt. 27:46; Mark 15:34), Jesus nevertheless demonstrated faith, "Father, into your hands I commit my spirit!" (Luke 23:46).[10]

The writer of Hebrews calls his readers to a faith based entirely on the faith-full life of Jesus, the "founder and perfecter of our faith" (Heb. 12:2). The dynamic faith that Jesus displayed in facing his death gives an example of perfect, human faith, but the news gets better. Jesus's faith-enabled obedience in suffering is exemplary to human faith, and it is also causative, foundational, necessary. Lane comments insightfully,

The poignant description as a whole points to Jesus as the perfect embodiment of faith, who exercised faith heroically. By bringing faith to complete expression, he enabled others to follow his example. . . . Jesus, however, is not simply the crowning example of steadfast faithfulness, whose response to God is cited to encourage the community to persevere in faith. His attainment of exaltation glory by way of faithful obedience in suffering was unprecedented and determinative, and not merely exemplary.[11]

Jesus's faith created the possibility for his followers to participate in a genuine, life-directing experience through faith. His dynamic obedience created the possibility for all humanity to experience redemption—the alignment of human hearts with the eternal heart of God. In Christ, human faith found its perfect expression. And the human heart is thus restored to follow this example.

## The Heart's Dynamic Faith

Faith plugs into the regular functions of the heart—what people think about, the things people want in life, the choices people make—and reroutes their entire day, week, month, and year. Faith in Jesus "reaches into the very soul and transforms one's life."[12] Faith, therefore, is lived out in daily life: It is not a Sunday thing. It is not an alternate state of mind people try to enter during a religious service. Faith is dynamically expressed in the way people intuitively respond to their everyday circumstances.

This is how the people of God have always lived. Hebrews 11 recounts stories of how the Old Testament saints lived by faith, a dynamic faith that restored their whole heart. Everyone in Hebrews 11 believed God's promises of a better homeland, valued that homeland more than the fleeting desires of today's comfort, and committed themselves to pursue that homeland against all opposition. Faith seeped through all the heart's functions. The author repeats the phrase, "by faith," numerous times, emphasizing the foundational nature of faith for the dynamic heart transformation demonstrated throughout the chapter.[13]

"By faith" the people of God "understand that the universe was created by the word of God, so that what is seen was not made out of things that are visible" (Heb. 11:3). This opening summary reveals the content of faith—the belief that God created the world with things that cannot be seen. This led the people of God to interpret the visible world in light of the invisible; earthly realities taken in by the senses and processed in the mind are done by faith in heavenly realities that are unseen.[14] These saints understood themselves to be "strangers and exiles on earth" (Heb. 11:13) and therefore were committed to "seeking a homeland" (v. 14) instead of taking the "opportunity to return" (v. 15); meaning, that if they did not believe beyond what was visible, their loyalties would not have gone past the borders of their earthly homelands.

Desire is strongly involved in faith, too, as the next verse makes clear, "But as it is, they desire a better country, that is, a heavenly one" (v. 16).[15] This desire was foreign to their natural values and was the direct result of their faith; it superseded their desire for other things. Acting "by faith" involves a renewed understanding of the self and the world, an affective longing, and a volitional dedication that supplants all other loyalties.

Some of the specific examples of people in Hebrews 11 demonstrate this dynamic faith well. Noah accepted as true God's testimony of what would occur (belief) and in reverent fear (feeling) constructed the ark (choice), thus showing his fundamental loyalty to God rather than the world (Heb. 11:7–8; see also Gen. 6:13–22; Luke 17:26; 1 Pet. 3:20).[16]

Moses also demonstrated the complexity of faith's dynamic. He "refused to be called the son of Pharaoh's daughter" (Heb. 11:24), meaning that he chose not to be identified with Pharaoh's family, a choice that reflected his heart's dedication to God's people.[17] His choice resulted in mistreatment alongside his people, which he valued more than the "fleeting pleasures of sin" (Heb. 11:25), a phrase that emphasizes the powerful emotional draw of the ease and comfort that Moses would have enjoyed had he stayed in Pharaoh's household. As Hebrews' author describes, "He considered the reproach of Christ greater wealth than the treasures of Egypt, for he was looking to the reward" (11:26); his desire for God's promises were greater than his desire for the pleasures of this world.[18] Moses believed in God, and his reward resulted in his affective desire for it that superseded his desire for the present benefits he enjoyed, resulting in his volitional rejection of Egypt and dedication to the people of God, even in their suffering. So many other observations of the dynamic nature of faith could be made from the rest of the chapter. This chapter shows the three-dimensionality of faith in living, breathing people.

## Faith and Righteous Function

Faith must be understood dynamically—meaning, it plugs into the created structures of the human heart: thinking, feeling, choosing. Once plugged into the human heart, faith restores its structures to imitate the righteous character of Jesus, whose perfect holiness fulfilled God's design for human experience. Righteousness may seem like an odd thing to bring up when discussing something as lively and routine as human experience, but human beings function optimally when their conduct, all the way to its colorful edges, displays God's righteousness.

That righteousness is granted by faith (Rom. 1:16–17). Jesus Christ became the author and finisher of human faith through his obedience (Heb. 5:8–9; 12:2). Believers are justified—legally declared righteous before God. But believers are also sanctified—righteousness actually characterizes their lives. Sanctification has an initial aspect being set free from the slavery of sin, so that it is no longer master (Rom. 6:6). It also has a progressive aspect, in which believers display in their lives the righteousness of Christ (2 Cor. 9:8–10). Righteousness is an animating force, made alive in the human heart by the presence of Christ himself. It declares believers righteous and transforms them progressively but decisively in righteousness, as Schreiner describes, "God's declaration of righteousness—which is a gift of the age to come invading the present evil age—is an *effective* declaration, so that those who are pronounced righteous are also transformed by God's grace;" therefore, it is rightly called "both gift and power."[19]

That power brings to life a structure dead in sin. By faith, the righteousness of Christ retakes control of the human response system that sin had hijacked. Righteous people become more human, more like themselves—that is, more like God originally designed them to be. Righteousness at work in people's hearts allows them to worship God instead of self. Righteousness is the animating force that makes the human heart alive with the presence of the resurrected Christ.

Just as sanctification has an initial and a progressive aspect, it also has a future aspect. The righteousness of Christ granted to believers finds its final completion only when they are resurrected, and thus made like their resurrected Savior (1 Cor. 15:53–56; Phil. 3:10–14). In this present life, righteousness will not characterize every aspect of human experience. Believers remain corrupted by sin morally, plagued by sin's effects physically, and influenced by others' suffering under the same conditions. Acknowledging the Bible's unblinking assessment of human incompleteness in this present life is vital. It tempers people's expectations and guides their approach to unfinished people.

The effects of righteousness in believers' hearts are sure, powerful, transforming as the Holy Spirit works initial, progressive, and future sanctification into their lives. The saints described in Hebrews 11 lived by faith in a Savior they did not yet know, and it changed the dynamic functions of their hearts. How much more can believers, indwelt permanently by the Holy Spirit, live out this dynamic faith in each aspect of their hearts? Such active righteousness displays itself in each heart function: thinking, feeling, and choosing.

## A Thinking Faith

Through faith, people begin to see the world as God sees it (Matt. 13:15). God grants Christians the mind of Christ so that they can discern spiritual truths they were incapable of discerning before Christ (1 Cor. 2:7–16). As Paul describes, the "knowledge of the glory of God in the face of Jesus Christ" shines into the heart (2 Cor. 4:6). The knowledge God reveals in Scripture about himself and his world are the interpretive lens by which people understand life. These beliefs affect people's understanding of meaning in the occurrences of their life, in both daily general patterns and life-shaping events.[20]

The apostle Paul regularly prayed for saints to be granted knowledge of Christ—while this knowledge involves more than accurate truth of who he is and what he has done, it certainly is not less. Paul prays that believers would be "filled with the knowledge of his will in all spiritual wisdom and understanding, so as to walk in a manner worthy of the Lord, fully pleasing to him, bearing fruit in every good work and increasing in the knowledge of God" (Col. 1:9–10). The knowledge of his will, spiritual wisdom and understanding, and the knowledge of God are all necessary components of a life of faith. Paul later refers to this as "the riches of full assurance of understanding and the knowledge of God's mystery, which is Christ" (Col. 2:2).

Similarly, the apostle John insists that faith involves the acceptance of a defined message, a report of truths both witnessed and proclaimed (1 John 1:1–5). This knowledge is a gift, as he says, "And we know that the Son of God has come and has given us understanding, so that we may know him who is true; and we are in him who is true, in his Son Jesus Christ. He is the true God and eternal life" (1 John 5:20).

Jesus redeems people's thinking by granting them new core beliefs that lead to an entirely new interpretation of their situations. Rather than understanding the world from a limited set of beliefs formed from the opinions of family and culture, observations made over the years, testimonies accepted as trustworthy, or the priorities of the media, the Holy Spirit helps Christians perceive the world from a different center of beliefs. Christians believe that a crucified and risen Galilean sits on the throne of the universe, ordering all things to glorify the triune God in a sweeping drama that spans all of human history. They believe that a good God makes the gracious effort to explain how people best function sexually, vocationally, relationally, and ethically. Christians believe that people are not the center of the universe, and their concerns are not the highest purpose of life. Christ re-centers people's deepest structures of belief around what God reveals as most important and most true.

When people place their faith in Christ, they dethrone old control beliefs and replace them with new ones. Christians have a battle within: old and new control beliefs play king-of-the-hill. As the Holy Spirit grows Christians in their sanctification, these new, Christ-centered core beliefs take their place at the top of the hill, and they affect all other beliefs as well. As Richard Lints aptly explains,

> When I believe in God, my way of thinking about the world is bound to undergo significant change. The shape of the lens is transformed not simply because a particular belief has been added to the noetic stock but also because this belief impinges upon other regions of the noetic structure. In that sense it may be more helpful to think of this belief in God not simply as one belief among many but rather as some kind of "control belief," since it asserts control over a vast number of other beliefs.[21]

These beliefs restore the native rationality for which God designed people. The Holy Spirit gives redeemed hearts, by God's Word, the core beliefs they need to discern truth from error in their own assumptions about the world.[22]

People who relate to God rightly by faith are becoming able to hear God's voice in his Word above the din of other voices surrounding them and within them. The Holy Spirit gives Christians an ability to undergo the rather arduous process of challenging deeply held beliefs about everything and anything. I call this process arduous because it requires both Scripture and the Holy Spirit's instigation to overcome the established structures of unbelief. The Holy Spirit uses Scripture to produce faith through regular human functioning. Faith is native to human beings; the knowledge that comes from faith qualifies as reasonable according to God's design for them. So faith should never be understood as some alternate state of mind or anti-intellectual experience.[23] No, Christians are able to hear God's voice in the regular way God designed them to think about their daily experience.

Because sanctification has an initial, progressive, and future aspect, no one's beliefs are perfectly restored in this life; all believers maintain some false beliefs, prioritize various accurate beliefs differently than God instructs, or remain ignorant of some beliefs they ought to have. Furthermore, redeemed people, even in the age to come, will always be finite in their understanding, with certain limitations to their knowledge. But redemption is nevertheless a fundamental shift of beliefs, a submission to the authority of God and his means of revealing himself. People will never understand their life the same way again.

### A Desiring Faith

Faith introduces a set of control values under which all other values are organized. Faith restores the heart to its native design to find delight in God above all things. As the psalmist proclaims, "Whom have I in heaven but you? And there is nothing on earth that I desire besides you. My flesh and my heart may fail, but God is the strength of my heart and my portion forever" (Ps. 73:25–26).

God becomes the control desire so that lesser desires do not rule the heart, and people's emotional responses to life display that fact. In suffering, believers mourn oppression, even as they look to God for refuge (Pss. 42—43). In distress, believers express their fear to God, anticipating relief from him (Ps. 13). Believers feel a newfound disgust for wickedness and a righteous anger toward idolatry

(2 Pet. 2:7–8; Ps. 31:6). Even enjoyment of earthly riches becomes Godward in its expression as thankfulness, rather than stopping with mere pleasure (1 Tim. 6:17–19). A believer's delight in God will also result in a delight for his Word above any earthly source of benefit (Ps. 19:7–11; 1 Pet. 2:2–3).

Just like the mind is renewed so that new control beliefs push out old false ones, so these new affections wage war against the old. Jesus taught that the affections were an essential aspect of following him when he famously said, "For where your treasure is, there your heart will be also" (Matt. 6:21). He knew that valuing money more than God would ground a heart from its eternal destiny. People created in the eternal image of God condemn themselves to become as short-lived as the money they love so dearly. Instead, Christ changes believers' desires so that life's joys and sorrows would not rise or fall according to small matters of personal wealth and pleasure, but they are anchored in eternal matters of significance.

Galatians 5:16–17 also describes faith as a battle of desires, "But I say, walk by the Spirit, and you will not gratify the desires of the flesh. For the of the flesh are against the Spirit, and the desires of the Spirit are against the flesh, for these are opposed to each other, to keep you from doing the things you want to do." The contrast in this passage is not between the beliefs or the choices of the flesh versus the Spirit, but rather the desires. The heart was designed to ascribe value to things external to it. The flesh and the Spirit completely disagree about which objects are desirable and which repulsive. A heart with dynamic faith will value things that God finds valuable and find offensive things God finds offensive.

When engineers changed the flow of the Chicago River, they had to flood the river with new water from Lake Michigan. The new water pushed the old sewer water away from the city, creating a new flow. Likewise, Christians need the Holy Spirit to flood their hearts with new desires, slowly turning the emotional tide in redeemed hearts. God designed people to value the pleasures of creation as God created them to be enjoyed, but in the fallenness of the flesh, human desires flow in the opposite direction: sexual immorality, jealousy, drunkenness, and countless iterations of all the works of the flesh (Gal. 5:19–21). The redemptive work of Christ Jesus, received by faith, begins to reverse the flow of the human heart's affections back toward God.

Believers do not only repent of old desires; they also ask the Spirit to help them value what he values, to find desirable what he says is good. Through submission to the Spirit, God himself becomes the control desire, shaping a person's perception of what is beautiful and good in life. This is how the fruit of the Spirit comes to characterize a believer's heart. They grow in their love for God's character, and are thus shaped to imitate him in love, joy, peace, patience, kindness, goodness, faithfulness, gentleness, and self-control (Gal. 5:11–12). Jonathan Edwards speaks of the pleasure that comes from desiring God's character to be displayed in one's own character as the exclusive privilege of a transformed heart,

> The believer may rejoice, and does rejoice, to see the image of God upon their souls, to see the likeness of his dear Jesus. . . . And if it be a great pleasure to see excellent things, it must be a sweet consideration to think that God of his grace has made me excellent and lovely. If they delight to see the loveliness of Jesus Christ, it must needs be matter of delight to see that Christ has communicated of his loveliness in their souls.[24]

Faith values God above all other objects in creation, even for things God created good. People can sinfully desire objects that are not in themselves sinful. People may value things that God himself values—a godly spouse, a secure means of employment, peace in a particularly difficult relationship—but the level of value they assign to it supersedes the value they place on God's promised presence through Jesus Christ. In other words, people may rather be married than have God's presence in their singleness. People may rather have a regular paycheck than God's nearness in a time they have to piece together an income. People may rather have an old friend be sorry for the hurt caused than God's closeness when they are alone. These desires lead to emotions that follow the trajectory of the objects they want. People may become characterized by feelings of depression in their singleness, overwhelmed by feelings of fear in their uncertain income, or gnawed by feelings of anger in their ruptured relationship.

Such emotions can take control and throw the heart off-center. People's hearts can value created things more than they value God's promises. When people do this, created things become the measure of their joy and the gauge of God's goodness to them. They begin thinking, *If God loved me, then he would* _____; or *I cannot find peace unless* _____ *is resolved*; or *God seems to be blessing him with so much* _____, *I wonder why he's forgotten me.*

Thankfully, faith does not leave the believer with off-center feelings. Faith in Christ is the check that keeps healthy desires healthy, for it orders desire for created good under desire for the Creator. What this means for believers' emotional life is that they are no longer exclusively characterized by the depression, fear, and anger that would overwhelm them apart from faith. Depression is injected with joy, fear is cut through with peace, anger is blunted by patience.

Faith in Christ does not make a person immune to depression, fear, anger, or any number of negative emotions. Negative emotions can be an appropriate response—*the* appropriate response—to a situation, since emotions are how people express their values. If a man loses his wife in a car accident, the sorrow he would feel accurately displays the value he had for her. If he were unaffected, everyone would rightly worry about either the state of his mind or the relationship he had with her. Likewise, if Christians experience depression, their feelings of depression are not merely the result of faithlessness. In the framework of their values, they may certainly be considering some things—like being married—more valuable than God's promised presence. But their feelings of depression may also show that they are accurately perceiving that life in this world is difficult and broken. Their depression just might indicate that they are learning to value eternal things in ways happier people do not: namely, a promised world that will finally be rid of the confusion, deprivation, and conflict that characterize this one. The people I know who struggle with depression often do a better job of longing for heaven than I do.

If this trajectory is accurate—that desires lead to feelings—then redemption of the heart by faith includes the redemption of emotions. Saying emotions are redeemed is not to say that Christians are only happy. Rather, it is to say that their emotional lives more closely reflect the values of God—himself supremely, and all good things secondarily.

## A Committed Faith

Along with control beliefs and control values, faith also inserts new control commitments. The Holy Spirit frees people to obey God willingly, whereas before they were volitionally bound to sin.[25] As Schnelle explains, "As a gift of God, faith always at the same time includes the individual factor of each particular person's life of faith and activates human freedom to *act*."[26] When the Holy Spirit calls people to faith in the redemptive work of Christ, a fundamental shift of commitment occurs. Before redemption, Christians were against God, but now they are under him: a willful submission of the heart both to acknowledge the truth of God and to agree with his supreme value. The new commitment results in choices that honor God. Redemption of the heart's intents, in other words, will result in obedience.

This is the necessary relationship between faith and obedience. All of the New Testament writers agree—even Paul and James— that a core element of faith is obedience. Paul said, "For we hold that one is justified by faith apart from works of the law" (Rom. 3:28) and James said, "So also faith by itself, if it does not have works, is dead" (James 2:17). Paul was arguing "against works as the basis of salvation" against "those who believed that works qualified them to receive the inheritance."[27] But Paul's letters argue that faith without good works is not faith at all (Gal. 5:6; Phil. 2:12–13;

2 Thess. 1:11–12), which was precisely James's point when he insisted that faith shows its presence in the human heart dynamically, in choices submitted to God.

The biblical writers appeal to the will of their Christian audience with the expectation that it has been changed through their coming to faith in Christ. Though faith is indeed an objective gift from God, when granted to the individual believer, it "comprises a new way of living that is appropriate to the people of God."[28] A command presents a necessary choice to be made: either submit or ignore. The biblical writers' persistent use of the imperative shows clearly that their conception of faith involves commitment and choice.

## Dynamic Righteousness from Dynamic Faith

Many passages exhibit the dynamic display of righteousness by faith, but I want to end this chapter with one of my favorites. First Peter 1:13–19 ties together all three aspects of the heart's function as it describes faith's operations. The context of this passage is the opening of the letter. In it, Peter celebrates salvation in Jesus Christ, secured for believers by God's power expressing itself in their faith (1 Pet. 1:5). This faith is proven genuine in the difficulties of their lives (v. 7) and has as its final outcome the salvation of their souls (v. 9). Then, Peter gives instruction, saying,

> Therefore, preparing your minds for action, and being sober-minded, set your hope fully on the grace that will be brought to you at the revelation of Jesus Christ. As obedient children, do not be conformed to the passions of your former ignorance, but as he who called you is holy, you also be holy in all your conduct, since it is written, "You shall be holy, for I am holy." And if you call on him as Father who judges impartially according to each one's deeds, conduct yourselves with fear throughout the time of your exile, knowing that you were ransomed from the futile ways inherited from your forefathers, not with perishable things

such as silver or gold, but with the precious blood of Christ, like that of a lamb without blemish or spot. (1 Pet. 1:13–19)

This is Peter's application of the gospel: a faith expressed dynamically. His instruction begins with a call to action. The phrase "preparing your minds for action" is the language of intention, commitment to "set your hope fully" on the grace that is coming (1 Pet. 1:13). As obedient children—meaning, willfully submitted to their new identity in God's family—they were no longer to be conformed to "the passions of your former ignorance" (1 Pet. 1:14). This phrase is a fascinating combination of feeling and thinking responses. Passion is desire, and ignorance is lack of knowledge. Faith rescues a believer from the desires that come from not knowing God.

Peter is showing how faith transforms thinking, feeling, and intentions in believers. Believers display in their dynamic functions a holiness that reflects the character of their heavenly Father (1 Pet. 1:15–17). They conduct themselves in deeds of holiness (v. 17a), accompanied by a proper affective stance of fear before the Lord (v. 17b), which is accompanied by confident belief in Jesus's personal work of ransoming them from their sinful ways (v. 18).

The human heart only works correctly when it follows the contours of Jesus's experience. His trust in the Father both models and enables human faith. Faith is the means by which people received the righteousness of Christ so that their hearts function according to God's masterful design. As we live by faith in Christ, all aspects of human experience are gradually (and sometimes quickly!) restored. Christ has provided to believers everything they need to respond rightly in the situations they find themselves. Jesus is the hope of human experience restored.

What does this look like in contemporary human experience? Imagine a teenage girl being pressured by her boyfriend to have sex. She was raised in a Christian home and was taught from Scripture that sex is a gift from God to be an act of intimacy in marriage. She considers herself a believer and wants to follow Christ. She also really likes her boyfriend Johnny—especially the attention he gives her, the social circles he gives her access to, and the peace of mind she has knowing she is not single. She manages to delay the decision by avoiding situations where sex would be possible and being noncommittal in the way she talks about it. But she knows this cannot go on forever, and she will have to make a choice. When that time comes, her choice will reflect which commitments of the heart are strongest. It is not a simple matter of commitment to Jesus versus commitment to Johnny. It is all the benefits Johnny represents to her—being valued by a socially important person, remaining included in his social circles, avoiding the undesirable situation of being alone. Is her commitment to her own desire for these benefits deeper than her commitment to her Redeemer?

If she has true faith, she has the ability to choose to turn away from sexual immorality because of a commitment to God's glory. Of course believers sin, and this girl could give in to temptation. But the point of a transformed dynamic heart means that the righteousness of Jesus frees her from lesser commitments, lesser desires. The righteousness of Jesus can display itself in teenage, feminine form, and she will be willing to part with the benefits Johnny brings. She will choose to obey. In this case, it would involve not only refusing to have sex but removing herself from a situation that makes provision for fleshly desires (Rom. 13:14). Perhaps this seems unlikely in today's world. It is. But is not that the point of needing a righteousness from Christ?

# CHAPTER 5

· · · ·

# THE DYNAMIC HEART IN CONTEXT

*There was no moment when a human being was
actually a solitary, autonomous, unrelated entity; self-consciousness
always included consciousness of one's relation to God, to each other,
and to one's place in the wider created environment.*

— *Michael Horton*[1]

Baffled hunters spotted a naked boy tearing through the forest, caught him, and carried him into town in eighteenth-century France. Victor of Aveyron had lived in the wild, presumably since infancy. He had no speech capacity as a twelve-year-old. In the 1960s, a southern California community was shocked when a thirteen-year-old girl was discovered in a local home, having been locked up in isolation since she was a toddler. Genie could not speak either, and has had extreme difficulty acquiring language and behavior skills in the years since her rescue. More recently, authorities discovered a ten-year-old Missouri girl who had never been seen by neighbors locked in a closet, weighing only thirty-two pounds. Little L. P. had no control over her bowels. History gives such mournful glimpses of what human experience becomes when deprived of its proper context. The cruelty of others has a lasting effect on the responses of these little souls. They are unable to do basic things everyone would consider human. Their personhood takes on a feral aspect, hindering them from what God designed them to be.

These examples are as extreme as imaginable, but they demonstrate undeniably a truth that is vital to everyday life: human beings are profoundly influenced by their context. The dynamic heart is strongly influenced by everything that surrounds it. God designed people that way. He structured the human heart and the human body to operate in an environment of relationships and circumstances, not in a vacuum. If babies were born into an empty space, even if basic nourishment could be provided, their brains would not develop without the sounds and touches of regular interaction, a linguistic system to shape the way they processes their experience, and the testimony of other human beings about who they are. In short, people are relational beings. And their relationality is not merely an implication of being created in the image of God but is essential to it.

Paying attention to how the human heart is shaped by the things surrounding it is a vital aspect of a theology of human experience. People respond to the hardships of life, the circumstances into which they are born, even the climate of their location. They believe certain things about themselves based on what other people say or certain incidents that happened. Even their perception of God is shaped by a number of things external to them—for instance, how other people in their lives talk (or do not talk) about God.

The dynamic functions of the human heart—thinking, feeling, choosing—are components of a response system, designed to interact with things outside a person. Just as the design of a telephone implies use beyond itself—it is a device of communication meant to interact with other similar devices and worthless by itself—so the design of the human heart implies interaction with things outside it. Thinking, desiring, and choosing beings influence other thinking, desiring, and choosing beings. Dynamic hearts are directly influenced by the dynamics that surround it.[2] People were made to influence one another, for the sake of their survival and flourishing. This is true from their earliest days and continues through adulthood. The operations of one person's heart influence the operation of another's—their perspectives, their opinions, their likes and dislikes. This is why people who listen to The Who always hang out in groups.

My point is, the heart was designed to be influenced by everything around it, and understanding that fact is vital to helping people understand their experience, in hopes of connecting Christ to the world in which they live.

This is the last of five chapters addressing how the human heart responds dynamically. In this chapter, I begin to transition to what the heart responds to. My goal is to consider the context of relationships and situations that shape a person's dynamic response. By recognizing these influences, people are better equipped to move from passive receiver to active responder. The primary point of this chapter is: A heart's dynamic response is profoundly shaped by surrounding conditions. Helping people understand how the active response of their hearts are influenced by their context is an important part of connecting their experience to Christ.

## Dynamic Hearts in a Dynamic Context: Conditions, Effects, and Responses

Consider for a moment: What makes people alcoholics? Is the cause genetic? Is it developmental? Social? Is it a matter of their own choices? Is it the vast multinational marketing scheme of commercial alcohol? Is it the tragedy that occasioned their first bout with drunkenness? All of these are the specifics of a more general question: How do external factors relate to internal responses? What is the cause of the alcoholism? The delicate interplay between what is external to a person and how it affects what is internal helps answer these questions.

I will attempt to handle this delicate interplay by describing what could be called a trajectory of influence. This trajectory is made up of three parts: external conditions, passive dynamic effects, and active dynamic responses. The first part, external conditions, are the contextual factors that create an ideal state for particular internal responses. Conditions are external to the individual's determination, and should therefore be understood as given. People, for instance, do not choose into what family they are born, what genetic characteristics they inherit, or what opportunities are available to them socioeconomically.

The second part of the trajectory of influence is passive dynamic effects: the imprint that external conditions make on the heart's beliefs, values, and intentions. They are passive in that the external influence exerts itself onto people, shaping their perception of the world imperceptibly and often without voluntary reception. A child growing up in poverty, for instance, will function from a different set of assumptions about the world than one born into wealth. These different assumptions are given, not voluntarily constructed. The more direct and extreme the external conditions, the more unavoidable the effect on the dynamics of the heart. God designed people as relational beings affected by their context. Jesus, for instance, acknowledges that others can inflict dynamic harm when he said, "whoever causes one of these little ones who believes in me to sin, it would be better for him to have a great millstone fastened around his neck and be drowned in the depth of the sea" (Matt. 18:6). Jesus recognizes that the words and behaviors of one person can have a tragic effect on others, particularly those positioned to be most influenced because of their vulnerability.

The third part of the trajectory of influence is active dynamic responses: the spiritual activity of a moral agent, determined by the individual to some varying degree of awareness. The dynamic heart is always active, response-able, and therefore responsible. In other words, as stewards of hearts created to image God's, people are culpable for their responses. Scripture addresses the heart, not the external conditions, as the direct cause of a person's response.

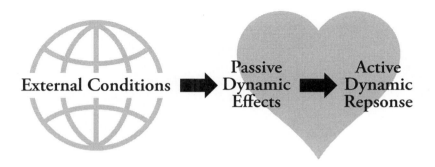

External Conditions ➡ Passive Dynamic Effects ➡ Active Dynamic Repsonse

This trajectory of influence occurs in extreme ways, like the opening examples illustrate, as well as in subtle ways. Some conditions have lesser influence, and some more. Getting cut off in traffic on the way to work would normally have a relatively low amount of influence. The conditions would create a state where some form of anger is more likely to occur, but the situation happens briefly, anonymously, and with little effect on a person's body other than a quickened pulse. Getting car-jacked is a different story. The alarm of being pulled from his vehicle, the threat of bodily harm, the shame of being left standing in the middle of a busy intersection is an extreme condition that will have lasting effects on his sense of safety. The lingering dynamic effects will likely include experiences like increased anxiety, difficulty sleeping, and even flashbacks. These dynamic effects are not caused by the victim of the car-jacking. They are passive imprints that put shape to what the victim is responsible for: their active responses to life from that point forward. For the car-jacking victims, a counselor helps them discern the difference between the passive effects and the active response. Victims should feel no guilt for the invasive thoughts and stalking fears that come from the situation, but neither should they passively allow these effects to control their responses. It is a delicate process.

Conditions are a vital consideration for ministering wisely to others, especially in more extreme cases. They are necessary for understanding heart responses with greater specificity and accuracy.

Seeing the distinction between external conditions, passive dynamic effects, and active dynamic response does not take away a person's culpability. Rather, it clarifies the phenomena and gives a clearer path to faithful response.

I will follow up that traumatic example with a more mundane one to illustrate my point and show its usefulness in caring for others. My wife is from a small town cushioned in the quiet fields of Indiana. Her parents' property adjoins a small farm with small horses, mini-horses to be exact. My kids love to feed these horses through the fence with the long grasses that border the property. They also know that the number one rule is that they must not climb the fence into the horse corral. I love them too much to see midget horses trample them.

A parenting dilemma arose on a springtime visit. One of our daughters rushed into the house, tearfully confessing that she had climbed the fence into the horse corral. We were immediately confused because this daughter, for whatever reason, loves rules. She is a queen bee who loves order in a chaotic world. I knew right away that some other factor had to be in play.

I asked her to tell me what happened, and she described the conditions it took to get her over that fence: My kids had been looking at the horses near the fence when their older, cooler cousins came over to play. These cousins are outdoorsman, comfortable anywhere, and they suggested a quick climb over the fence. My daughter resisted, citing the rule. Her cousins, however, pressed her with how fun it would be. Again, she said no. They pressed her again, but this time with the most devastating logic possible, "We thought you were our friend." Persuaded, she climbed the fence, set one foot on the other side, and promptly climbed back over to run to the house proclaiming her transgression.

Thus, the parenting dilemma: does my daughter get punished for climbing the fence? That question is really the practical outworking of a prior question: What was the cause of her breaking that rule? Was it her own choice, or was it her cousins' pressure? External conditions and active responses are in delicate interplay here, and wise parenting will address both.

On the one hand, the conditions brought about behavior that would not otherwise have happened. I would bet my life savings (which is not much) that my daughter would not have climbed that fence had her cousins not shown up that day. The unique pressures that led to my daughter's disobedience include a few factors. The cousins were local, more familiar with the territory, and thus had more knowledge than my daughter about the horses. They were older and able to wield the influence of their age. And perhaps strongest of all, she did not get to see them much and knew they wanted to play on the other side of that fence. Without these conditions, my daughter likely would have been content to follow the rules and keep trying to feed the uninterested horses. It is right for me to acknowledge that with her.

On the other hand, the cause of my daughter's climbing the fence was her own choice to do so. No one took control of her choices, sending neurological signals to her arms and legs against her conscious will, causing her body to climb a fence. She voluntarily participated in breaking the rule meant for her safety and happiness. She needs to be held accountable for her behavior with the appropriate punishment.

Considering this trajectory of influence is vital for me to serve my daughter well in this situation. If I simply punished her behavior in this situation, I might sweepingly conclude, "You climbed the fence because you wanted sin more than you wanted God." This statement is true in a generic way—like saying someone fell off the roof because of gravity. But it is too generic to be helpful. Instead, acknowledging the external conditions helps me better explain her internal responses. I want her to have a deep understanding of her heart in that situation so that she can have a greater appreciation of her need for grace.

As my daughter and I talked through what happened, she realized that the conditions had exposed certain things in her heart. She did not disobey because she wanted to break a rule. For her, in that situation, her disobedience came from a heart more concerned with how her cousins felt toward her than with trusting her dad and, by extension, the God who gave her a dad to protect her. She valued the opinion of her cousin more than the instruction of her dad. By acknowledging conditions, she was able to see better why she chose to climb the fence.

Those who want to help others in personal ministry need to acknowledge this trajectory of influence. They must learn to recognize conditions as those external factors that create an ideal state for particular internal responses, then detect what they are in real-life situations. This interplay between the dynamic heart and its dynamic context is delicate and not easily discernable. But knowing the three-part distinction between external conditions, passive dynamic effects, and active dynamic responses will help. The reason this task is so important is that it allows us to apply theology wisely to human experience. In caring for others, a wise counselor will learn to read how strongly certain conditions have influenced people's responses, and advise them appropriately.

### Embodied Conditions

So far, I have spoken of conditions primarily as those external contexts that surround people. But in a book about human experience, I must address the basic fact that part of all people's situation is their God-given physical body. God designed the dynamic heart to function within a physical body—the immaterial and the material beautifully woven together so that unseen spiritual activity correlates with observable physiological activity. People are psychosomatic unities.[3] This means that spiritual activity is expressed by means of the body, but the body also conditions spiritual activity. I wish to show in this section that people must steward their heart responses in part by maintaining awareness of bodily conditions unique to them.

I have tried many ways of diagraming how the spiritual activity of the dynamic heart relates to the body. If I diagram how cognitive, affective, and volitional functions relate to one another (as I do on page 17), where would I put the physical body? I think the best solution is to consider the paper on which the diagram is printed as the body. The page readers can touch and tear is the necessary platform for the concept to be expressed.

People's bodies are both a part of who they are as well as the circumstances they have been given. People do not personally determine the most significant characteristics of their body. From hair color to mental capacities, people do not choose the features of their bodies, but their bodies are subject to God's providence and the fall's corruption.

When considering bodily realities as part of the conditions of a person's experience, counselors should recognize, at the very least, how age, personality, and mental/physiological capacities may be significant factors in how people are responding to their present situation. In each of these areas, a person will have some intact features that, because of common grace, function properly according to God's creational design as well as some defective features that, because of the corruption of a fallen world, fail to function according to God's creational design. So for each of these areas, a counselor considers, *what unique realities does this person have to respond to? What is functioning according to God's creational design and what is not?*

**Age.** For age, these realities change with time. An adolescent boy faces hormonal and social realities quite different from the seventy-year-old married man. The teenager is faced with the challenges of rapid bodily transition, the awakening of new physical urges, and the awkwardness of disproportion. For his part, the seventy-year-old married man faces the financial and health implications of an aging body, the loss of basic abilities he once assumed, and new types of pain that are not accompanied by the youthful hope of conquering. The adolescent boy is facing the difficulties of stewarding his potentiality, the old man of stewarding his legacy. People should be approached differently according to the present circumstances of their stage in life, as seen modeled in Scripture (Titus 2:1–5).

**Personality.** Entire industries try to classify the different characteristics of people's behavior and thought. No two theories agree entirely on how to classify personalities or on how those personalities are exactly formed (cue the whole nature/nurture debate). These tests may provide helpful insights into tendencies people have in approaching the world. For instance, the Meyers-Briggs Type Indicator is a popular test for schools to use in their career guidance department. Like all tests, it is based on certain theories of personhood; in this case, Jung's four principle psychological functions. The deficiencies of the test are the same as the deficiencies in the theory. The tests may describe people well in a general sense. For example, I was labeled ENFJ, with a recommended career either as an educator or as clergy. I do both. However, the tests cannot describe the core of who people are as a moral agent before God.

At best, these tests describe the style with which people tend to approach the world, but they do not establish a determined trajectory of those responses. Personality is important for the counselor to consider because it is the shape of their counselees' spiritual response—the way they tend to think, the way they tend to feel, the way they tend to make decisions. Some folks tend to be highly relational and able to understand the experience of others, but they cannot process theoretical information well. Others can retain impressive amounts of information, but have little creative capacity. Some are quick to make decisions; some are slow. Some are task-driven; others are relationship-driven.

These tendencies are, at least in part, given. I have five children, and each emerged with different personalities. Each one was designed to know and love God, but how that love will express itself will be unique to each. By unique, I mean unique in expression. One may love God as a person who tends toward quiet reflection, another one as a person who is always looking to accomplish the next task, and still another as a person who loves to chatter on about the joy of life. My parenting has to account for these unique forms.

Counselors similarly adjust their approach upon understanding these unique tendencies. They help people see how the condition of their personality can be used in ways that glorify God or in ways that do not. One personality is not any more righteous than another in itself; it is all in how that personality is uniquely directed by faith to display the righteousness of Jesus Christ.

**Mental and Physiological Capacities.** For mental and physiological capacities, a counselor or caregiver needs to consider the unique stewardship each individual has been given. They should seek to understand both the capacities and incapacities that make up a person's embodied condition. Some folks have high mathematical and logical intelligence, and others have high body and kinesthetic intelligence. Some are skillful at building relationships; others are skillful at building visually beautiful structures. Some people's brains function in the range of normal, others' do not. Whether that is a native capacity or one affected by the conditions, the reality nevertheless stands. A counselor should not assume everyone is capable of the same responses at the same pace, as if everyone has the same set of capacities and incapacities.

Applying the question of what conditions are intact and what are defective requires counselors to acknowledge that God's masterful design of the human brain was corrupted by the same futility that marks the rest of this dysfunctional world. Though faith restores the heart to respond in worship to God, people still await the new creation when corruptible bodies are made incorruptible (1 Cor. 15:35–56). An obvious example of this would be individuals with Down syndrome. A chromosomal condition means that they are given certain mental incapacities. No one can be counseled out of Down syndrome. But people can be counseled to respond in faith according to the capacities and incapacities given to them. For some of my friends with Down syndrome, their capacity to understand and respond to Scripture is high, and their caregivers help them understand what types of behaviors or words are honoring to God and what are not. Others with more severe forms will have a much more limited range of possible response. Part of people's dignity before God is their responsibility before him, yet God knows the limits of their capacity in a fallen world.

While the case of Down syndrome is clear because it is physically observable in everything from facial features to chromosomal makeup, other physiological conditions are less clear because they are less physically observable. These conditions are what culture typically refers to as mental illness, which includes many different categories of disorder, from psychotic to personality. I believe that physiological dysfunction happens to spiritually functioning beings. Both sides of the equation are vital to maintain. On the one hand, mental illness is a conceptual construct describing patterned abnormalities in mental and emotive states, dispositions, and behaviors that commonly occur in association and suggest strong physiological influence. On the other hand, mental and emotive states, dispositions, and behaviors are inescapably spiritual in nature.

Extreme patterns of mental, emotional, or behavioral problems are not either spiritual or physical. They are both, though I recognize a sliding scale of influence. I can appreciate how a diagnostic schematic like the DSM-5 at times accurately describes physical symptom clusters and gives some direction to appropriate medical intervention. Insofar as the DSM-5 or any other diagnostic scheme helps accurately identify how physical conditions are defective of God's designed order, these schemes may help identify what unique physiological factors are distinct in this person's experience from what others may experience. Some troubles may be more neurologically engrained, thus requiring close medical attention, such as those troubles that fit under the label neurodevelopmental disorders or schizophrenia. Other troubles involve relatively normal neurological function, but they are conditioned through repeated use for disruptive purposes, such as many of the impulse-control or conduct disorders, like oppositional defiant disorder or internet gaming disorder.[4]

Nonetheless, the DSM-5 and the like fall short in describing physiologically verifiable trouble in two important ways: First, the diagnosis is based on theory that does not include a theological vision of humanity, which understands people to be active spiritual agents made to reflect the righteous personhood of an unseen God. DSM-5, therefore, defines dysfunction primarily in terms of what is distressing to the individual or harmful to others. The observations are not simple, bare acknowledgments of truth, but interpreted according to a framework of belief. That is not a problem in itself, of course. However, the short-sighted beliefs of any culture constantly change, thus shifting opinion of what should be considered distressing or harmful. Second, no amount of neurobiological ingenuity in medical treatment can overcome the corruption of living in a fallen world. Physiological troubles will never be eliminated in this world, but Christians can respond to them in faith.

In summary, a theology of human experience needs to take seriously the possibility of defective mental conditions so that the dynamic functions of the heart can be addressed realistically. The dynamic expression of faith will look different in every person, and those suffering from unique physical deficiencies will need unique compassion. Realistic expectations, appropriate to the given conditions, help counselors love people well through the change process. Being aware of physiological conditions helps establish appropriate expectations. The response of faith does not completely neutralize the physiological condition, but it gives hope for establishing new patterns of action that, for embodied creatures, brings more stability than would otherwise be. This is hopeful news for people waiting for their broken bodies to be made new on that future day when Jesus returns. Complete healing will not occur before that bright day. Waiting is not passive resignation to present conditions; rather, it is active determination to seek promised grace despite them. Jesus loves those burdened by various forms of mental illness, and his grace is sufficient for them to respond to him in faith, even in the turmoil of their experience.

## The Contexts of Human Response

Understanding people's conditions is a vital consideration in helping them see how they are called to uniquely glorify God in the distinct situation where he has placed them. Ministering to others as if conditions are not a significant factor in their experience is an unbiblical form of Gnosticism that denies the goodness of God's creation. Gnosticism treats human beings as if life in the physical body, positioned in a particular life situation, were a separate consideration from some sort of spiritual existence or true self. Gnosticism acts as if people should act from an independent platform of self-direction, uninfluenced by any external reality.

The Bible gives a far more satisfying understanding of people. To be a person is to be in communion with other things. This was true from the very beginning of human experience. Adam and Eve awoke from their creation immediately aware that their surroundings involved a number of different pieces that interacted with one another. The first thing that happened to people was God interacting with them, and their receiving his instruction (Gen. 1:28). Through this interaction, God made them aware of their surrounding circumstances, the purpose of their own presence within those circumstances, and their relationship with one another. Creation belonged to them to care for as representatives of God in cooperation with one another. They were designed to respond to God with an accurate understanding of self, of one another, and of the circumstances in which they had been placed. Adam and Eve never understood themselves apart from their relationship to everything else. To be human is to be in context.

*Section 2*

# The Context
# of Human Experience:
## What the Heart Dynamically Responds To

To continue this celebration of human experience, I now turn attention from *how* the heart dynamically responds to *what* the heart is responding to. The goal of this book is to equip caretakers to understand the experience of those they are helping. Understanding the heart's internal response system is not enough. We also have to pay attention to the external factors that are unique to every individual. This section will explain how the dynamic heart interacts with the various components of a person's situation. Helpers need to take an honest look at the interchange between the two in order to give insightful guidance. What people respond to can be roughly categorized as four components: The dynamic heart responds to God, to self, to others, and to circumstances. These four contexts are vital to recognize when considering a person's experience of the world.

The most important context of the heart's response is God himself. A. W. Tozer got it right when he said, "What comes into our minds when we think about God is the most important thing about us."[1] The heart was custom-made for worshipping God, and the closer it comes to that design, the better it works. In fact, when the heart responds rightly to God, it will respond rightly to everything else. People were created to worship God in thought, desire, and choice.

The remaining three contexts—self, others, and circumstances—are where a heart daily operates in the visible world. Regarding self, people operate out of a sense of identity, a perception of who they are and what role they ought to play. What people believe about themselves, the values by which they measure themselves, and their personal commitments make up their identity and determine how they respond to life. Change in people's lives occurs in part through addressing their sense of identity.

Regarding others, people are both influenced by and exert influence on others. God designed people this way as relational beings whose dynamic functions exert evident effect on one another. Helping people change requires considering key relational influences on their life.

Finally, regarding circumstances, people are shaped by the events and situations in which they find themselves. Significant, memorable events shape how people perceive the world, as do the countless invisible factors of people's existence, like their socioeconomic or cultural situation.

The next four chapters are dedicated to each of these contexts respectively. Unpacking someone's experience, then measuring it according to Scripture's categories requires considering the beliefs, values, and commitments of the heart as expressed in these contexts.

# The Dynamic Heart in Relationship

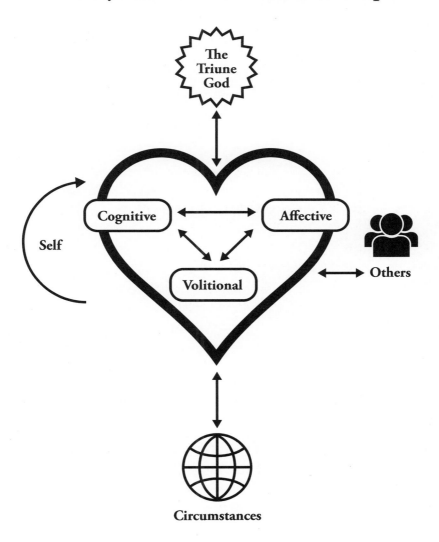

# CHAPTER 6

. . . .

# GOD AND WORSHIP

Ah my dear angry Lord,
Since thou dost love, yet strike;
Cast down, yet help afford;
Sure I will do the like.

I will complain, yet praise;
I will bewail, approve:
And all my sour-sweet days
I will lament, and love.

— *George Herbert, "Bitter-sweet"*[1]

The world becomes a strange, mad, painful place,
and life in it a disappointing and unpleasant business,
for those who do not know about God. Disregard the study of God,
and you sentence yourself to stumble and blunder through life
blindfold, as it were, with no sense of direction,
and no understanding of what surrounds you.
This way you can waste your life and lose your soul.

— *J. I. Packer*[2]

God is like the dawning sun over the eastern sea. Every morning it emerges in precisely the same way, yet no two sunrises are exactly alike. On some days, the sun emerges to display its hot potential immediately, clear and distinguished in a cloudless sky. The water reflects its intensity from the outset, rolling out before it a dazzling carpet of light. Morning shouts for joy on such days, without a bit of subtly to the sun's introduction.

On other days, the sun announces itself sideways—in the pink and orange fingers of peripheral light, caught by the underside of scrolling clouds that hang silently across the horizon. The sun is most playful and clever on these days, bouncing its emerging light off the deep dimensions of the atmosphere, which comes alive with ethereal color. Morning sings on such days, the sun seeming most concerned with displaying its capacity for delicate beauty rather than triumphant heat.

On still other days, the sun is almost a background presence, discernable, but only by the gradual realization that the sky is slightly less dark than it had been. Deep purple is slowly diluted into a softer pink. Eventually the sun becomes distinguishable only as a vague orb, able to be directly gazed into because of the thick veil covering it. You notice the sun's quiet approach only long after it has been present. Morning merely lingers on such days. It seems an entirely different sun from those bold or playful mornings.

The varying dawns are a fine illustration of how God relates to his creation, and specifically to people. The sun remains fixed in the center of the solar system. Its core still burns with the same incalculable combustion. The temperature of the sun does not change. So why does its temperament change in the differing dawns? The sun's essence does not change. The conditions do. To be more specific, the sun's immutable presence is simply responding to variable conditions.

Why is this observation of God's interaction with the world important for a theology of human experience? How God interacts with his creation is central to a biblical theology of human experience, since people were created to reflect his personhood in theirs. God made human hearts to function in the same way his does.

This is the first of four chapters addressing the contexts to which the dynamic heart responds. The purpose of these chapters is to equip counselors and caregivers to understand the experience of the folks in their care. The primary point of this chapter is this: The dynamic heart was made to imitate God's. As people respond in faith to God, they take on the shape of his character in the way they think, in what they want, and in the choices they make. Caring for people involves addressing how their heart is relating to God.

## God's Experience Is Unlike Ours in Many Ways

The similarity between God and his image is, of course, not total. Any discussion of God's experience is directly related to a discussion of his attributes, which theologians helpfully classify as either communicable or incommunicable. God shares his communicable attributes with people: wisdom, love, holiness, and so forth. God does not share his incommunicable attributes with people: eternality, independence, omniscience, and so forth.

People must understand God's experience as outside their immediate ability to imitate because of his immutability, omniscience, and independence. God's immutability means his character is unchanging, unlike people's. He does not vacillate, as if he might approach things differently on any given occasion. Nor does he develop, as if he were not always at his fullest potential. God is solidly, squarely, wonderfully the fullest breadth of who he was, who he is, and who he will always be. Biblical writers appeal to the unchanging, independent character of God as reason for great confidence in him (Num. 23:19; Ps. 102:24–28; 2 Tim. 2:13; James 1:17).

God's stable character is foundational to how people relate to him. God's immutability means people enjoy relational stability with him. In fact, God's unchanging stability undergirds the very concept of relationship. Even when creation is thrown into tumult—including personal circumstances—God remains confidently untouched and in charge. God's faithfulness does not change according to human faithlessness. God will not change his gospel, but will lend every grace for the journey to the lasting city. People may confidently approach God in faith, knowing he will not be in a foul, ungenerous mood.

Unlike people, God's character cannot change, for it is perfect and complete. Unlike God, people are dependent beings and are therefore in need of various aspects of creation—physical provision, personal relationships, regular use of their brains, communicable languages—in order to express their personhood. And, unlike God, those factors influence and steer the formation of their personhood as their heart actively responds to them in various ways. So, people's characters change as they respond to the things around them—everything from God to other people. As created beings, people are dependent upon and therefore influenced in their personhood by God and his creation.

God's omniscience means that, unlike people, God has immediate access to the full breadth and depth of who he is. He understands immediately his own experience in ways people do not understand their own. God understands himself completely whereas people are often a mystery to themselves and to others. God dwells in perfect command of himself, for his experience is the direct emanation of his omniscience, omnipotence, and omnicompetence. He immediately and accurately understands the plethora of his own responses to the countless situations occurring in the world he has made. God's understanding is complete, seeing every angle and context. His decisions are beyond human ability to assess (Isa. 40:28; Rom. 11:33). Unlike people, God is unlimited in his capacity, capable of having an infinite number of experiences simultaneously. People are limited to a singular experience. They can have mixed emotions or a multitude of scattered thoughts, but there is still a single stream of consciousness running through their minds, but people cannot limit God to their conscious experience, constrained by their finite capacities.

Finally, God's independence of his creation means his activities are not merely responses to his creation. The Trinity existed in joyful, dynamic fellowship long before they formed the seas and land. He had a personal history prior to anything we can now see or imagine. God functions independently from creation; his interaction with it is only part of his experience. He has a set plan independent of creation, one that orchestrates all of creation's unfolding. God's determination is prior to creation's input and response, both chronologically and relationally. He made choices before there was anything existing to respond to (Eph. 1:4), and he has no counselor whose input he needs to make decisions (Job 36:22–23; Isa. 40:13; Rom. 11:34; 1 Cor. 2:16). Human beings are always responding to God, but he is not always responding to them. He was around far before people were, and has dealings with things far beyond human imaginations.

Despite the differences between people and God, the unchanging, omniscient, and independent God has genuine interactions with his creation according to his personhood. Isaiah 57:15 says, "For thus says the One who is high and lifted up, whose name is Holy: I dwell in the high and holy place, and also with him who is of contrite and lowly spirit, to revive the spirit of the lowly, and to revive the heart of the contrite." The dynamic God meets with his dynamic image bearers. He draws near to people, and the following section considers how people are like God in their experience.

## God's Experience Is Like Ours in Many Ways

Scripture also describes God as relating in different ways to different circumstances. The way he interacts with his creation is dynamic. Like the rising sun relating to varied atmospheric conditions, God genuinely responds to the various situations in his creation. This dynamism of God gives important insight into the human heart's dynamism. The way God functions in relation to his creation is a paradigm for how people function as his image within his creation.

In Exodus 32, the narrator presents an exchange between God, who is angry and intent on destroying Israel, and Moses, who intercedes on Israel's behalf. This passage is a good example of how God functions in relational response to his people. God had invited Moses up to Mount Sinai to give him the law, and the people impatiently and lustfully built a golden idol. "And the LORD said to Moses, 'I have seen this people, and behold, it is a stiff-necked people. Now therefore let me alone, that my wrath may burn hot against them and I may consume them, in order that I may make a great nation of you'" (Exod. 32:9–10).

Notice the complexity of God's response. First, "I have seen" (v. 9). God observes the actions and hears the words of the people. He draws a rational conclusion regarding them: they are "stiff-necked" (v. 9), which is a negative moral judgment of the type of people they are based upon the evidence of their behavior. This aspect of his response is the paradigm for human thinking—the ability to utilize a rational process of observation and reasoning toward a conclusion.

God displayed strong emotion in response to what he saw. His moral judgment was not just a coldly reasoned conclusion but also a hotly felt passion. God said, "My wrath may burn hot against them" (v. 10). God's deeply held value for his own holiness resulted in strong emotion. If he did not care so deeply for his own holiness and his people's sharing in it, then his response would not have been so strong. This aspect of God's response is the paradigm of human feeling—the ability to desire something and display it in their emotions.

In addition to his reason and his emotion, God's response included his intention: he planned to take action based upon the conclusion he drew and how he felt about it. God concludes, "Therefore let me alone . . . [that] I may consume them" (v. 10). His response was completed with a coordinating act of the will. In response to what he concluded to be wrong, the emotional energy he felt from the wrongness, God also intended to do something in response. God's intention is paradigmatic of human volition—the ability to choose or determine action.

Moses understood that within God's response was a reasoned perspective accompanied by an emotive response and a determined intention. In fact, in acknowledging God's emotive response, Moses asks him to call to mind a different thought that might change his intention. Moses pleads with God, saying, "Turn from your burning anger and relent from this disaster against your people. Remember Abraham, Isaac, and Israel, your servants, to whom you swore by your own self, and said to them, 'I will multiply your offspring as the stars of heaven, and all this land that I have promised I will give to your offspring, and they shall inherit it forever'" (Exod. 32:12–13).

Notice how the conversation between God and Moses was genuinely interactive. God was not playacting. The timeless God was genuinely relating to the timely situation according to his unchanged internal character. Since God's internal experience infinitely transcends people's, the biblical writers describe his internal experience in ways more suited to people's finite version of that experience. God is described anthropomorphically[3]—biblical writers use language to describe God that accommodates human's finitude.

So for instance, the passage continues, "And the LORD relented from the disaster that he had spoken of bringing on his people" (Exod. 32:14). It appears by this conversation that Moses introduces a bit of information that the Lord had not properly weighed in his reasoning—namely, his promise to Abraham, Isaac, and Israel to multiply their offspring and not to destroy them. However, other portions of Scripture teach that God cannot change his mind like a man, "God is not man, that he should lie, or a son of man, that he should change his mind. Has he said, and will he not do it? Or has he spoken, and will he not fulfill it?" (Num. 23:19). Saying that God changed his mind was the biblical writer's way of describing God as a being who thinks, feels, and makes decisions in a way that is like the way people do these things, but unlike them in their finite capacity.

Notice also the simple fact that Moses knew how to interact with God. Moses did not need an alternate language or alien state of mind to interact with his Creator. Moses had all the skills he needed as a human being to have meaningful interaction with God. Moses's automatic and immediate response to God indicates his familiarity with the various factors at play in God's response. Moses assumed that the general way he functioned would make sense to God, just as God made sense to him. Moses could relate to God's complex response because he was made to function the same way. As previously discussed, God designed Moses's heart theomorphically:[4] the functions of the human heart are reflective of divine internal functions.

The dynamic heart as instrument of thought, desire, and choice is analogous to God's internal experience, and therefore a reliable means of knowing him. This claim is no small thing. At one point in church history, some thought it blasphemous to claim the ability to know the almighty, inconceivable God. Aquinas countered this mystic conception by the idea that there is some definite level of correspondence between the mind of God and that of human beings. He called this correspondence *analogy*, a concept that unpacked further Augustine's teaching on the relatability of God.[5] Augustine believed that there was a correspondence between the human spirit and God because people were made in God's image. This is precisely the doctrine upon which the knowability of God rests: People were created with corresponding functions that allow them to relate to God, and more than that, to imitate him. People's entire experience of daily life rests on this wonderful doctrine: they can understand and relate to God because they were created to be like him.

## Imitating God as the Purpose of Human Experience

All people reflect God in the structure of their hearts, but not all people imitate him in the use of that structure. In other words, all people reflect God in their personhood, but only those who belong to him by faith in Jesus Christ can imitate him in character. Imitating him in character is not only acts of obedience, but hearts that think like him, value what he values, and share the same priority of commitments. Character means having emotions that reflect God's in what angers them, what grieves them, what delights them. As one scholar puts it, "God's emotions are always in line with his holiness and moral character. God's emotions are always correct, righteous and moral because he is always correct, righteous and moral."[6] So human emotions follow a similar value system of righteousness. Imitation also means understanding the world from God's set of concerns, seeing it as he sees it. It means making the kinds of decisions that he would make in the same circumstances. In other words, this imitation is dynamic.

The problem is, people generally do not know how to relate to God well, and it starves their dynamic hearts of the power to function rightly. Faith is the means by which the heart relates to God rightly, resulting in love for him and others. People were custommade, top to bottom, to respond in relationship with God in such a way that shapes their response to the rest of the world. When people rightly relate to God, they rightly relate to themselves, others, and the world. Consider the structure of God's law—his revealed will for how human beings ought to function. God begins the Ten Commandments with a statement about himself, "I am the LORD your God, who brought you out of the land of Egypt, out of the house of slavery." He follows with instruction as to the only proper response to who he is, "You shall have no other gods before me" (Exod. 20:2–3). Three more commands show his people how they ought to act toward him—not to make a visible image to worship, not to use his name without honor, not to work seven days as if God were not God. Then, he instructs them about how to relate to everything else. A heart that honors God will respect the authority of parents, not angrily harm others for personal gain, not misuse others sexually, not take resources from others for selfish gain, not misrepresent the truth of God's reality to injure others, and will not brood jealously over valuables belonging to others (Exod. 20:4–17).

Jesus confirms this connection between people's relationship to God and their relationship to everyone else when he summarizes, "You shall love the Lord your God with all your heart and with all your soul and with all your mind. This is the great and first commandment. And a second is *like it*: You shall love your neighbor as yourself. On these two commandments depend all the Law and the Prophets" (Matt. 22:37–40, emphasis mine). The phrase "like it" expresses commonality of purpose—the primary command correlates necessarily with the second command. The apostle John later puts this in reverse. If people are relating destructively to others around them, it is a clear sign they are relating destructively to God. John says, "If anyone says, 'I love God,' and hates his brother, he is a liar; for he who does not love his brother whom he has seen cannot love God whom he has not seen. And this commandment we have from him: whoever loves God must also love his brother" (1 John 4:20–21).

Only a heart relating rightly to God will relate rightly to others. This is apparent in every relationship imaginable. Without a heart anchored solidly in God's love, a teenager will likely respond to the social pressures of high school in unhealthy ways. Maybe he will be intimidated and anxious, or maybe he will be dismissive and judgmental, or maybe he will avoid and escape. When an employer is not personally surrendered to God's glory, she will likely use her employees to seek her own glory through various motivational tactics that spur them toward her personal agenda. When a husband is not submitted to God, he will be cowardly or controlling, distracted or harsh with his wife. In all of these situations, people need to build others up in love so that they are lifted up toward God. This is the key to healthy human relationships.

The same pattern exists for how people relate to circumstances in general. A prime example of this is the theme of wisdom—living skillfully according to God's design of reality. The Old Testament's wisdom literature captures how God designed the dynamic heart to live in daily life. A thesis statement of sorts for the book of Proverbs is, "The fear of the LORD is the beginning of knowledge" (Prov. 1:7), and this statement links the heart's proper relationship with God to its proper relationship to God's world. The phrase "the fear of the LORD" may sound strange to modern ears, but it is a rich, comprehensive idea that people live most successfully in the world with affectionate awe for God's holiness and majesty. Such reverence is the starting point of all accurate knowledge of the world and how it works.[7] The heart will relate to the world in thought, desire, and choice only when characterized by such a reverent posture before God.

How people respond to God is, therefore, the most important thing about them. Imitating God by faith means that his Word shapes the dynamic functions of the heart. Scripture directs control beliefs around which all other beliefs are arranged, the control desires around which all other desires are shaped, and the control commitments around which all other commitments are positioned. God is the central piece of reality that determines the rest of the system of meaning.

## Practicing Dynamic Imitation

It is one thing to point out that people were designed to imitate God by trusting him. It is a whole other thing to describe how that imitation is practiced. Faith's expression is described in a whole landscape of verbs that stretch across Scripture: ask, seek, knock, obey, listen, heed, bow, abide, return, rejoice, trust, put off, put on, believe, clothe yourself, hold fast, love, consider, fear, strive, draw near, prepare, hope, overcome, and countless more. These are the actions of faith, and each gives a unique hue to the colorful spectrum of the dynamic heart's pursuit of God.

I could not possibly cover the whole color palette here, but perhaps I can give some of the basic groupings on the color wheel. The Bible describes the privilege of relating to God dynamically in at least three ways. Being knowledgeable of these three practices will allow people to seek God when they might be uncertain about how to do so.

First, faith is expressing the raw contents of the heart to God. Second, faith is submitting the raw contents of the heart to what God said about himself. And third, faith is acting in the present situation on what God says is true, valuable, and worthy of commitment.

### Faith involves expressing the raw contents of the heart to God.

The crown of dynamic expression to God is the Psalms. They capture the dynamic heart expressing itself in the first-person, giving people an experience they can directly imitate. Even better, the Psalms ultimately point to the faith of Jesus, the messianic King who imitated God perfectly.[8] Jesus not only reconciles people to God, but he also shows his people how to relate to him. So people can think of the Psalms as living pictures of how to have faith like Jesus—and Jesus expressed his heart to God constantly.

Imagine if the Psalms were subjected to a rationalistic theological editor with a big red pen. This imaginary editor would butcher the literary and theological beauty of expression. Just think what he would try to do to Psalm 13.

> Verse 1, "How long, O LORD? Will you forget me forever? How long will you hide your face from me?"
>
> [Comment: Theologically inaccurate. The omniscience of God precludes his ability to forget. One would expect the speaker, in his function as representative of the covenant people of God, to understand this. Change or Delete.]
>
> Verse 2, "How long must I take counsel in my soul and have sorrow in my heart all the day?"
>
> [Comment: Theologically inaccurate. "Counsel" here is a synecdoche of wisdom, and the psalmist is claiming he has been externally compelled to self-referential wisdom due to the failure of covenantal wisdom. Still worse, this is accompanied by sorrow, which is an inappropriate emotional response for anyone who understands accurately the omniscience of God. Change or Delete.]

To do this would be to miss the function of these verses. The primary function is to express. Specifically the psalmist expresses his perception of his situation—or more specifically, his perception of God's relationship to him in light of his situation. This expression is raw and honest. The act of expression to God is the psalmist's faithful attempt to process his experience before God. The psalmist knew that God had designed him to need this. His expression is a sign of the strength of his faith—he is not self-referentially mulling over his problems. He is not seeking some alternate plausibility structure. He is not distracting himself with some other concern. He is taking his experience directly to God and expressing it before him. This expressive prayer was his only hope in shaping his heart after God's.

Some people from a Western culture marked by individualistic pragmatism will have a difficult time with this aspect of faith's expression. Such a culture values relationships that are efficient. Communication should be a simple exchange of information for the purpose of accomplishing some necessary task. I was raised in this culture and find that the way I relate to God is often as a business exchange. I need him to give me grace so that I can obey him. So my approach is often acknowledging what I ought to be doing and asking him for the strength to do it. I often skip the task of prayerfully expressing my heart to God to move on to other things. I do not have time to process its raw contents before him. I have other things to do for him.

But God's concern in prayer is to shape a heart that trusts him with everything. Faith is expressing the raw contents of my heart to God. What I mean by raw is the unprocessed, unedited truth about what I am believing, what I am experiencing, what I am wanting, or to what I am committed. Or perhaps even the fact that I am not even sure what I am believing, what I am experiencing, what I am wanting, or to what I am committed. It is an expression of what is actually there inside me, unrefined by what I know it ought to be. What often keeps me from such honest expression is my misunderstanding of what it means to respect God. I think I should only say what ought to be true of my heart rather than what is true. And by shying away from this process, I am actually erecting an illusion of my own respectability as I approach God. But I am not respectable. A raw expression of my heart will betray the fact that I am poor and needy, self-centered and distrusting. I do not see things as God does. I do not value what he does. I am inadequately committed to his ways.

Some may skip this task in pride, wanting to move quickly on to corrective action. Other may skip it in fear, thinking of God as disapproving and unapproachable with the truth of what is inside them. Part of believing the gospel of Jesus Christ is believing that God receives all who trust in him, and believers are therefore safe to process before God the raw contents of their hearts. Scripture models honest interaction between the Lord and those he loves. Relating to God is a living, unguarded conversation.

Having said this, God is not a silent receiver in the conversation. He is not an equal conversation partner, there to affirm everything people say to him. He receives people's rawness for the purpose of conforming their responses to his. This is primarily for his glory— meaning, the way he responds is more glorious and true than the way people respond. For this reason, faith is not just expressing, but also submitting.

**Faith involves submitting the raw contents of the heart to what God said about himself in his Word.**

People find it quite difficult to submit to God because it requires them to repent of beliefs, values, and commitments that fall short of his will. Being willing to give up such preciously held things requires a miracle—a miracle called faith. Faith is a miracle of the Holy Spirit working through his Word, particularly in perceiving God as he is and not who people prefer him to be. The greatest hindrance to submission is often a misperception of God: viewing him through the lens of personal desire. A 2005 study on the religious life of American teenagers revealed a sad view of God they lived according to, now famously summarized as "moralistic therapeutic deism."[9] Basically, teens think of God as a creator who watches over the world, wanting people to be nice to one another and to be happy, with no particular need to be involved in a person's life except to offer help in time of need. Teens who hold such a view are largely carried along by the values of the culture and unaffected by the alternate vision of life found in Scripture. Such a softly-conceived being requires no submission.

That weak vision of who God is may be characteristic of a large swath of America, but other competing visions are as numerous as the stars in the sky. This is why counselors must carefully consider the cultural and religious background of the individuals they counsel—along with the books they read, the talk shows they watch, the political partnerships they have. Everyone has a vision of God that is biblically deficient in some way, and that deficiency will have consequences in their lives. Counselors have to be aware of common misperceptions of God in their culture so that they can recognize how their counselees might be thinking. Helping folks understand God as he is revealed himself to be as opposed to God as preferred by the individual is necessary for genuine submission to him, along with all the benefits that come through such happy submission.

To submit to God, then, is to take him at his Word. To submit to God is to love him as he has revealed himself to be, to trust him according to the way he describes himself in the Word. In fact, the love of God is accurately understanding who he is, valuing him as supreme, and submitting to his will. And this is only done by faith in his Word. The Holy Spirit alone can bring about the miracle of faith, and he does so, "from hearing, and hearing through the word of Christ" (Rom. 10:17). His words have always been God's way of bringing life to humankind. Scripture is the means by which God "extends his action, and therefore himself, into the world in order to act communicatively in relation to us."[10] God's Word is the touch point for rightly relating to him in this world.

Consider for a moment the basic purpose of why God reveals himself to people. What is God's intended effect of Scripture on human experience? He intends to be believed. God spoke in various ways in order to reveal his glory in Jesus Christ (Heb. 1:1–4). Jesus's person and work is the gospel, which benefits a hearer only when received by faith (Heb. 4:1–2). The pattern of God's revelation is one that both demands and enables faith.[11] Thus, the central purpose of Scripture for human experience is to elicit faith in Christ, to the eternal benefit of the receiver.

Some of the most poetic words about love in all of Scripture are written by the apostle John, "Anyone who does not love does not know God, because God is love" (1 John 4:8). This is one of the most quoted verses in Scripture, and for good reason. It states in profound simplicity a basic fact of human identity: To know God, the essence of love, is to be a person who loves like him. But the foundation of John's instruction to love, carefully laid throughout the entire letter, is that Christians are able to love by believing the message of his love for his people (1 John 5:3–5). Faith is the victory that overcomes the world and makes believers lovers of God and of others.

All of this means something quite simple: people can only love God by believing what is true about him, and they know what is true of him from his Word applied to the heart by the Holy Spirit. For fallen human beings, believing what is true about God is not a singular act, but a continual series of acts. Believing is not merely a static, established belief, but also a continual process of submission. Yes, people have to read the Bible and understand its meaning, but they also have to surrender the remaining beliefs, values, and commitments that rival what they find there. This is a living, active, expulsive faith instead of a static, inert one.

This is why the Word of God is powerful to those who have the Spirit of God living in them. Faith is the initiative of the Holy Spirit in people to enliven their heart to receive God by means of his Word. Faith, then, is relational at its core.[12] It is the continual re-submission of people's beliefs, values, and commitments to God's Word; and such a massive structural reorientation requires the Holy Spirit's strength and nothing less. The Holy Spirit enables personal faith in God's Word to conform people's thoughts to God's, shape people's values around what they find precious, and establish godly priority of commitments. Faith changes everything.

The vision of God portrayed in Scripture demands the full attention of anyone who dares approach him. He is infinite in his wisdom. God knows every fact and every possible interpretation of those facts. He is infinite in his power. God has never needed anything for which he has not provided. He is infinite in his holiness. God is the definition of morality, and has never had a single thought or desire contrary to himself. He is infinite in his joy. The unmixed source of all happiness is the burning delight of God's heart.

Such a tremendous God is the most relevant fact of every human experience in every part of the world at any point in history. Faith means believing what God says about himself so that I value him as worthy of my deepest commitment. So, when I express the raw contents of my heart to him, I readily submit my thoughts, my desires, and my choices to worship him in my situation. I may not know exactly what I ought to do, how I ought to feel, or what decision I ought to make in the situation swirling around me, but I do know that God's person is always worth my supreme attention, and his intention for my life is trustworthy.

The psalmist again models this dynamic faith. Psalm 119 is a tour-de-force of dynamic submission to God. The epic song puts color to this task of submission.

> How can a young man keep his way pure?
>     By guarding it according to your word.
> With my whole heart I seek you;
>     Let me not wander from your commandments!
> I have stored up your word in my heart,
>     that I might not sin against you.
> Blessed are you, O LORD;
>     Teach me your statutes!
> With my lips I declare
>     all the rules of your mouth.
> In the way of your testimonies I delight
>     as much as in all riches.
> I will meditate on your precepts
>     and fixed my eyes on your ways.
> I will delight in your statutes;
>     I will not forget your word. (Ps. 119:9–16)

Consider how close to the surface the dynamic expressions of the psalmist's heart are. He seeks the knowledge of God in his Word, his commandments, his statutes. He delights in them, more than all other riches. He seeks diligently, begging God not to let him wander away. This picture of submission is alive—rousing, stabilizing, smart. It shows how God is worthy of people's attention over the raw contents of their hearts, whatever they may be.

Psalm after psalm gives an animated picture of people expressing their concerns to God about their present situation, then acknowledging God as the highest consideration in any of it. Even Psalm 13, which showed the honest expression of a heart that feels God's abandonment, nevertheless concludes, "I will sing to the LORD, because he has dealt bountifully with me" (Ps. 13:6). Even without a clear indication that the psalmist's situation changed from the beginning to the end of the psalm, he gives a clear indication that his heart's response did. This is not magical, nor is it automatic. It is the process of faith working through the dynamic functions of the heart.

Submitting to God, therefore, requires commitment to him above all. It echoes Jesus's faith when he said, "Father, if you are willing, remove this cup from me. Nevertheless, not my will, but yours, be done" (Luke 22:42). Notice the interplay between expression and submission: Jesus requested that God spare him from the agony coming. He was expressing his personal desire to God. Closely following, however, he submitted that desire to God's superior value, the eternal salvation of his people, a prize of great cost to both of them. Submission is accurately perceiving God's perception as superior, and releasing one's own in favor of it. Jesus submitted to God because he loved God for who he is. Likewise, Christians will only submit to God as they understand him to be as grand and good as he says he is in Scripture.

**Faith involves acting in the present situation according
to what God says is true, valuable, and worthy of commitment.**

The situations of people's lives are the canvas on which God creates. He is making a people of his own possession who are zealous for good deeds (Titus 2:11–14), even in the difficult cultural and relational situations they find themselves (Titus 1:10–12). Situations demand active responses, and the responses of a submitted heart are earth-shifting.

Once people have expressed the raw contents of their hearts and submitted them to God, there is nothing to do but to act. Submission to God happens in the active responses to life. A person cannot claim to trust God and fail to act on it. Imagine Abraham claiming to submit to God's direction, but then refusing to go up the mountain with Isaac. His willingness to act was proof of his submission (Heb. 11:17–19; James 2:21–24). Jesus made this point in the parable of the two sons. A father asks them both to work in the vineyard for the day. The first son says, "no," and the second son says, "yes." But when it was time to clock in at the vineyard, the first was ready with his punch card, while the second was nowhere to be found. Which one submitted to his father? Like so many of Jesus's brilliant riddles, the answer is mysteriously obvious (Matt. 21:28–32).

The psalms also model a commitment to action as the necessary culmination of submission. When David was in the situation of fleeing from his son Absalom, he expressed his deep fear to the Lord (Ps. 3:1–2), submitted his perspective of the danger around him to the superior truth of who God is (vv. 3–4), and took the appropriate action, which in this case was to lay down and sleep securely (vv. 5–6). Prior to that, when David was in the situation of Saul coming after him, his actions were much different. With the same expression of fear to God (Ps. 18:6) and the same grand vision of a formidable God (18:13–19), he was equipped with the strength to go to war and win (18:31–45). In yet another situation, when David was in enemy territory in Gath, that same expression of fear (Ps. 34:4) coupled with submission to who God is (34:8–10) lead him to act like a crazy person as a tactic of escaping King Abimelech.

Faith in God is expressed as action in a situation. These relational tasks are impossible apart from reflective prayer and careful study of Scripture. Hearing God's words and responding to him in prayer have always been the means of faithful activity in the world. People imitate God by believing what he says, valuing what he assesses as good, and making decisions that show commitment to him. For fallen creatures, this imitation will be clumsy and inconsistent; but for creatures also redeemed, it will nevertheless be true. Made possible by Jesus, the author and finisher of faith.

# CHAPTER 7

. . . .

# SELF AND IDENTITY

The world may be filled with
technological innovations undreamt of fifty years ago—
cyberspace devices, social media networks and advanced medical
technologies—but the reality is that the greater change
has occurred in how we relate to our world,
what we think about ourselves and, last but not least,
the ways in which religious faith has been transformed.

*— Richard Lints* [1]

In his sanctification man is freed from his egocentrism
and renewed to an ex-centric life, oriented to God,
his neighbor, and the world.

*— Hendrikus Berkhof* [2]

There's a fat kid inside us all. We all have various perceptions of ourselves. Some of them are carried from a long time ago, some forming more recently. These opinions of self develop and change according to the influences around us—what is celebrated and what is mocked. In junior high, the athletic kids with good complexions usually ruled the day (although they too struggled with insecurities). The fat kids got the short end of the stick. The athletic kids and the fat kids alike knew the pecking order, and they also knew exactly where they fit into it. Such identities are not native, but constructed. In adult life no less than in junior high.

This is the second of four chapters addressing the contexts to which the dynamic heart responds. The purpose of these chapters is to equip counselors and caregivers to understand the experience of the folks in their care. The primary point of this chapter is this: The dynamic heart functions from a personal identity constructed from various sources. Caring for people involves addressing how their constructed identity compares to their given identity.

Every person operates out of some kind of identity. This is another way of saying that people operate from some perception of themselves that involves their beliefs, values, and choices. Our dynamic hearts operate vis-à-vis ourselves. Consider this self-assessment: what do you recognize that you believe about yourself? Maybe you are no good at math; you are a male; you are more generally more responsible than your brother. These are all beliefs about yourself. You also hold yourself to certain values: Maybe you feel slighted when you are not invited to a certain dinner party. You feel discouraged that you should have accomplished more by your age. You are glad you do not look like that family in sweatpants coming out of Long John Silver's. These are all desires by which you measure yourself. You also make choices to act according to the beliefs and desires you have about yourself. As soon as your eyes open in the morning, you begin choosing according to your deepest dedications—to your job, to your family, to your hobbies.

People operate from different levels of identities simultaneously. Some are vital to self-perception, others not so much. As an example, I have a number of identities I operate from—with varying degrees of importance. I am a Cleveland Browns fan. I am a father and a husband. I am a son and a brother. I am a pastor. I am a professor. I am a middle-class white American. I am a Baptist. I am a Christian. I think that I am funnier than most of my friends. I am a crummy athlete. All of these identities are true of me, at least, as I conceive of them, but they do not all relate directly. Being a Cleveland Browns fan does not contradict being a Baptist, or a lot of Clevelanders would have to rethink their doctrinal statements because they are not going to rethink their professional sports loyalties. Likewise, being a crummy athlete does not correlate with being a pastor, as my fellow pastor, John Kimbell, could demonstrate on the soccer field.

People operate out of many layers of identity. Not everyone has the same layers, so they cannot be universally categorized—as if there were a "sports fan" category and a "vocation" category. Nonetheless, these layers of identity generally correspond with people's cultural circles. Everyone fills a role in each circle, and thus have an identity in each. This occurs in vocations (I am a UPS pilot), our families (I am a mother), personal gifting (I am a singer), personal accomplishments or aspirations (I am a college graduate), nationality (I am Haitian), ethnicity (I am Hispanic), church affiliation (I am Presbyterian), community (I am a Texan), and any other key association (I am an Ohio State Buckeye; I am chair of the local chamber of commerce; I am a Freemason). Each identity circle matters for how people perceive themselves.

## The Importance of Self-Conception

What people believe about themselves determines the shape of their life. God made people that way. Some of the most refined thinking through the ages has been dedicated to understanding how people experience the self. Even John Calvin claimed that without knowledge of self there is no knowledge of God, and without knowledge of God there is no knowledge of self.[3] How people conceive of their role in their environment will largely determine how they respond to life around them.

The reason for this is theological. God designed human beings to operate out of an established self-conception. That self-perception, ideally, correlates to their true identity as God designed them, but this is never entirely the case for fallen humanity. Human beings, from the beginning, have been given everything they need to construct an accurate self-conception, one that correlates with their true identity as divine image bearers. God gave people the one thing they need to understand both who they are and why they experience the world the way they do: He spoke to them. More specifically, he spoke to people about themselves. A biblical understanding of the human individual insists that unseen realities are the most determinative of a person's identity and function in the world.

The very first thing God did to the newly created human race was to bless them and speak to them. What was the topic of his first words to these newly formed people? God said, "Be fruitful and multiply and fill the earth and subdue it, and have dominion over the fish of the sea and over the birds of the heavens and over every living thing that moves on the earth" (Gen. 1:28). The subject of God's inaugural statement to humanity was about them. The first thing God said to Adam and Eve was not a description of angels or of him, nor was it an explanation of why he made the trees and stars. No, the topic was Adam and Eve, and how they could carry out his purposes in this new world. The Lord God was forming Adam and Eve's self-perception around the central purpose of his existence: to rule the world as a happy agent of God.

Adam and Eve would function out of this identity, until an alternate voice suggested a different one. Satan constructed a different understanding of self he wanted to implant: that they could not enjoy life under God's command and that they would not die if they broke free from that command (Gen. 3:4). And so began Satan's construction of the rival identity that echoes in every human soul since. Instead of, *I am a dependent being using my capacities to rule God's world for his purposes*, it is now, *I am an independent being using my capacities to rule my world for my own purposes*. Pride hijacked Adam and Eve's identities and made its permanent home in the human heart.

Within every human heart, there is a given identity and constructed identity.[4] People's given identities are simply who God has designed them to be and how God has designed them to function in the world. To put it in the first person, a given identity is *what God says about who I am*. But as finite creatures (and fallen ones, at that), people do not automatically operate out of a given identity. Adam was not born with a pre-understanding of his design and function in this new world. He had to be instructed verbally in order to form his subjective understanding of his proper role in the world. This subjective understanding is constructed identity: people's established self-image, made up of a complex arrangement of various beliefs, values, and commitments about who they are and what role they play in the world. It is, to phrase it again in the first person, *what I say about who I am*. The more people's constructed identity conforms to their given identity, the healthier their self-conception will be. In other words, people with healthy self-perception allow what God says about them to determine what they say about themselves.

A given identity is determined by God, and thus remains unchanged by people's perception. People form their constructed identity as they adopt various beliefs, values, and commitments. Those who work with people must understand the delicate interplay between constructed and given identity, because accurate self-conception is vital to spiritual and mental health.

## Constructed Identity

People's constructed identity is their established self-image, made up of a complex arrangement of various conceptions, values, and commitments about who they are and what role they play in the world. A constructed identity is not intrinsically bad; in fact, it is necessary. Where it goes bad is if the perception becomes inaccurate. To make things even trickier, people are often unaware of their constructed identities. People do not consciously choose their constructed identity in every way, but they listen to the atmosphere of voices about what they ought to be and slowly absorb those values. Then, people make the little decisions that, over time, reinforce these layers of identity until it solidifies and becomes less penetrable the more packed in it becomes.

People can be inconsistent in their self-perceptions and constructed identities. The ideas people have about themselves are often a jumbled mix of accuracies and inaccuracies. People can be supremely arrogant, yet plagued by self-doubt. People can have incredible professional gifting and use it to tremendous advantage in business, but they can also be blind to the relational weakness everyone around them sees. People might be convinced they are no good at something, when they are actually quite accomplished. People are inconsistent, and so need both compassion and directness when discussing issues of identity.

The sources of building material for a constructed identity are innumerable. People construct them from many different sources in their experience—the way caretakers respond to them, what teachers expect from them, the way siblings and friends do the same, the perceived successes and failures of their efforts, the tone and shape of the culture around them, the history of events that occur in their life, even the particular language system they learn first.

Some of those layers are vital to self-perception, others not so much. My layers include being a Cleveland Browns fan, a father, a husband, a pastor, a professor, and so on. Not all of them have the same degree of truth-quality. Not all of them say the same things, so they contradict one another. Many of them also contradict what God says is most important. The result is that every person under the sun has a constructed identity that is a rickety framework of accuracies and inaccuracies, muddled together.

Scripture reveals God's understanding of who people are; thus, it should be the primary building material for a constructed identity. Given identity sets the limits and priorities of constructed identity. I understand myself as a husband accurately only as I understand myself to be, for instance, created to worship God and not myself in the way I fulfill my roles as a husband. My identity as a husband is a temporary aspect of my status as disciple of Christ—so I do not idolize my marriage, yet I remain fully committed to my wife's eternal good because it is part of God's call to honor him in the situation he has placed me. God's understanding of me holds authoritative weight over my opinion of myself in vocation, in social status, in family heritage, in sports loyalties, in political allegiances, and even in racial and cultural conventions.

Breaking up constructed identities and re-forming them according to God's Word is no quick task. Understanding and changing a constructed identity is possible but difficult work. The gospel works literal miracles, but the means by which this miracle takes place may be lifelong. This is, perhaps, most true at the level of identity. And a necessary step in this process is simply raising people's awareness of their own self-perception.

## Given Identity

"We may say without much fear of contradiction," writes Berkouwer, "that the most striking thing in the Biblical portrayal of man lies in this, that it never asks attention for man in himself, but demands our fullest attention for man in his relation to God."[5] People's given identity is God's universal design of humans to be in relationship to him. All human beings share in this design, though specific variances in capacity and context are unique to every individual. God sovereignly orchestrates both the original design and the unique context of every individual. He originally designed people to be agents of worship who reflected his personhood in this brand new world (given identity), and he meticulously arranges the unique native tendencies and contextual influences that will shape each individual's particular expression of personhood (constructed identity).

God still verbalizes what is most vital to people's self-perception, the core components that are necessary to a healthy, growing understanding of self. People are obligated to submit their self-conception to God's conception of them, and his divine conception has been unfolded in a story, a sweeping narrative that includes all human beings and their personal experiences. It is a story with four acts, all vital to understanding everyone's personal story. People were created, but have fallen, yet may be redeemed, and are awaiting a new creation. These four components are aspects of people's given identity as discussed in Section 1.

Excluding any one of these elements results in a skewed vision of personal identity. For instance, if Christians exclude the biblical recognition of their sinfulness and God's displeasure on them, they will blind themselves to the growing sin they are tolerating in their life. If Christians exclude the recognition of their beloved status as children of God, they will grow fearful of approaching the God they were designed to be near. If Christians do not understand themselves in light of the tension between their present righteousness in Christ and their future fulfillment of that righteousness, their expectations of themselves and others will be so high they will end up burning out in frustration. A view of self must be grounded in the full breadth of God's view, as revealed in Scripture. These key elements of a given identity are important enough to explore.

### I am created, and therefore both eternally valuable and inescapably dependent.

Even set against the backdrop of incalculable stars and distant worlds spinning, human beings are God's highest delight in all of creation (Gen. 1:31; Ps. 8:3–9). They are of infinite value because God considers them so, and he considers them so because they alone share the infinite characteristics of God's personhood. Even though they have bodies that locate them in one place and time, their inheritance as the image of God is more important than even the bright, bodiless angels (Heb. 1:4, 14). Every person is of infinite worth to God, since he has shared with them alone a part of his own infinite worth. Therefore, human value is derived from God's character and estimation, not an individual's internal uniqueness, as Western individualism suggests.

People are valuable because they were created to reflect God. That createdness has many core aspects vital to their self-conception. I will highlight the three that make the strongest appearance in the account of humanity's creation. First, God created people male or female. The creation narrative embeds gender into the very fabric of the image of God, "So God created man in his own image, in the image of God he created him; male and female he created them"

(Gen. 1:27). The beauty of this poetry lies in the contrasting, yet progressing lines: God created man individually as his image, God created man collectively as male and female. Gender is grounded in given identity, not constructed identity. God's glory is displayed in people as either male or female, and which gender they are is assigned by God, not determined by personal experience. God made each with glorious, differing roles that are aspects of an individual's given identity (Gen. 2:18, 21–24; 1 Cor. 11:7–9; 1 Tim. 2:12–14). In some difficult situations, people's experience of gender does not perfectly match their given biological sex. Such a situation is a real example of constructed versus given identity. In a culture that rejects human createdness, and thus the limits and distinctions of a design given to them, people can suffer all the more.

Second, God created people as capable of receiving an accurate understanding of the world. God gave knowledge to Adam for him to craft his own self-conception (Gen. 1:28–30; 2:15–17). Adam was capable of receiving that knowledge through language, and then capable of applying that knowledge to the world around him by the way he conducted himself. His faculties, in other words, were sound and reliable. Why mention this? Because, contrary to the postmodern intellectual undercurrents of Western culture, people can think of themselves as able to understand the world around them in a way that corresponds with reality. Indeed, they must think of themselves this way, or they will all descend into a relativistic, nihilistic, throw-up-our-hands approach to the problems of life. This would be disastrous at the societal level ("If morality is only a cultural construct, who are we to get all flustered about the genocidal activities of ISIS?") and at the individual level ("If love is only what I construct in my mind, then why should I stay committed to this marriage when I don't feel like it anymore?"). People's ability to accurately perceive reality is not an indication of their independence, but quite the opposite. People are utterly dependent on their design as God's image to function in a way that corresponds with reality, and they are without excuse when they do not (Rom. 1:18–20). People are created with the capacities to understand the world in a way that reflects God's understanding.

Third, God created people with limits to their capacities, and these limits are not just moral. Adam and Eve had limits prior to God forbidding them to eat of the tree of the knowledge of good and evil (Gen. 2:16–17). In verse 15, "The LORD God took the man and put him in the garden of Eden to work it and keep it." The Lord authoritatively placed Adam where he wanted him, as a located being with a specific purpose. Adam had to eat in order to live, and had to exert himself to accomplish the work he was purposed to do. He needed rest, he needed companionship, he needed revelation. From the very beginning of their existence, humankind has been limited and utterly dependent, in contrast to God who is unlimited and completely independent, as he says, "If I were hungry, I would not tell you, for the world and its fullness are mine" (Ps. 50:12, see also Ps. 104). Human limitedness is a part of their worth, since it is the means by which human beings attach themselves to God in dependence. God created people with limitations so that they might depend upon the God who is without limitations.

**I am fallen, and therefore both bad and broken.**

Given identity is certainly complex. In God's understanding, people are of infinite value. But people are also tragically corrupted, and that corruption is the explanation for all of their turmoil—both internal and external. People must understand themselves as suffering from this corruption in two distinct ways that often intermingle. People are bad, and people are broken.

People are bad, which is another way of saying they are sinners. When people accurately perceive God by faith, they draw immediate conclusions about themselves in contrast, as the apostle Peter did when he witnessed Jesus perform a miracle for the first time, "But when Simon Peter saw it, he fell down at Jesus' knees, saying, 'Depart from me, for I am a sinful man, O Lord'" (Luke 5:8).

Furthermore, people are not theoretically sinners, but actively and inescapably so. Sin is not just an occasional thing people do, but a decay within who they are, so that their glorious capacities that were meant for the worship of God are used to worship self. And self-worship estranges people from themselves, because it abandons the original purpose for which they were designed. People are voluntarily estranged from themselves, and they do not like to recognize this fact. Scripture portrays the wicked person as one who "flatters himself in his own eyes that his iniquity cannot be found out and hated" (Ps. 36:2), an amazingly insightful observation about the self-conception of those who are wicked. And since, according to Scripture, every person born (save One) falls into the wicked category (Rom. 3:9–23), every person needs to face this tendency to construct an identity different from their given identity. The apostle John refers to this as being self-deceived (1 John 1:8) and the writer of Hebrews to being "hardened by the deceitfulness of sin" (Heb. 3:13). Scripture shows that people are particularly eager to build around this aspect of their identity. They construct a thousand other explanations for why they are such an angry person or what drove them to that affair. But if people have an accurate self-conception, it must include this uncomfortable fact: they are fallen into sin, which means their motives and actions are bent toward self-worship at the expense of others.

People are not just bad, but they are broken as well, which is saying something different than merely that they are sinners. Being bad emphasizes their voluntary participation in their estrangement from self, and being broken emphasizes the involuntary victimhood of their self-estrangement. Saying people are broken means that all people suffer from damage inflicted upon them by their original parents when they disobeyed and invited upon the human race the fear of one another, of God, of a new harsh world (Gen. 3:7–19). Futility and chaos now toss about throughout all creation, including in the soul of every person born.

The futility of existence stalks people until they are cornered into recognizing it for what it is, "All things are full of weariness; a man cannot utter it; the eye is not satisfied with seeing, nor the ear filled with hearing" (Eccl. 1:8). Even those who seek the wisdom of understanding human life conclude, "It is an unhappy business that God has given to the children of man to be busy with. I have seen everything that is done under the sun, and behold, all is vanity and a striving after wind" (Eccl. 1:13–14). The whole world, including the people who are commissioned to lead it, are in a condition of being less than its original design. The book of Ecclesiastes is a prolonged lament of, and multifaceted attempt to cope with, the preacher's own brokenness and the brokenness of the world.

This futility marks people's inner life, dis-integrates the functions of the heart. Emotions do not line up with what people believe to be true; desires do not follow their commitments; thoughts contradict one another without their realization. People grow tired and weak; they find themselves at a loss of what to do next; they get confused, forgetful, and short-sighted. On top of this, physical bodies no longer function optimally—including people's brains. Neurological functions get caught up in dysfunctional patterns, hormone levels spike or tank without explanation, nerves fray and muscles strain. People are broken, both body and soul. And so, a necessary aspect of self-conception is people live in a broken world as a broken person, and thus they are weaker and less able than they wish to be.

**I am redeemed, and therefore forgiven and loved.**

All people share the first two aspects of their given identity: all people are created eternally valuable, and all people have fallen into corruption. But the next two aspects divide humanity into two, eternally distinct categories: the redeemed and the unredeemed. Those who are purchased by the blood of Christ, and those who are not. Those whose names will be read from the Book of Life, and those whose names will not be. And while the distinction between these two groups is not plainly known until that future day of judgment, that distinction nevertheless makes itself plain in the way each group conducts themselves in the present (Matt. 25:31–46).

Christians find their redemption identity even more precious than their created one. They are created in the image of God, and therefore of eternal worth. But far better, they are redeemed from their sin and into an even more intimate relationship with God—the image of his beloved Son. Christians are valued by God in their createdness, and dearly loved by him in their redemption. To those who believe the gospel of Jesus Christ, the apostle John declares, "See what kind of love the Father has given to us, that we should be called children of God; and so we are" (1 John 3:1), and this position as children is given because "your sins are forgiven for his name's sake (1 John 2:12). Following John's lead, I will feature two aspects of a redeemed identity: being forgiven and being loved.

Personally identifying oneself as forgiven is vital to Christian identity, because only when sin is forgiven can a relationship with God be reestablished. And further, only a re-established relationship with God will bring a re-established relationship with self. Human beings are born estranged from themselves—each have an internal mechanism of self-critique that comes from being made to image God but failing to live consistently with that image. That mechanism of self-critique is called the conscience: people's internal witness against their own hearts, making them aware that things are not functioning properly. The result is shame and self-condemnation. It is the dissociative pain of knowing something is wrong, but being unable (and often uninterested) in finding a resolution. People find this witness intolerably painful, so they come up with many schemes to rid themselves of it—they ignore it, distract themselves from it, modify it to the cultural climate around them. But the internal witness was placed there as a conduit of God's opinion of sin, and only God can allay it. And he does so by dealing justice for those sins on his own Son, so that he can declare anyone who trusts in Jesus to be completely forgiven (Rom. 3:21–26). Christians are no longer personally separated from the kindness of God by their sin because of Jesus Christ.

Being forgiven is not an end in itself, but part of the larger identity of being loved by God. God's love restores people to whom God made them to be. In his high priestly prayer on behalf of his rag-tag followers, Jesus asked his eternal Father something universe-altering. He asks for things that constitute a new, eternal identity for these fishermen and tax-collectors. Jesus asked his Father to "keep them in your name" (John 17:11) since "yours they were, and you gave them to me, and they have kept your word" (John 17:6). If his language of being named and kept by God were not clear enough, Jesus ends his prayer by saying, "I made known to them your name, and I will continue to make it known, that the love with which you have loved me may be in them, and I in them" (v. 26). In receiving the word of salvation by faith, a person becomes loved with an intra-trinitarian love. The same love shared between the persons of the trinity—eternal, consuming, pure, and core to divine identity—the Father shares with those who believe in Christ Jesus. United to Christ, people can experience no higher privilege, no greater identity, than being loved by the all-valuable God. Christians are loved with the same delight the Father has for the Son.

**I am newly created, and therefore both cleansed and waiting.**

"If anyone is in Christ," the apostle Paul announces, "he is a new creation. The old has passed away; behold, the new has come" (2 Cor. 5:17). A correlating identity with being forgiven and loved is being newly created. When people come to faith in Christ, they are made citizens of an undying kingdom, an escape from broken creation awaiting destruction (2 Pet. 3:7). Redeemed people have a new master in this present life—their slavery to cruel sin is broken, and their slavery to kind God begins; one pays with death, the other pays with life eternal (Rom. 6:22–23). This citizenship is already granted and not yet finalized. The reality is that Jesus's kingdom is both present and future, and thus, citizenship in the kingdom has a present and future aspect.[6] The kingdom is here, but it is still coming. The biblical writers constantly speak of believers as new creations who await a new creation in the final sense.

This tension between the already and the not yet is a significant factor in the Christian's identity in that Christians are both cleansed and waiting. They are freed from the power of sin now, but they await the time when sin will have no power whatsoever. Recognizing this tension is the only way to make sense of New Testament instruction. For instance, Paul insists that believers, who were once sexually immoral, are already "washed, you were sanctified, you were justified in the name of the Lord Jesus Christ and by the Spirit of our God" (1 Cor. 6:11), and yet immediately instructs them to flee sexual immorality as a sin against identity with Christ (1 Cor. 11:17–18). Beliefs, desires, and intentions that are directed toward sinful objects remain within believers (James 1:12–15); yet, God promises to provide the ability to escape any temptation (1 Cor. 10:13). Christians may experience overwhelming sorrow over losses in their lives (Phil. 2:27); yet, they can be content in Christ in any situation (Phil. 4:13). To put it simply, believers belong to Christ completely, but are not yet completely like him, not until they see him.

The apostle John lays out this tension in a grand theological vision of Christian identity, "Beloved, we are God's children now, and what we will be has not yet appeared; but we know that when he appears we shall be like him, because we shall see him as he is. And everyone who thus hopes in him purifies himself as he is pure" (1 John 3:2–3). Those who identify themselves as God's children know their incompleteness, but place such active hope in the day of their completion that they strive for it now. Expectations of human life are tempered by an individual's given identity. Even redeemed people remain limited by creation, corrupted by sin, and incomplete in the present age. Yet, because they are redeemed, they are accepted by God and promised the power they need to live by faith in response to any situation. Christians are incomplete and waiting to see Jesus Christ, which gives me hope to be like him now.

## Submitting Constructed Identity to Given Identity

This given identity has many implications for Christians' self-conceptions. There is a healthy form of self-interest and self-love because God declared his creation, "good." G. K. Beale offers helpful insight, saying,

> But there *is* a good self-love that seeks what will truly make us happy; it is loving ourselves by desiring to become what God wants us to become. More precisely, we love God, and in the process of loving him, we become what God wants us to become. Loving God, paradoxically, is the best expression of self-love, for in loving God we are truly happy.[7]

God values people as beings he created with the special purpose of reflecting his own personhood. Because of the fall, God is displeased with people as beings who direct their personhood to their own destructive ends. God delights in people as those cleansed by the blood of his Son. And he is patient with their incompleteness in the present age. All of these estimations are simultaneous. Of course, God's understanding of people is infinitely more complex than anything I could describe, but he at least sets the primary categories in place. Thus, to properly value self is to prioritize these concerns as the anchor of one's constructed identity.

By faith, a healthy self-conception flows from a wholehearted understanding, consent, and commitment to God's given identity. As faith grows, people's identities are increasingly shaped by God's perspective. More specifically, the beliefs, values, and commitments people measure themselves by increasingly resonate with God's perspective. Thus a central theme in the New Testament is the faith necessary to give access to one's true identity in Christ.[8] This faith is the only way to construct a self-conception that is ultimately true.

Saying Scripture lays the authoritative layers of human identity does not mean it is easy for people to then assess the various layers of identity functionally motivating their conduct in real life.

Deciphering different layers of identity or competing identities is quite complex, but a few questions can help. The various layers of a person's identity can be measured on at least three scales:

1.  Source: What voices in a person's life are serving as building material for this particular layer of identity? Is the source reliable?

2.  Center: Is a particular layer too close to the center of a person's identity? Is it dis-ordered in wrong priority?

3.  Purpose: What is the end goal of a particular layer of identity—independent glory or derived glory?

## 1. Considering the Source

God designed people to need material from outside themselves to build those constructs of self-perception. Adam did not come pre-loaded with accurate self-knowledge prior to God's input. And that self-perception remained unchanged until Satan's tragic input. This simple observation teaches something important about self-perception: Self-perception is not fixed, but is constructed from material outside the self. To use a building metaphor, the structure of self-perception is built from materials taken from a wide variety of stockyards. This does not imply that people are passive in the formation of their self-perception. The narrative direction is quite the opposite, actually. Adam and Eve were held accountable as active agents because, instead of being satisfied with God's stockyards, they borrowed material from a rival one.

Individuals are always active in the construction process, even if they do not choose what stockyards are available to them. Different cultural values, different family expectations, different access to opportunities—these are the stockyards of material for self-perception. People do not choose the culture, family, or opportunities into which they are born, but they are nevertheless active in the acquisition of the beliefs, values, and commitments that make up their opinion of themselves.

Take, for example, a girl raised in a wealthy family, whose father was largely disengaged and whose mother was an insecure socialite. Her teenage years were a stream of luxurious social engagements, extended trips, and elite schooling. Her father related to her as he would an expensive doll—he pampered her, but with little relational interaction. His particular manner of treatment is material for his daughter's constructed identity. Her mother, on the other hand, would both promote her as an object of accomplishment and cling to the social benefits of it. Her particular manner of treatment is also material for her daughter's constructed identity. The available stockyards only had some pretty shoddy material: Her dad displayed his opinion of her as someone to supply, but not personally associate with. Her mother displayed her opinion of the girl as a tool to gain the admiration of others. And because she is an active agent in the construction of her identity, we can imagine a number of dynamic responses: She could transition to adulthood feeling quite admired, but not loved. Maybe this would lead to self-loathing for not being more pleasing to her father or for not being able to stand up to her mother. Or maybe, quite the opposite, she would be quite satisfied with being admired as long as it involved such a luxurious lifestyle that doesn't demand much from her.

Identify the sources people use in constructing their identity. Unreliable sources must be actively identified and undermined. A teenage girl battling depression might consider if the angst-laden music she listens to every day is partly why she views herself as a poor, tortured soul. The preoccupied professional needs to assess if the books on leadership and success are reliable sources of truth regarding what he ought to be. The single woman in her forties needs to consider if the cultural pressures to be married are saying something true about her value. The adolescent boy caught up in his online role-playing game must consider how the digital marks of progress and respect hijack his sense of identity. Caring for people who live in worlds full of potential sources of identity, means always asking, *Who is speaking to them most strongly about who they are? What does*

*Scripture say about the messages they are receiving? How can the unreliability of the source be exposed?*

## 2. Considering the Center

Regardless of the outside material, people actively construct their identity as a statement of the deepest longings of what they wish to be. Even as you read this, if I were to ask you what you most wish were true of you, you would begin to reveal some of the central aspects of your constructed identity. For '90s kids, no one said it better than Skee-Lo, "I wish I was a little bit taller. I wish I was a baller. I wish I had a girl who looked good, I would call her. I wish I had a rabbit in a hat with a bat, and a '64 Impala."[9] Played from car stereos, watched on TV, caroled in the locker room. If you were to ask my teenage self what I most wished were true of me, I would have sung these lines at you. Of course, if I were in a discussion at youth group, I would have known to start with the Christian virtues, but I would eventually move on to what I could only secretly acknowledge seemed more valuable to me: some skills, a girl, a phone, and of course a ride. These are the values that made a man complete. The radio said so. My friends said so. And I said so. I had imbibed the values around me and reflected them in my own self-conception.

As much as people might not want to admit it, the identity issues do not change much after the teenage years. Adults may wonder why teenagers are as obsessed with where they fit into the social circles of their local high school, little recognizing their own obsession with where they fit in wider circles. These concerns are not intrinsically evil—wanting to be in a relationship, wanting to be successful according to the measurements of your culture. Nor is it evil to have as part of one's self-concept those other layers of identity I mentioned in an earlier chapter—a Cleveland Browns fan, a banker, a sister and mother, a brother and husband, a Brazilian, a killer scrapbooker. Well, maybe that last one was a bit extreme. My point is, these layers are kept in order of relative importance by how closely they conform to God's priorities. If God said my profession is more important to him than the gospel making it to new parts of the globe, then I would be right to be more alarmed by professional failure than by the unreached millions. But I know from his Word that this is not true, and thus I am accountable to conform my self-perception to God's values.

When helping people, then, consider what beliefs, values, and commitments they have absorbed into the center of their identity. Consider the source of these values, and also consider which have become most central, most self-defining for a person. Not everyone's constructed identity emphasizes the same concerns. The values by which a middle-aged professional man judges himself might be based on financial success. The defining values by which a village elder measures himself might be his standing in the community or his legacy as a great warrior, unlike a medieval monk who may gauge his value based on his austerity and dedication. Regardless of the counselee's situation, counselors are always asking, *What standard are people using to measure themselves? How closely does that standard conform to God's? How are they prioritizing their standard above God's?*

### 3. Considering the Purpose

Every layer of identity has a promised end. It moves toward something, has some outcome intrinsic to it. Elite athletes arrange their existence around their sport in hopes of championship glory. Gang members seek the protection and prestige of being the dominant presence in their space. Academics pursue their studies to establish preeminence in their field. Regardless of the specific of a certain identity, each serves the greater purpose of establishing glory. That glory will be either self-serving or God-serving. John the Baptist understood his identity well when he famously said of Jesus, "The one who has the bride is the bridegroom. The friend of the bridegroom, who stands and hears him, rejoices greatly at the bridegroom's voice. Therefore this joy of mine is now complete. He must increase, but I must decrease" (John 3:29–30). Jesus elsewhere says of John, "among those born of women there has arisen no one greater," yet this privileged role was not for the purpose of his own glory, but to prepare the way for the glory of Jesus, who was establishing a kingdom of people even greater than John (Matt. 11:11). John understood well that the purpose of glorifying self and the purpose of glorifying Christ are mutually exclusive.

The chief end of every layer of identity is only to glorify God as he has revealed himself. In both the permanent and temporal aspects of who people are, they worship God. The permanent aspects of their identity stretch into eternity—they are embodied creatures, made male or female, born into certain tribes and languages, and these unique aspects of individuality are designed for the very purpose of glorifying God, as we see in the cosmic diversity of those who worship in God's eternal throne room (Rev. 7:9–12). But the same is true of the temporary layers of identity that make up a person's situation in the present life, those that will pass away in the age to come. In temporal identities, people purpose to glorify God in the uniqueness of their situation: in their identities as husband or wife (Eph. 5:22–33), as child or parent (Eph. 6:1–4), as slave or free (Eph. 6:5–9), as unmarried or widowed (1 Cor. 7:6–8), as soldier or tax collector (Luke 3:10–14), as poor or rich (James 2:5; 1 Tim. 6:17–19). All of these layers of identity will not pass into the next epoch of human destiny. They are nevertheless valuable as earthen containers of God's glory in the present. As counselors help people consider the layers of identity in their lives, they are always asking, *Is this layer of identity—whether permanent or temporal—precious to them for the sake of their own glory, or God's? What are indicators of either possibility?*

# CHAPTER 8

. . . .

# OTHERS AND INFLUENCE

You are the average of the five people
you spend the most time with.

— *Jim Rohn*[1]

The company we keep, and the books we read,
insensibly form us into the same likeness.

— *Andrew Fuller*[2]

While Jim Rohn is overstating his case, the celebrated businessman perceives something vital about life. He recognizes the power other people have to influence someone's conduct and outlook on life. Rohn aims to set up a culture for personal success by bringing the right confluence of people together. He is right, but there is far more to it. Andrew Fuller, an eighteenth-century Baptist, recognized the same dynamic. He recognized how people shape others, in whatever form their actions or words take. As Fuller noted, the influence can happen without discrete choice. The ability to interact in spiritually significant ways is an important part of being made like God. God gave people dynamic hearts in order to represent him on earth, and the way people do so is primarily through interacting with others.

This is the third of four chapters addressing the contexts to which the dynamic heart responds. The purpose of these chapters is to equip counselors and caregivers to understand the experience of the folks in their care. In this chapter, I will consider how the heart responds to others. The primary point of this chapter is this: The dynamic heart is strongly influenced by many voices in a person's life. Caring for people involves addressing the voices that are most significant in shaping their understanding of life.

People made to image the triune God are inescapably communal.[3] God made human beings with the capacities to shape one another dynamically, for the purpose of spreading his worship across the globe. This is a privilege that cows and trees do not have. In all of creation, humanity is unique in his ability to interact in eternally significant ways. Even in a fallen world, people nevertheless go on influencing and being influenced by one another in ways that will echo into eternity.

Biblical narrators seem to recognize intuitively the shaping influence that people have on one another. Eve was powerfully influenced by the wiles of Satan, and in turn influenced her husband to share in her tragic decision (Gen. 3:1–6). The barren Hannah was provoked to envy and sorrow by the cruel treatment of her fruitful rival Elkanah (1 Sam. 1:6–7). Solomon's 700 wives had such a collective influence on him that the text makes the influence explicit, "His wives turned away his heart" (1 Kings 11:3). Such is the power of others to influence the dynamic functions of the heart.

Ancient proverbial wisdom has recognized the influence as the proverb explains, "Whoever walks with the wise becomes wise, but the companion of fools will suffer harm" (Prov. 13:20). This is a statement of influence through association. Walking with wise people shapes a person's perception of the world, what's valuable and reasonable. Walking with fools will do precisely the same thing, "Make no friendship with a man given to anger, nor go with a wrathful man, lest you learn his ways and entangle yourself in a snare" (Prov. 22:24–25). This proverb focuses on the specific attribute of anger, but the principle can be applied to any human attribute. People "learn the ways" of one another through association and imitation. Like iron in direct contact with iron, people with dynamic hearts have a sharpening effect on each other (Prov. 27:17). This is why "bad company ruins good morals" (1 Cor. 15:33), and just like a little leaven infiltrates all the dough (1 Cor. 5:6).

God designed people to mimic what others believe and value, what they choose, how they behave from their earliest days. God's primary instruction to people—the center of his will for human-kind—is that they love him with the full breadth of their hearts and teach their children to do the same (Deut. 6:4–5). When people believe God's Word, value his character, and submit to his will, they will influence others with whom they interact while sitting in their house together, walking in the street, lying down and rising up, coming in and out of the gates (Deut. 6:7–9). What people primarily love in their hearts shapes others under their influence.

The power of relational influence is seen in the imitation/ example motif used throughout the New Testament, particularly in Paul's letters. Paul frequently instructs believers to imitate him. In 1 Corinthians 11:1, he says, "Be imitators of me, as I am of Christ" (see also 1 Cor. 4:16). Paul unabashedly tells his readers, "Brothers, join in imitating me, and keep your eyes on those who walk according to the example you have in us" (Phil. 3:17) as a means of maintaining citizenship in heaven. He goes on, "What you have learned and received and heard and seen in me—practice these things, and the God of peace will be with you" (Phil. 4:9). He praises the Thessalonian believers' imitation of him and the other churches (1 Thess. 1:6; 2:14), adding specific instruction about imitating him further in providing for the needs of others (2 Thess. 3:7–9). Paul also acknowledges the powerful influence of faith that Timothy's grandmother Lois and mother Eunice had on him (2 Tim. 1:5), and in turn tells Timothy to "set the believers an example in speech, in conduct, in love, in faith, in purity" (1 Tim. 4:12).

Other New Testament writers urge their readers to imitate. The writer of Hebrews instructs believers to imitate others more established in the faith. He particularly sees those whose faith animates them to pursuit of God as well as those who shepherd God's people as worthy of imitation (Heb. 6:12; 13:7). Similarly, the apostle John tells Gaius to imitate those who do good, not those who do evil (3 John 11).

Imitation is an effective means of spiritual formation as people model themselves after others who embody a full-hearted faith. The instruction to imitate is based on the assumption that the beliefs, values, and commitments that flow from genuine faith are passed on to others through active embodiment. The true influence of instruction in the faith is relationally weighted. The gospel message for Paul was not merely knowledge content to be transferred, but also a life to be lived in light of that knowledge. People learn what that life looks like by seeing it. This is true for gospel instruction as well as all human instruction, even negative instruction.

Imitation can have negative effects as well. In a relationally charged letter, Paul writes to the Corinthians, alarmed that they seem more influenced by the super-apostles than by him. At first glance this might seem egocentric on Paul's part; Paul knew that to accept the relational influence of the super-apostles was to accept their gospel (2 Cor. 11:1–6). He spends much of his letter defending not just the core elements of the gospel, but his relationship to the Corinthian believers (2 Cor. 1:12—2:4; 5:11–15; 6:3–10). At one point, Paul makes a personal plea, saying, "We have spoken freely to you, Corinthians; our heart is wide open. You are not restricted by us, but you are restricted in your own affections. In return (I speak as to children) widen your hearts also" (2 Cor. 6:11–13). Paul was adamant to maintain his relational influence over the believers because he knew it would lead to eternal life in the gospel. The super-apostles' relational influence would have led the Corinthian believers to death.

Many other portions of Scripture display the negative influence of relationship, specifically as people lead others to destruction. Jesus himself warned "whoever causes one of these little ones who believe in me to sin" would be better off dead (Matt. 18:3–6). Paul warns that believers who disagree on matters of conscience "not pass judgment on one another any longer, but rather decide never to put a stumbling block or hindrance in the way of a brother" (Rom. 14:13) which could actually result in a person being "destroyed" (1 Cor. 8:11). The reckless actions of one person can cause destruction in another person's life—not just externally, but internally. A person's actions can injure other people's bodies as well as undermine their faith.

## Two-Directional Influence

God designed people to function dynamically in relationship to other dynamic beings.[4] A single morning watching three-year-olds in the church nursery would convince anyone of this. If one child takes notice of an unwanted toy in the corner of the room, then all children converge around it as well. Witnessing someone else playing with the old toy elicited desire in the hearts of other children. This, by the way, is the only explanation for people wanting haggis.

Because people are made in the image of God, all human beings both influence and are influenced. One person's cause is another person's condition. The things I believe about the world, the values by which I measure others, the commitments I demonstrate in my personal life—all of these shape the people closest to me. The things that others believe, the values by which they measure their lives, and the commitments they display also shape me. I affect their trajectories, and they affect mine.

To use a category from Scripture, people imitate one another's desires. People do the same with beliefs and commitments, too. People imitate one another's daily intuitions. If one employee feels depressed about the viability of the company in a tough market and expresses this to other employees, they will be more likely to feel the same. Or if the employee expressed confidence in the company weathering the storm, that would result in the others finding it easier to be confident as well. Imitation is a part of God's good design of human beings in his image.

Without the influence of other image bearers, people do not develop but digress. Without the influence of others, people become less human, because they turn inward in a dangerous way. This is not the case just for the hermit in the woods, but also for people who isolate themselves in less extreme ways. Isolated thinking becomes idiosyncratic—self-referential in a way that repeats itself over and over, becoming less and less penetrable by the ideas of others. Soon, people's minds can only follow certain established ruts of thinking. Those ruts can wear so deep that thoughts about other topics or passion for other concerns becomes impossible. People need the regular interruption of other people's thinking and values to keep theirs in check. People need to observe others' choices to rightly situate their own.

The dynamic functions become dangerously self-referential without disruption from others as they did with my former neighbor. He is a salty gentleman, retired from factory work. He lives alone with relatively little contact with others, though not necessarily by his choice. When I visit him, I notice that the conversation falls into certain tracks every time. No matter the opening topic, the ending topic is always the same: the country is going to hell in a hand basket. If we are talking about heirloom tomatoes, my children's first day of school, or the water main break down the street, all of it relates somehow to the fiery descent of America. I am sure many factors go into this, but the easiest explanation lies in a simple consideration of his daily interactions: the only voices he hears regularly besides his own are those of cable news channels. He constructs a narrative of the world based on this limited input, and rolls it over again and again in his mind.

The two-directional influence of others to self and self to others is a necessary and good thing, but it can have an intentional or an unintentional process. There are many times when influence is consciously intended. People try to change other people's minds about a decision or opinion. Teaching is the intentional effort to shape students' perspective of the world with vital new knowledge or a new perspective about existing knowledge. People influence their significant others' understanding of their relationship when they say, "I love you." The purpose of all such communication is clear: I want you to change in some way I think will be beneficial.

But many times, the consequences of one person's influence on another are not always intended. The influence is often insensible even to the one doing the influencing. The pattern of response people intuitively display in front of others tends to influence their own responses. People express frustration with their boss to their spouse merely intending to vent, but the effect on their spouse is an altered opinion of the boss and likely a mirrored frustration. People who are thankful to God and say so influence others to be grateful as well.

Intentional or unintentional influence can steer others toward good or toward harm. The difference lies in the purpose of the communication: To what end is this influence directing a person's heart? Is it being used for God's purposes in designing human relationships, i.e., increasing a faith in Christ that expresses itself in love for him? Or, is relational influence being utilized for some other end, i.e., erecting some belief, elevating some value, deepening some commitment that rivals this central purpose for the human heart?

These are questions people can apply as a litmus test to all human relationships: Who are the significant voices shaping people's perspective of life? In what ways are others influencing them toward an accurate, biblical understanding of life? In what ways are they not? People, through self-reflection and self-awareness, can distinguish the difference between the helpful and the harmful influences.

Imagine a college student seeking counseling for anxiety. He is in an engineering major at an elite university, and only the highest in the class get the kind of internships that lead to the best jobs. He constantly feels the pressure to distinguish himself from the pack, but is wearing down under the strain. A wise counselor will consider what the important relationships in his life might be telling him about himself.

These voices will at times say things that compete, agree, or are entirely unrelated to one another. This college student has an English major roommate whose constant advice to him is to slow down and enjoy more reflection on life. He has professors who are friendly as they deliver the material, but have little personal concern whether he or some other classmate gets the internship. He has that one rival classmate who is the perennial favorite in his major and never seems stressed. He has parents who help him pay for school and tell him regularly how proud they are of him. He is also regularly on social media, observing what everyone implies about what makes life worthwhile with their pictures and comments.

A counselor should help this college student understand his anxiety as his own response, but the counselor will also help him see how the input of others is an ingredient in that response. Not all of these voices are equally important. The way he perceives the world is always in some way responding to this input: the parents' hope in their boy's success is a value he adopts himself, his professors' lack of interest in him except in measuring his academic performance, the intense drive of his rival toward certain goals, his roommate and the social media world valuing the prolonged adolescence of the college experience. None of these people set a personal goal to teach this young man to place his confidence in his performance, both as an engineering student and as a socialite. Their treatment of him displayed certain patterns of value and belief that he integrated into his own. By helping him recognize this influence, a counselor gives this young man a chance to make a conscious determination of what he will do with the values being pressed on him.

The student must assess them in order to determine whether to accept or reject them. The standard of assessment is God's perspective of human life as described in Scripture. If the particular beliefs, values, and commitments being patterned for him align with God's perspective, then the influence is healthy. If these beliefs, values, and commitments do not align with Scripture, then they are dysfunctional. The answer is not to start cutting off all relationships that impose a foreign value system (Good luck finding one that does not) but to consciously submit to Scripture the values adopted from other people.

## Orbits of Relationship

A person is greatly influenced by the expectations and values of his surrounding family, church, workplace, social circles, economic strata, ethnic background, and countless other cultural expectations, and these personal relationships exert influence to varying degrees. Some voices are highly influencing and some are less so. Which ones are stronger and which are weaker is different for everyone. As people grow in self-awareness, they can understand these orbits of dynamic influence on their perspective and behavior.

Not everyone is influenced by the same categories of relationship in the same way. Some people are powerfully shaped by social circles, others less so. Some are influenced heavily by the opinions of authority figures, others not so much. While there are general patterns of greater and lesser influence, an accurate gauge is simply whether a person holds a relationship in high regard or low regard. The higher the regard an individual has for someone's perspective, the more influence it has on the heart. The lower the regard, the less influence.

By regard, I mean that an individual considers another person's or group's perspective as authoritative. A teenage boy is more influenced by the opinion of an NBA all-star on which shoes are the highest quality than by the researchers at Consumer Reports; his parents are influenced in exactly the opposite way. A young professional may be more influenced by reading a biography of Steve Jobs than by his pastor's sermon from Job on Sunday. In the various orbits of relationship, then, the more the regard people have for the perspective of another, the more influence it will have over their own perspective.

There are various types of orbits people should consider in the web of relationships that stretch through their lives. When people understand the level of regard they have for the various relationships in their lives, then they can consider how Scripture stands authoritatively over the relationships, affirming some aspects and challenging others. Some of the possible orbits of relationships include culture, family of origin, present family, vocation, social circles, and media.

## Culture

Culture describes any group's shared expectations about the world. More specifically, culture is a collective system of beliefs, values, and commitments that act as the organizing logic of a group of people. Culture is established as a pattern of communal response. One person's response increases the likelihood of another person responding similarly, and when repeated countless times by people in close proximity to one another, a typical pattern emerges. Therefore, culture is a significant voice in how people understand themselves, circumstances, relationships, and God.

People's nationality, ethnic background, and even pop-cultural engagement influence their dynamic heart, shaping their understanding of meaning and purpose, the types of accomplishments or possessions they find desirable, the loyalties that shape their sense of identity. For example, my Asian friend was served divorce papers because someone in his family insulted someone in his wife's family. As a Westerner, I could barely wrap my brain around it. Yet, I have seen plenty of Americans served divorce papers because the spouse no longer felt fulfilled in the relationship. I have a feeling my Asian friend would barely be able to wrap his brain around that. He was from a culture more oriented to think of the collective good, whereas I was from a culture that thinks more individualistically.

Meeting folks from other cultures reveals the cultural influences of which people may or may not be aware. For example, I do not like my face being close to someone else's when having a conversation, but my gradual withdrawal mid-conversation seems evasive to my Middle-Eastern brothers. Close-talkers encroach upon my personal space, thanks to my American Midwest upbringing. Imagine how

I feel when burly Italian men kiss my cheeks in greeting. To them, my mild revulsion is a sign of priggishness. Cultures share a general approach to everything in daily experience, such as clothing, work schedules, food, and manners. All of these factors have an influence on individuals. A man growing up in China would feel odd wearing a turban, and a woman from Afghanistan might feel ashamed wearing pants. These are culturally conditioned expectations.

Considering a person's cultural backdrop is no simple task, since everyone lives and breathes in a number of cultures at a number of different levels simultaneously. Sociologists speak of macro-cultures and micro-cultures: On the largest scale, they observe differences in Western individualism from Eastern collectivism. From there, they zoom in on different language groups, down to certain cities, down to certain neighborhoods, and even down to certain families. Larger cultural realities, like national and ethnic identities, somehow interact with smaller cultural realities, such as family, social community, church affiliations. Some of these macro-cultural influences are inescapable, since they characterize almost every significant voice in a person's life: Think of a person born into a Hindu culture as a member of the Sudra caste. Everyone from his parents to the local priests will treat him as a peasant, inferior to the Vaishya landowners, but superior to the street-sweeping Untouchables. So, he will almost automatically understand himself in terms of these categories. The narrow set of opportunities offered him throughout life in his culture will only reinforce this conception. The way each of these layers of culture influence an individual is through key voices that speak to him. Culture does not influence an individual by osmosis. It does so through communication and embodiment: cultural ideals are expressed in people who represent them.

If one of the goals of counseling or personal ministry is to help individuals understand their own experience, then a helper needs to point out the cultural voices that seem most influential over a person's perspective. In Western culture, determining culturally significant voices is complex because of the great freedom individuals have to assimilate divergent cultures into a personal hodgepodge. People are walking mash-ups of different cultural ideals. A teenager's outlook on life may have elements of his parents' Christianity, but also the values of the online gaming community with whom he spends many of his waking hours. A retired military officer may have vestiges of the hippie culture he grew up in mashed up with years of military ideals forged into him professionally. The point is: try to discern what cultural influences determine a person's present perspective of their troubles. Then, a helper considers how Scripture stands authoritatively over every culture's values, affirming some aspects and challenging others.

### Family of Origin

"He's got daddy issues," I heard a friend reflecting about our mutual friend. I had never heard the expression before, but I immediately knew what he meant. Fathers who are constantly displeased for haphazard and unjust reasons leave devastating effects in their children's lives. The constant guessing at his mood, the withering criticism, the guilt-induced gifts, and the obvious disinterest had a strong influence on our friend's perception of himself, of relationships in general, and of God. Best-selling literature and award-winning movies are full of very intelligent folks wrestling with the lingering effects of parental influence, good and bad. Apparently, a lot of writers have daddy issues.

People's caretakers have the single most significant voice in shaping their outlook on life. Significant voices in the formative years are mysteriously powerful in determining the shape of a person's dynamic responses to life. Attitudes, beliefs, habits, and emotive patterns begin their development in childhood, and caretakers largely influence that development. While the Scripture does not indicate that what occurs in childhood is determinative of how adults behave, it does give an overall picture of people as continuous beings. What that means is a twenty-eight-year-old is the same person she was at eight years old, though she has grown and developed in countless ways.

What a person understands as normal, desirable, and good is shaped by the regularities of the family's life, the interests they pursue, the standards upon which they insist. As with every other aspect of a person's culture, family influence stands under the authority of Scripture, which acts as the standard by which all family values are measured. Where family values are determined to be against God's values and thus detrimental to the individual's soul, he will need help finding his way out of them.

**Present Family**

While people's families of origin are important, so are their present family situations. If married, each spouse's family of origin exerts influences. Singles also face unique challenges as a family unit of one. Every new family situation forms its own unique set of expectations and standards. How a family spends its time, the topics of conversation that seem normal at the dinner table, the work ethic displayed in both parents, the level of awareness of each other's thoughts and feelings—all of these are elements of a family culture. Like other levels of cultural influence, the unique culture of a family becomes invisible to them.

Several key questions can help people become more aware of these invisible influences. Every family has a functional approach to God—is he important to the regular considerations of family life, and how? How are members of the family positioned to think of themselves in relation to the whole—as beloved members with valued contributions to make to the whole or as largely independent entities held to certain arrangements-from-convenience? What are the expectations and values by which people are measured in their present marriage and family?

**Vocation**

Vocation is a precious and vital aspect of identity in a Christian theology. Vocation is God's unique call upon a person's life to work for dominion over the world. All human beings share the call to care for God's world, but they do so in their own unique way. Various personal, geographical, and societal factors go into people discerning the best vocation for them. Some are called to be skilled laborers, some educators, some managers, some farmers, some child-rearers.

Every vocational group has its own pecking order, its own promises of glory. Every vocation has its own set of standards by which a person is measured as successful. One vocation's standards are foreign to another's. If a person's present pursuits are schooling, then the standards applied follow the contours of academic performance, the opinions of his professors, and the network of connections in the field for desirable opportunities. If he is in sales, then it is in hitting certain revenue standards, number of sales, expanded client base, and ability to communicate clearly with superiors. If child-rearing, then the standards are more along the lines of the human product being produced, so the standard of measurement is how well educated or musically trained a child is and how orderly the house can be kept all the while.

## Social Circles

From church friends, to social cliques at school, to groups of friends, to common interest groups—the web of social relationships people find themselves in will shape what they want from life. In some circles, the prime value is social popularity; in some it is athleticism and victory on the field; in some it is bookishness and erudition; in some it is plain old hedonism. In all, social influences are a multilayered combination of many values. People have an internal logic of the social circles in which they are most embedded.

Some questions to explore that internal logic include: Who are the most important friends in people's lives? What are people's safe relationships, the kind of comfortable friendships where the exchange of ideas is unthreatening and welcomed? Sometimes, husbands are more open with their buddies at the bar on Friday nights than they are with their wives. College kids may be more comfortable sharing with their soccer buddies than they are with their parents. It is important to know the values shared on the soccer team. If an old lady is more concerned with the opinions of her quilting group than those of her adult children, anyone helping her make decisions must recognize this influence.

## Media

Media is a mash-up of thousands of voices, all elbowing each other for an audience, wanting to draw attention to their prized issues. These favorite issues compete with one another for occupancy in people's brainwaves. Media battle among themselves for the prize of determining what is worthy of the public's attention. The one who wins the battle shapes beliefs and values. Media competes for the power to ascribe worth.

Consider how television, movies, print magazines, tabloid publications, blog sites, and news sites work. They have limited space on a homepage, front page, or screen time, and so they have to place in that space only the most valued issues or narrative themes. To what they draw attention directly reveals what the writers and producers find most worthy or assume the consumer finds the most worthy. To what these voices ascribe worth will shape the values and beliefs of those who listen.

Such media shapes people's intuitions in ways they are not aware. Beale observes masterfully, "Though this worldly media mindset affects us subtly and sometimes unconsciously (i.e., we are not bowing down before the television set, radio or computer), if we do not overtly and consciously evaluate it for what it is, then it can affect us *as if we were* intentionally committed to imitating it [emphasis mine]."[5] Being a regular consumer of *Men's Health* will make people more likely to measure themselves by the standards of physical attraction and performance displayed on its glossy pages, likewise for *Self*. Watching *The Bachelor* will enforce a certain scale of measurement for what makes a potential partner desirable. Watching most reality TV shows pulls viewers into the mud-fight of human stupidity, shaping them to value the amusement that comes from self-righteous shock.

The same is true of social media, although the sources differ. Instead, people's friends and social networks decide what is worthy of attention. Consider this: Certain values are emphasized and worldviews promoted in the twittersphere; the constant stream of status updates and pictures are a direct reflection of what people find worthy; and consuming social media will influence the heart to conform.

People are quick to measure themselves against any standard they see others valuing. It only takes a few pictures of perfectly executed homemade crafts to make a mom condemn herself as uncreative and disengaged. An image of friends crowded into a picture from last Friday's big party is enough to make a twenty-something feel downright lonely. A few articles about things-you-wouldn't-believe-celebrities-did-in-third-grade is enough to dumb the sensibilities of the most sober minded. People are that fragile. The stream of information edits a perspective of life, makes people concerned about things that they would not be otherwise. Social media is documented awesomeness, displayed for the world.

## The Church as Alternate Community

In a sense, church belongs in the same category as other spheres of relationships. Every church, after all, has a culture, a set of shared expectations for what happens within the walls of its building on a Sunday morning (or Saturday evening!) as well as how community plays out throughout the week. Whether hands are raised or are pocketed in singing, how much windows allow natural sunlight or are blacked out for light control, the regular content of public prayers, the expectations on children in the main gathering, the normal characteristics of the preaching—all of these are elements of a church's culture, and by extension any denominations or associations of churches. Besides this, churches can be captured by worldly values that negatively influence members—materialism, moral laxity, cultural crusading—and so function in much the same way as any other relational sphere.

But the church is an alternate kind of community—God designed the church to be a supra-culture, a community whose shared beliefs and values are shaped by the Word of God and characterized by the Spirit of God. People do not leave their regular culture to be a part of the church. Christians do not cease to be influenced by those other orbits of relationship, but the church becomes the centerpiece of Christians' social influence.

Believers understand themselves to be part of a collective body. However imperfectly, the individuals collected into Christ's church are fellow citizens and saints, members of the household of God, the temple of the living God, the pillar and buttress of the truth, the children of God shining as lights in the world (Eph. 2:19, 21; 1 Tim. 3:15; Phil. 2:15). The church is made up of parts that comprise the whole, like the individual parts of the entire human body. Thus the function of one part directly affects the others (1 Cor. 12:20). People who love God with individual dynamic hearts collectively influence one another toward him. The church's love for one another, through faith, reflects the image of Christ, who is the goal of human design (Eph. 4:16).

An individual Christian will only have a healthy faith when influenced by other Christians in the context of church. The writer of Hebrews makes this clear when he instructs, "let us hold fast the confession of our hope without wavering." He then directly commands, "let us consider how to stir up one another to love and good works, not neglecting to meet together, as is the habit of some, but encouraging one another, and all the more as you see the Day drawing near" (Heb. 10:23–25), linking the concepts of holding fast in the faith with meeting together with other saints.

The Christian faith is a collective faith. Individual Christians contend "for the faith that was once for all delivered to the saints"

(Jude 3). Faith is dynamic in the individual, but reinforced through the display of that same faith in the church, the only community of people who are learning to influence one another for lasting good. Genuine faith allows one person to love another without being either controlled by each other or closed off from each other. Church is where people learn to submit their values to God's, and thus not measure one another by the standards of the world—an impartial and sincere acceptance for the purpose of growth. It is a community where one person's commitment to an unseen God strengthens another person as they pull away from the lesser commitments. Church is a community where one person's view of normalcy is molded a little closer to God's priorities by watching the regular conduct of a godly friend.

## Dynamic Transformation in Relationship

People express love with dynamically transformed hearts influencing one another in their thoughts, emotions, and intents. In terms of thoughts, loving others means people will think regularly about the interests and concerns of those around them rather than dwelling on their own. They will be open to thinking in categories not native to their own orbits of concern in order to enter into those of others. An openness to how others think means valuing their thoughts and perspectives as important to, and possibly even corrective of, one's own. This humility recognizes the value of others' thoughts for rightly understanding life, relationships, God, and Scriptures. It also recognizes the importance of sharing healthy, biblical thinking with others in order to influence their thinking to more accurately conform to God's, as revealed in Scripture.

In terms of desires, faith works through love by helping believers have proper desires and emotional responses in relationship with others. As desires for various self-exalting goals or objects give way to faith, a believer is freed to have a genuine desire for the good of others. These desires will change the emotional impact of interactions. A believer's emotional life will serve others through empathy. For instance, Christians may find themselves experiencing sadness at the misfortune of others, even those whose interests have nothing to do with their own, whereas previously, they only experienced sadness from some sense of personal loss. Also, as God-exalting desires increasingly influence the heart, a believer is better prepared to respond to hostility without destructive emotion. Faith expresses itself in emotional orientation to the concerns of God for others.

In terms of commitments, faith works through love by helping believers choose to do what is relationally beneficial rather than relationally destructive. In a fallen world, human relationships are difficult and require dedicated effort. Only the gospel of Jesus Christ, received by faith, can bring about true submission to God's will. Faith purifies the intentions of the heart when interacting with others, undermining ulterior motives that do not correlate with ultimate commitment to God. Jesus demonstrated better than anyone that faith makes people willing to serve others instead of being loyal to their own interests.

# CHAPTER 9

. . . .

# CIRCUMSTANCES AND MEANING

The world's a wonderful place,
If you don't mind laughing at your mistakes,
If you don't mind feeling like you've lost your brakes,
And if you don't mind
A touch of hell
Every now and then.

— *Harrod and Funck, "Come Clean"*[1]

The mind is its own place, and in itself
Can make a Heav'n of Hell, and a Hell of Heav'n.

— *John Milton, "Paradise Lost"*[2]

Humans instinctively assign meaning to everything around them: the sun and moon, the wind and sea, birth and death, plague and bounty. We are explainers because we want explanations. This has been true as long as the earth has been round. Every culture has a mythology that gives meaning to the world, and those mythologies are themselves shaped by the events and circumstances that people group endures. Human experience is one continuous act of interpreting what on earth is going on. We cannot not assign meaning to the things that occur in our lives. (Double negative intended, and not apologized for.)

In various fiction writing workshops I have attended over the years, instructors always remind would-be writers of the basic components of a good story: plot, setting, character, point of view, theme, and other variants. But even with all those reminders, amateur writers tended to make the same mistake: focusing on the characters so exclusively that the setting was paper thin. Ironically, without a detailed setting, our characters were flat—not convincing, likeable, or complex. We had failed to create a world rich with pressure and opportunity, forcing characters to reckon with things they were not expecting—a world with an external logic of its own, where events occurred outside the direct causality of the characters. A good story is about characters trying to make sense of what is happening around them. Likewise, human experience is about people forming beliefs, shaping values, strengthening commitments in response to the circumstances swirling around them.

This is the last of the four chapters that covers the contexts of human response. I have covered how the heart responds to God, to self, and to others. In this chapter, I will address how the heart responds to circumstances as part of our ongoing purpose of equipping counselors and caregivers to understand and help folks in their care. The primary point of this chapter is this: The dynamic heart responds to circumstances by assigning meaning to the significant events and general routines of life. Caring for people involves addressing those meanings in light of the larger meaning Scripture gives to life.

## Active Response and Control Beliefs

People tend to be unaware of why they interpret the facts of life in the way they do. People automatically process the events occurring around them according to their established framework of belief. Why does one mom interpret her son's drug addiction as an indication of her poor parenting while another mom in the same situation interprets it as a commentary on the state of young people today? They usually are not aware of why they perceive a certain meaning in the event because they are not aware of beliefs and values that control them.

Fighter pilots have no such luxury. My uncle, a retired Lieutenant Colonel in the US Air Force, introduced me to a concept called "situational awareness."[3] Unlike people walking around in regular life, pilots have to be aware of their own process of interpreting circumstances. In order to make good decisions behind the controls of a multimillion-dollar jet streaking through the atmosphere at high speeds, pilots have to maintain an active knowledge of the variables of their environment as well as the baseline of knowledge they are using to interpret these variables. Notice the two vital elements here: First, pilots have to recognize the various elements of their environment—location, altitude, tactical status of threat aircraft. Second, they have to apply their aeronautical knowledge to properly interpret their meaning and make a decision—*I have not arrived at the designated coordinates; I am flying too low for my planned maneuver; or threat aircraft is in attack position, and I need to counter maneuver.* Being either unaware of the circumstances or unable to interpret their meaning from accurate knowledge would result in a loss of life and machine.

As complex (and awesome) as flying a fighter jet is, regular human experience is no less complex (though admittedly less awesome). People in regular life have to maintain situational awareness of their circumstances and interpret them correctly according to accurate beliefs. Pilots train their instincts by sound knowledge of aeronautics. For people in regular life, their instincts need to be trained by sound knowledge of God's purposes in their lives.

The interpreting God designed human hearts to interpret. Human beings never experience the facts of life as bare facts. People actively receive facts, not passively. People automatically deposit facts into a system of understanding, like a new book being delivered to a library. That book does not sit independently on a shelf. Librarians integrate it into an existing system of call numbers and subject headings. If the book were not in the system, patrons could not access it, and it would be forgotten. Therefore, folks in library science apply their best theories to position the book in relation to other books. If library visitors came across *A Tale of Two Cities* in the self-help section, they would think someone made a mistake. (Even though Dickens's brilliant novel is more instructive for self-reflection than any self-help book I have seen.) In the same way, people position facts in relation to each other, categorized under subject headings. This is a loose and imprecise process, but it is nevertheless a process that is constantly active.

To use dynamic heart language, people's control beliefs will determine how they interpret circumstances; their control values will determine how they feel about circumstances; and their control commitments will determine what choices they make in response to circumstances. These structures are the catalog system for arranging the library of facts about life. Thus, helping people renew these structures is the key to helping them rightly understand the events of their lives.

Either God's perspective or someone else's will shape those core beliefs, values, and commitments. Only a Godward perspective of life can bring about healthy responses to circumstances. I use the term Godward to describe an orientation to trust God's unseen purposes in the visible events of life. Wisdom is one of the major themes of Scripture regarding people's understanding of life, and wisdom is the fear of the Lord operating in the way people understand the world and live in it (Prov. 1:7). Wisdom means that people understand their life, trusting that God's purposes are at work. Some of those purposes are revealed in Scripture, others remain hidden. The general purposes of history are revealed, while the specific purposes in the details of life are hidden. Only faith allows people to understand their life in light of both.

## A Godward Perspective

The portions of the New Testament that most directly display a Godward perspective of circumstances demonstrate this faith perfectly. Paul's ability to be content in any and every circumstance because of his confidence in the provision of God (Phil. 4:11–13), which closely follows his encouragement for believers not to be anxious in any situation because of God's nearness (Phil. 4:4–7). Or, his similar encouragement to give thanks in all circumstances because it falls within God's will in Christ Jesus for his people (1 Thess. 5:18). Or, the promised grace sufficient to respond rightly "in all things and at all times" (2 Cor. 9:8). These are the little daily applications of large theological truths, like God's wisdom, sovereignty, nearness, and grace. All of them deserve a spot in Christians' core convictions as they think about their circumstances.

These passages show that God's perspective of human life is what matters. A Godward perspective interprets an individual's life in light of the larger purposes of God in redemptive history. God is doing things in a world that was created good, has fallen into corruption, and awaits the redemption of people along with the new creation that accompanies it. Let me unpack that statement a bit further: First, God created the world and declared it good. Therefore, God's kindness and wisdom providentially direct people's circumstances. Second, man's rebellion against God corrupted the world. Therefore, people's circumstances are characterized by suffering and futility. Third, the world awaits the redemption of God's people, which means a person's circumstances serve the purpose of God in preparing believers to be like Christ. Fourth, the world will be destroyed and made new, which means a person's circumstances are temporary and anticipatory of something far better.

A central passage that establishes these themes of existence is Romans 8. In difficult circumstances, Christians love to cite verse 28, "And we know that for those who love God all things work together for good, for those who are called according to his purpose." And for good reason—the purposes of God to use pain for good purposes is the only redeeming thing about the tragedies of life. But the problem is, Christians often cite this verse one-dimensionally. In other words, they recognize redemption, while not positioning it in the context creational goodness, sin's harsh reality, and heaven's future hope. The full logic of Romans 8 is vital for understanding verse 28.

Paul begins with honestly acknowledging the brokenness of a good creation (Rom. 8:18–22). The brokenness of creation is directly linked to the brokenness of people as creation's crowning glory, "And not only the creation, but we ourselves, who have the firstfruits of the Spirit, groan inwardly as we await eagerly for adoption as sons, the redemption of our bodies" (Rom. 8:23). Paul refers to this reality of waiting with one, simple concept: hope. He says, "Now hope that is seen is not hope. For who hopes for what he sees? But if we hope for what we do not see, we wait for it with patience" (vv. 24–25).

The created goodness of the world, the fallen corruption of it, the anticipation of something better—these are the necessary backdrop for understanding present circumstances in light of redemption. Circumstances—even difficult ones—become servants of God in his purpose to train believers to "be conformed to the image of his Son" (v. 29). To put it differently, faith displays itself in the dynamic imitation of Jesus Christ in every circumstance of life. This process is what ennobles every circumstance. Whether Christians were born into a poor family with limited vocational options or a wealthy one with endless possibilities, they can embody the beliefs, values, and commitments of Jesus in that place. Thus, a Christian becomes a unique representation of Christ in the circumstances God has assigned to them.

If believers' understanding of life is shaped by their culture's ideas of what is meaningful—comfort, prestige, safety—then they will respond to their circumstances wrongly: perhaps in bitterness and discontent, perhaps in pride and manipulation. These are the kinds of responses that people languish under, sometimes for years, before they seek help. They get caught into patterns of response and begin to assume that until the circumstances change, nothing can. But the burden of those who care for hurting people is to help them understand the difference between the circumstances and their responses to those circumstances. The remainder of the chapter will be my attempt to put a hand on the various aspects of people's circumstances, in order to help them assess their responses to those circumstances.

## Considering Circumstances

In order to establish situational awareness for the key factors of a person's circumstances, I distinguish between two broad categories: shaping events and general routines. By shaping events, I mean significant, life-altering events that occur to a person. These shaping events may move them along in life or stunt their growth. By general routines, I mean the daily atmosphere of a person's situation—the schedule, the pressures, the comforts, the opportunities of their unique existence. Both shaping events and general routines are vital to understand in people's experiences.

### Shaping Events

The men of the sunken whale ship *Essex* spent months at sea in a few small boats, with little water, depleted rations, and no prospect for rescue when one of their shipmates died, forcing a decision they would never have to make in almost any other circumstance. Should they eat their friend or bury him at sea? Everything in their Nantucket upbringing, with its Christian heritage, had taught them that cannibalism was wrong. But their dire circumstances had a powerful sway over their held beliefs and values. The wrenching hunger, the hollowing thirst, the hopeless repetition of the sea—it suddenly began to seem foolish not to make use of caloric material that would nourish their bodies. Their desire for food overwhelmed their natural and culturally conditioned aversion to what had to be done in order to harvest the meat. The circumstances had compelled these men to

operate in ways they would never have imagined in regular circumstances.[4] The survivors' eventual return to Nantucket did not heal
the trauma of those months at sea. They were never the same again.

Most people have not gone through the particular trauma of
starvation and voluntary cannibalism. But they may have gone
through trauma no less life altering. A child being torn from the
home of negligent parents, an adolescent girl being sexually molested
by a trusted uncle, a young family losing a child, a troop exposed to
life-threatening danger, a refugee fleeing from her burning village,
a city terrorized by a hurricane. These circumstances become the
external conditions that have dynamic effects on the heart, resulting
in patterns of response that would not have been there otherwise.

How specifically do such events shape new responses? Such
events provide new data that compels some kind of change in existing
beliefs and values—by adding to them, altering them, or replacing
them. An adolescent being molested by an uncle opens an entire
world of experience she was not prepared for, and in the most tragic
of ways. This new experience adds knowledge—about the male
body, about her own body, about the dark side of power dynamics,
about the feeling of fear mixed with confusion and guilt. This alters
her understanding of life as more complex than she had recognized,
of males as more dangerous than she had realized, of herself as more
vulnerable than she could have fathomed. This replaces the feelings and beliefs she used to have—toward her uncle, toward herself,
toward life, and toward God. She used to feel secure, now she is fearful. She used to understand herself to be healthy and growing, now
she feels dead and decaying. She experienced sin from the helpless
perspective of a victim, and her outlook on life was altered. Though
I have made the case that circumstances are not determinative over
certain responses, no amount of "heart management" could have
prevented the tragic influence of these circumstances on her patterns
of response. The trajectory of influence is powerful.

Where is the hope for victims of such horrific abuses? Even the
most tragic influences can be mitigated, altered, opposed. Significant

events of the past are significant mainly because of their lingering effect on the way people respond to the daily circumstances of the present. People cannot change the facts of what occurred, but they can change the meaning they assign to those facts, and this begins the glorious process (sometimes arduous, sometimes succinct) of restoring the emotional or behavioral patterns that formed as a consequence of the meaning they originally assigned to those facts.

The Bible gives victims new knowledge that alters the old: God validates the horror of sin, and he grieves its evil effects. God places guilt upon the perpetrator alone. God seeks justice both in this life through the civil authorities and in the next life through eternal damnation. Also, the way the Lord expresses his sovereignty over the evil things that occurred to her is entirely different than the way he expresses his sovereignty over the good. His relationship to evil events is indirect: he withholds the common grace of his righteous character directing the actions of people created to be like him. His relationship to good events is direct: he shares the common grace of his good character directing the actions of people create to be like him. These and countless other truths will help her re-interpret what happened to her.

Such knowledge, received by faith, adds to, alters, or replaces the old. Eventually, this new knowledge establishes itself in new patterns of emotion. Healing may take a lifetime, as feelings of shame or fear do not melt away without a trace. Instead, those feelings will be crowded by the added company of new emotions, like hope in the God who receives the broken and binds their wounds, who has not forgotten them in their circumstances.

The adding, altering, or replacing of values is a constant process—people are dynamic beings ever forming. Victims of molestation are not locked into a static status of victim, but grow and change in their perception of that victimhood. When faith in Christ is actively directing their perception, they find greater freedom to live faithfully in the present. The same is true for the troop shaken by the horrors of combat, the grieving parents reminded of their lost child every birthday, or the refugee seeking a new norm in a foreign land.

## General Routines

The vast majority of days are sort of boring—completely void of the type of incident that would radically alter people's course. Most days are only incrementally significant, and they are the context for a person's regular responses.

People are often unaware of how general routines influence them until they meet someone with a very different routine. I remember, as a kid, traveling to Haiti with my dad. When the Haitian kids dug into their food without washing their hands, I looked up at my dad to see what we were going to do. In the moment, I was feeling some level of distress, due to beliefs about germs. My middle class American circumstances, which included readily available running water and commercials peddling antibacterial soap, largely conditioned these beliefs. My intuitions regarding cleanliness were invisible to me until I met folks who did not share those intuitions, and they were just as healthy and happy as I was. The routines of people's context affect relatively unimportant things, like how closely people stand to one another when speaking, to very important things, like how men should treat women.

Counselors need to understand how the problems people face are in some way their response to their present circumstances. Working through present circumstances does justice to the human experience as God has designed it. When helping people understand their experience, what general routines should people pay attention to when considering the regular daily context of life? Think of the quiet components of their day. The person they wake up next to, the demands that must be answered for the day, the mode of transportation they take to work, the expectations of their profession, the amount of wealth they have, the tightness of their schedules. All of these factors, and countless more, make up the contextual settings to which people respond, and over time, those responses form into characteristic patterns.

Once people identify what general routines they face, they can explore how their responses are shaped by these general routines. While organizing the totality of a person's experience into fine categories is impossible, perhaps I can give two general ones: opportunities and responsibilities. These two simple categories can guide an exploration of the unique circumstances of a person's experience.

**Opportunities.** People's situations have particular advantages and disadvantages, including the opportunities afforded them by their socioeconomic, cultural, and family position. People born into urban, single-parent, working-poor homes will have a different set of opportunities before them than people born into a middle class, two-parent home. It is easy to spot the disadvantages: less income stability, less social stability, less access to quality education, less parental investment. The circumstances they are responding to are quite different than a person born into great wealth and family stability.

A more advantageous situation with better opportunities does not cause healthy responses. Plenty of folks from privileged situations respond poorly to the opportunities before them while people from disadvantaged situations respond in healthy ways. Greater access to education does not inherently lead to greater learning or learning for the good purposes of serving others. Greater access to technology is often addictive, warping the brain. Greater access to food, drink, and entertainment is often the context for indulgence and dissatisfaction. Greater power means greater opportunity to manipulate and abuse others.

Considering people's unique matrix of opportunities will help a counselor do two things: First, understand how people's beliefs, values, and commitments have been shaped by the opportunities available to them. Second, set a realistic vision of what faithful response would look like in those circumstances. A man born as the sixth son of an immigrant family will have a unique perspective of the world shaped by his family's difficulties acclimating to the culture or perhaps by his father's primary investment being in the oldest son's education. He will not think like the only child of a well-established family in town, who never had to acclimate to a different culture or compete with any siblings for parental attention. In whatever difficulty this might cause the immigrant son, the goal of the counselor is not to help him respond like the other guy from the established family, but rather to respond in faith to the unique set of opportunities afforded to him by a wise and loving heavenly Father. Perhaps for him, dynamic faith means being freed of a false value system that esteems being integrated into the dominant culture more than it esteems being included in the beloved of God. For the other guy, maybe faith looks like using the opportunities at his fingertips to benefit others rather than indulging himself.

**Responsibilities.** To be human is to have responsibility. After the breath in their newly formed lungs, God gifted work to Adam and Eve (Gen. 1:28). The responsibility to use God-given capacities for the good of others in the care of creation is one of the crowning honors given to human beings. So responsibility is a daily, not occasional, aspect of a person's experience and a necessary expression of the image of God.

In a fallen world of limited resources, I find the main source of people's fear, distress, relief, or triumph is their various responsibilities in life. I have found it helpful to think of responsibilities in concentric circles of obligation. The circles closest to the center are for obligations that fall most exclusively on a person, such as family or vocational responsibilities. Moving outwardly, perhaps close friendships, then community, then country. For a Christian, the community of God's people ought to be close to the center, as well as an obligation to the poor and unbelieving world.

Considering how people's unique responsibilities and pressures shape their heart responses is a necessary task. People may not be aware of how circumstantial responsibilities are shaping their heart responses, but the experience of being overwhelmed for a homeschooling mother of five will be different than the experience of being overwhelmed for a divorced executive in her late fifties. A young man addicted to video games may need help seeing how his fear of failure characterizes his general approach to the responsibilities of life, thus provoking him to flee into what is safe and amusing. A derelict father might need to see the same thing in the way he is responding to the demands of raising children well.

A faithful response to responsibility acknowledges the created goodness of work, the futility that characterizes all human efforts due to sin's corruption, the unique privilege of all work as an expression of a redeemed heart loving others, and the hope of a world to come where people will immediately perceive the cosmic meaning of their work. These core commitments help people respond to their circumstances in healthy ways, prioritizing the various circles of responsibility in a way that reflects God's priorities.

## Section 3

# Counseling from a Theology of Human Experience

Theology demands practice. A theology of human experience has necessary implications on how people respond to and approach others. Section 3 will outline a methodology for counseling people with dynamic hearts living in the unique situations in which God has placed them. If I were to summarize this process in one (overly complex) sentence, it would be this: People must know God to change. Knowing him relationally involves increasing in the knowledge of who he is from the Word (cognition) in such a way that addresses deeply held values or strongly felt emotions (affection) and calls them to submit to God as responsible moral agents (volition) in the various contexts of their experience (self, others, and circumstances).

The following method most directly applies to counseling, a relationship that is temporarily arranged around the task of helping people respond to particular difficulties that have arisen in life. Counselors bear a heavy responsibility. Their words may lead to either a wise or an unwise understanding of how best to respond in the situation. To give wisdom, the counselor needs to understand the situation adequately, process it biblically, and speak to it skillfully.

Nonetheless, the Bible encourages countless modes of discourse that can be used for transformation, and more people than counselors will find the outlined methodologies helpful. Scripture gives a comprehensive view of life as one, long talking point about

God. People address one another as dynamic human beings all the time, whether catching up with a college friend on the phone or speaking with a grieving neighbor. Thus, the principles of dynamic human experience can help people speak wisely and realistically to others—whether they are parenting children, managing employees, or preaching to a congregation.

I have found it helpful to think of this process as involving four tasks. I use the term tasks, not steps, since they can occur in a flexible order that nevertheless interrelates. Steps work well in a repeatable process, like baking. A cake recipe has a series of steps that are distinct from one another and occur in sequential order. Step one: mix the dry ingredients. Step two: mix the wet ingredients. Step three: combine wet and dry in mixer on medium speed for two minutes, etc.

Counseling is not like baking; it is more like raking. Autumn is beautiful for everyone except those with mature trees on their property. If people are given the job of raking a yard like that, at first they think in terms of three main steps: rake 'em, bag 'em, haul 'em. But quickly they must abandon all hope that the job can be broken into distinct steps. When people are actually in the situation, they discover the dynamics going on: different areas of the yard will have wetter leaves that take more time, trees drop their leaves at different rates, bags tear open (especially the terrible paper ones), sticks get in the way, leaves behind bushes are infinitely harder to gather, and so on. People learn quickly that the day will be filled not with distinct steps, but necessary tasks that accomplish the goal. Yes, there is raking and bagging and hauling, but they occur in an overlapping cycle of aching labor. While there is a certain order that makes sense—people cannot haul bags that have not been packed with raked leaves—this is occurring in a number of cycles around various parts of the yard.

Likewise, the tasks of counseling cycle and occur at various stages throughout the counseling process. Let me briefly introduce these tasks. Please forgive the alliteration. I too am suspicious of lists that all start with the same letter.

## 1. Read: Hearing People's Hearts

Listening is a key feature of counseling since counselors are seeking to understand how this dynamic person is functioning in this particular context. Without listening, counselors understand neither the person nor the context, and thus the process of applying theology becomes impossible.

## 2. Reflect: Helping People Understand Their Heart Responses

Self-awareness is not automatic. Helping people see how their intuitive responses in life reflect deeper structures of belief, value, and commitment is a necessary part of the change process. Without greater self-awareness, people cannot challenge their instinctive responses to life.

## 3. Relate: Looking to Jesus, the Author and Finisher of Faith

As people become more self-aware of their heart responses, they will better perceive their need for help to be what God has designed them to be. That help comes in the form of Jesus Christ, the only man to fulfill God's will for dynamic human life. As people learn to trust Jesus Christ for salvation from their sin, they also learn to trust his help with the dynamic responses of the heart.

## 4. Renew: Calling Them to New Responses from Faith

Learning to walk is a practical matter. Heart change occurs as it is lived out, shaping and reinforcing new values and commitments. A counselor has to help people strategize about how to respond differently in their context. While a counselor's instruction does not begin and end with behavior, it certainly addresses behavior with specific, practical instruction and accountability.

The following four chapters expound on each task, beginning with reading. This task is mentioned first because it must happen early and often.

# CHAPTER 10

. . . .

# READ: HEARING PEOPLE'S HEARTS

You never really understand a person . . .
until you climb into his skin and walk around in it.

— *Atticus Finch*[1]

When people pouring out a slew of details about the problems
that brought them in for counseling, I have often wished for a
Holy Spirit o' Meter to plug into their heart so I can have a direct
reading of what's going on inside there. But, alas, counselors have
no such instrument. What we rely on to understand the contents
of people's hearts is to listen for how they respond to the world
around them.

Listening well involves both letting counselees talk and directing
them with questions that draw their attention to important things. A
good counselor will listen to where people go, how they interpret the
events that surround them, what they emphasize as important, what
they fail to mention, and where they are most emotionally tender. In
all their talk, a counselor is looking for clues as to how their heart
is responding in context. And so, questions ought to come from a
theological framework for human experience as counselors listen to
how counselees' hearts are responding cognitively, affectively, and
volitionally to the various contexts around them—to God, to self, to
others, and to circumstances.

To say the same thing a bit differently, a counselor is trying to discern the interplay between what is inside a person and what is outside a person. In seeking to understand people's experiences, counselors cannot have a singular focus on either the situation or the response. Counselors must address the way people are dynamically responding to a situation, and they must consider the factors of the situation that are provoking the difficulty. Ignoring one or the other will result in lopsided counsel. For example, a counselor could instruct a counselee to work fifty instead of seventy hours a week to reduce anxiety while failing to address the fears of the heart. Or vice versa, a counselor could spend all of his efforts addressing the inner experience of anxiety while ignoring the oppressive situation that provokes it.

Another way to be guilty of lopsided counsel is to ignore one or more of the dynamic functions of the heart. If counselors only pay attention to what counselees are feeling, then counselors will miss important control beliefs that need to be challenged. If they only focus on the choices people make, then counselors will miss the control desires that are driving choices. If counselors only focus on correcting false beliefs, they will not adequately appeal to counselees about making new choices.

One of the greatest challenges for counselors is being comprehensive in their approach, while recognizing key themes that emerge in the way a counselee is dynamically responding to the various factors of life. My hope is that the framework of human experience I have laid out in this book will help counselors recognize what is going on in a person's heart in real time.

I will attempt to lay out this framework of human experience in a way that is useful in the counseling room. I will do this visually first, with basic questions that consider how the heart responds cognitively, affectively, and volitionally to each of the four aspects of a person's situation: God, self, others, and circumstances. The graph for each task will be identical in format, but different in content, since the purpose of each task is different.

These graphs are intended to give multiple entry points rather than an exhaustive list of questions a counselor has to ask. Each graph contains a summary of the questions a counselor will need to consider at each stage. These questions help counselors and other ministry leaders know what insights to anticipate. Then, I will unpack this graph in the rest of the chapter by supplying questions counselors might pose directly to a counselee.

# 1. Read: Hearing Their Heart

| | Cognition: Thought and Belief | Affection: Desire and Feeling | Volition: Will and Choice |
|---|---|---|---|
| *What circumstances (past or present) seem most important? How are they responding?* | | | |
| **Circumstance** | How are circumstances conditioning their responses? What do their interpretations reveal about their core assumptions about life? | How do they respond emotionally to their circumstances? What do their feelings indicate about the values they're operating by? | What choices are they making in response to their circumstances? What do those choices reveal about their core commitments? |
| *Who are the significant voices in their life? How do they respond to others?* | | | |
| **Others** | How do the beliefs of others shape their own? In what ways is that influence being exerted? | How do others influence their emotions? How do the value systems of others influence their desires? | How do their commitments reflect the culture around them? What do their choices indicate about their commitments? |
| *What seems to be their source of identity?* | | | |
| **Self** | What do they think about themselves (generally and specific to the situation)? What do they believe God thinks of them? | How do they feel about themselves? What is their "ideal me"? By what value system do they measure themselves? | How do their actions reflect their beliefs and values about self? How does their dedication to self relate to their dedication to God? |
| *How do they involve God in their story?* | | | |
| **Triune God** | What do they believe about God? Consider functional vs. theoretical belief. | How do they feel toward God? Does their life demonstrate a dynamic desire for him? What do they wish God would do for them? | Does their life demonstrate dedication to God? Is obedience a burden or a joy? What do they pursue hardest in life? |

## Reading Their Responses to Circumstances

What circumstances (past or present) seem most important? How are the clients responding? How are circumstances conditioning their response? Think about both significant events and daily situation. Regarding daily situation, think about both embodied conditions and the opportunities/responsibilities of their situation.

### Listen to Their Experience

#### Cognitive

What do their interpretations of the situation reveal about their core assumptions about life? What do they pay most attention to in describing their circumstances? What's their overall take on the problem with which they want help?

*Questions to Ask*

This situation seems very important to you. Why do you think it is important? What do you think it means?

- What do you think this situation shows about the way God runs the world?
- What do you believe would be better circumstances for you? Why?

#### Affective

How do they respond emotionally to their circumstances? What do their feelings indicate about the values from which they're operating? How have these values been conditioned by significant events in their life? How have these values been conditioned by their unique, daily situation?

*Questions to Ask*

This situation seems like it has affected you emotionally. How did this situation make you feel at the time? What about now?

- Why do you think you were so distressed/moved by this situation?
- What do you wish were different? Why are those differences attractive to you?

**Volitional**

What choices are they making in response to their circumstances? How do these choices establish patterns of behavior? What do these patterns reveal about their core commitments?

*Questions to Ask*

We are always making decisions on the fly in any situation. What did you do in response to this situation?

- What aspects of this situation feel like they're outside your control? What do you do in response to the helplessness you feel?
- How do you typically act when you're in (or reminded of) this situation?
- Have you made any decisions you regret in response to this situation? Why?

## Reading Their Responses to Others

Counselors consider how other people treat their counselees as well as how their counselees are treating others. Counselors are seeking to determine who are the significant voices in their clients' lives, and how those voices exert their influence. They need to think in terms of both actual relationships and cultural influence. How are they being shaped by the thoughts, desires, and commitments of others? Counselors will also need to consider how their counselees exert influence over others through their own responses.

### Listen to Their Experience

#### Cognitive

Who are the most important shaping influences in their life? How do the beliefs of others shape their own? In what particular ways is that influence being exerted—condemning words, affirming words, randomly expressed opinions? What layers of culture are most prominent in shaping their assumptions about life—from social media, to mass media, to family, to specific vocational industry, etc.?

*Questions to Ask*

Our outlook on life is shaped by the way others see the world. God made us this way. Who would you say has shaped you most? Has that influence been good or bad?

- Help me get a feel for the people in your life whose opinions matter most for your well-being? Think in terms of family, social circles, church, job.
- How do those opinions shape what you believe about everything, from God to yourself to your situation?
- What do you think is motivating [specific person] to treat you like that? How do you respond?

**Affective**

How do they respond emotionally to other people? Whose opinions seem most important to them? Who are the people who bother them most, make them happiest? How do the values of others affect their own values? In other words, what desires are they mimicking from the people around them? Remember, this is general cultural voices (media, etc.) as well as close personal relationships (family, friends, etc.). How do their emotions shape their responses to others? Consider their words and actions toward others, and what it indicates about what they want from the relationship.

*Questions to Ask*

We are emotionally affected by other people, negatively and positively. What people in your life tend to affect you most, either way? Remember, this applies to people close to you and to people you may not know, but read about or listen to over media.

- Why do you think they're so influential?
- What might your emotions show you're wanting from them? Does that emotion drive you to respond in a certain way?
- If you could change something about how [specific person] treats you, what would it be?

**Volitional**

How do their commitments reflect the commitments of those around them? To what are they most loyal in the relational circles where they live? How do their choices in relationship show these loyalties?

*Questions to Ask*

The choices of other people directly affect our own. Whose choices have affected you most in this situation, and how have they affected you?

- If you could change something about how you treat [specific person], what would it be?
- What would you say are both good and poor choices you've made in response? Why do you consider them good or poor?
- Why do you think you made those choices?

## Reading Their Self-Perceptions

Everyone operates out of some kind of identity. That identity is a mix of accuracies and inaccuracies. Because of estrangement in a fallen world, people's given identity—who God says they are—does not entirely shape their constructed identity—who they say they are. A major part of helping people understand their experience of various troubles is to understand the identity that drives their responses.

### Listen to Their Experience

**Cognitive**

What do they think about themselves, both generally and specific to the situation? You're looking for what they believe about themselves. A good way to uncover this for those who believe in God is to ask them what they think God thinks of them. This often reveals some of their truest self-conceptions.

*Questions to Ask*

Whether we realize it or not, all of us carry around opinions of ourselves. Generally speaking, what is your opinion of yourself?

- If I asked for the three most important things you believe about yourself, what would you say? If I asked your [spouse/close friend] what they think you believe about yourself, what would they say?

- If you could perch at the edge of God's mind for a moment and observe his thoughts, and someone mentioned you to him, what would you observe? What does he think of you?

### Affective

How do they feel about themselves? Feelings reveal desires, so what do they most wish were true of themselves? What is their "ideal me," a construction they are measuring themselves by? Or, said differently, what value system are they measuring themselves by?

*Questions to Ask*

We are always self-evaluating, whether we recognize it or not. There are things we like and do not like. Let me ask, what do you wish were different about yourself? Why? In other words, describe for me the "ideal you."

- What are the things you feel generally satisfied with about yourself?

- If I were to ask how you typically feel about yourself, what would you say?

- What do you see in other people that you wish were true of you? What have you been told is deficient in you? If you could change two or three things about yourself, what would those be?

### Volitional

How do their actions reflect their beliefs and values about self? What does their pattern of behavior—their weekly use of time, their interactions with others, their media intake—reinforce in their self-perceptions? How does their dedication toward self relate to their dedication to God? In what ways is the one stronger than they other?

*Questions to Ask*

All of us act out of an identity. What would you say your typical pursuits show about how you view your role in this world? What wraps up most of your time?

- What causes or issues would you say you're most dedicated to in life? How does the dedication show itself in your pursuits?
- Tell me about your career goals and how that drives you in the workplace.
- What do you use your free time to pursue? What do you ideally wish you used your free time to pursue?
- What types of media [music, TV, books] are your go-to favorites? Why are they appealing to you personally?

## Reading Their Responses before the Triune God

Whether people realize it or not, their story is not primarily about them, but about the God who made them. People were created with the supreme purpose of loving God with the full extent of their dynamic functions; so every use of those dynamic functions can be measured by how it conforms to this supreme purpose. But the sad presence of sin makes people's hearts inclined away from God. They do not naturally perceive God rightly, nor do they see him as important to their daily experience. So as counselors read people's story, they are listening for how their clients involve God in it.

### Listen to Their Experience

#### Cognitive

What do they believe about God? Is he unimportant or irrelevant to the way they talk about their problem? Is he angry and disapproving? Is he causal and permissive? Is he distant and uncaring? Or, perhaps their view of God is biblically accurate, but seems to be a theoretical instead of functional belief?

*Questions to Ask*

What does God have to do with the trouble that brings you in here?

- If you could describe who God is and how he acts toward you in a few words, what would you say?
- How do you learn about God?

## Affective

How do they feel toward God? Feelings reveal desires, and people tend to measure God by their own desires, either using him to confirm their own wants or being upset with him for withholding their own wants. Does their life demonstrate a dynamic desire for him, or do desires for other things seem more dynamically active? What do they wish God would do for them?

*Questions to Ask*

How do you feel about God most of the time? When do you feel closest to him? When do you feel most distant?

- If you were to guess what emotion God feels toward you most often, what would it be?
- How has God cared for you amid this trouble?
- If you could have a guaranteed yes to one or two requests to God, what would they be? Why do you think he hasn't granted them to you?

## Volitional

Does their life demonstrate dedication to God? What core commitments seem to motivate the person, and how do they align with those God prioritizes? What do they pursue hardest in life, a slot reserved for God alone? Is obedience a burden or a joy in the way they talk about God's expectations of them?

*Questions to Ask*

What would you say is the greatest commitment of your life? What do you pursue hardest in your life in the way you use your time, your words, your money, your efforts?

- If you would say God is your greatest commitment, then how is this demonstrated in your pursuits?
- Do you like the thought of obeying God? Why?
- Do you think God deserves your highest commitment? Why?

# CHAPTER 11

. . . .

# REFLECT: HELPING PEOPLE
# UNDERSTAND THEIR RESPONSES

"I know it's very wrong in me to says so, miss,"
continued the girl, ". . . but she do dress herself out so,
and go on in such a manner to get noticed, that—
oh—well, if people only saw themselves!"
"What do you mean, Phib?" asked Miss Squeers,
looking in her own little glass, where, like most of us,
she saw—not herself, but the reflection of some
pleasant image in her own brain. "How you talk!"

— *Charles Dickens*[1]

If the first task of counseling is to understand other people's heart response, then the second task is to get them to understand it for themselves. People generally do not knowingly choose their response, and this is vital to understand in counseling. They do not choose to be hurt by a friend's comment. They do not decide in the moment which jokes they find funny and which they find offensive. They do not choose to feel so overwhelmingly depressed that the thought of going to work seems like climbing a brick wall. Intuition is an important concept because it explains how people act in the way that comes most natural to them, and what is natural to them is indicative of how their heart is functioning cognitively, affectively, and volitionally.

People are hurt by their friend's comment not because they have decided to be in that moment, but because they believe certain things about their friend's motives (like, the friend should be more understanding), or they want certain things from their friend that the friend is not giving them (like, approval), and they are committed to certain things in that conversation (like, a certain sense of self that the friend's comment undermines). People laugh at one joke and get mad at one another, not because they decide to in the moment, but because the jokes either confirm or deny their beliefs, value or devalue their loves, and affirm or mock their commitments. This is why people can be simultaneously offended and amused by a joke—the joke devalues some things they love, but affirm other things they recognize in the world. Likewise, people are not depressed by choice, but out of the overflow of the beliefs you hold about the world (like, life is pointless without accomplishment), the values they measure themselves by (like, I am not successful), and the commitments they hold (like, my life ought to be better than this).

When counselors recognize this trajectory of intuition, they can appeal to people to take responsibility for their responses in a wise and understanding way. I have attempted to hold two truths in tension regarding the way the human heart works. On the one hand, change is not a choice, in terms of conscious, discrete decisions in a given moment: When you become angry, choose not to be. When depressed, choose happiness. When you feel desire for something unhealthy and sinful, choose not to want it. Such advice ignores the complexity of human experience. On the other hand, change is a choice. Not only can people choose to do the right thing in a given moment despite what they are naturally experiencing, but they also can use the opportunity to look inwardly to seek better understanding of the deeper dynamics that lead to that particular spontaneous response. In other words, people are stewards not just of their immediate response, but of their heart conditions that lead to those responses.

## 2. Reflect: Helping Them Understand Their Responses Biblically

| | Cognition: Thought and Belief | Affection: Desire and Feeling | Volition: Will and Choice |
|---|---|---|---|
| *What framework of meaning might they not realize is motivating them?* | | | |
| **Circumstance** | How are their assumptions about life leading to a misperception of their circumstances? How do these core beliefs fall short of God's ultimate purposes in their circumstances? | What desires do they need to recognize as the source of their emotions? Think both in terms of immediate desires (e.g., circumstances changing) and the deeper value that desire represents (e.g., rest). | What commitments do they need to recognize in their responses to the situations at hand? Do their pursuits match the priorities that they claim, particularly regarding God? |
| *How are others influencing them in ways they're aware of and in ways they're not?* | | | |
| **Others** | In what ways are they unaware of being shaped by the beliefs of others? How can they recognize better the particular ways that influence is exerted? What key relationships do they need to reconsider? | What do their feelings show they're wanting from people? How are they not seeing the connection of their emotions to the values adopted from culture? How might they feel differently if their values aligned more with God? | In what ways are they unaware of being shaped by the priorities of others? How do they come across relationally in ways they're not aware of? How are they motivated by self-interest in their behaviors? |
| *What do they need to acknowledge about their constructed identity?* | | | |
| **Self** | What do their interpretations indicate about their beliefs about self? Do they understand self from biblical categories or some rival standard or judgment? If believers, how aware are they of their identity in Christ? | What do their feelings indicate they want about self? How do their feelings about self reflect a biblical or a rival value system? How does their "ideal me" compare to the priorities of their given identity? | How does commitment to a particular constructed identity show in their words and behaviors? How would Godward commitments reshape these self-commitments? |
| *What do they need to see more clearly about their understanding of and disposition toward God?* | | | |
| **Triune God** | What does their understanding of this trouble indicate about their beliefs about God? How does Scripture affirm or challenge those beliefs? What attributes of God or the gospel of Christ are not adequately present? | What do their feelings indicate they're wanting from God? How do their feelings toward God fall short of those modeled in Scripture? What rival value system are they measuring God by? | What do their choices indicate about their commitment to God? How do these choices pattern themselves as pursuits? How do these pursuits square with Scripture's instruction? |

## Helping Them Be Aware of Their Response to Circumstances

What framework of meaning might they not realize is motivating them? How are they making sense of the story of their life? What are the main events, the main goals, the main direction? In other words, what do they assume life ought to be for them, and what do they understand to be the main obstacles to their ideal life?

### Listening for Self-Awareness

#### Cognitive

How are their assumptions about life leading to a misperception of their circumstances? How are their assumptions about life leading to an accurate perception of their circumstances? How do these core beliefs fall short of God's ultimate purposes in their circumstances? How do these core beliefs align with God's ultimate purposes in their circumstances?

*Questions to Ask*

The way we understand a problem situation is based on certain beliefs we bring into it, beliefs we often aren't aware are operating. Earlier you said [statement] about your circumstances. What are some of the assumptions about life that might be part of that statement?

- How do you think that belief lines up with what God thinks?
- Where might we go in Scripture to get an idea of God's perspective of this? Specifically, what he would want you to believe?

#### Affective

What desires do they need to recognize as the source of their emotions? Think both in terms of an immediate desire (e.g., circumstances to change) and the deeper value that desire represents (e.g., rest).

*Questions to Ask*

Our emotions in some significant way reveal our desires. Why do you think this particular emotion has such a hold on you? What desires might be more active than you're recognizing?

- If you could have one thing that would make you feel better, what would it be? Why would that make it better?
- Do you see that your answer to this question shows what you might be placing your hope in?

### Volitional

What commitments do they need to recognize in their responses to the situations at hand? Do their pursuits match the priorities that they claim, particularly regarding God?

*Questions to Ask*

Our choices in the moment show the deeper commitments of the heart. What commitments do you think were active when you responded to the situation in that particular way?

- Why are those commitments so important to you?
- Would those commitments line up with the priorities that God would want you to have? How do you know?

## Helping Them Be Aware of Their Responses to Others

Relationships are often where people are most blind to the beliefs and desires that drive them. How are others influencing them in ways they are aware of and in ways they are not? Or, what quiet motives make them respond certain ways toward others. What are they wanting from the various people in their lives, and how do those wants shape the way they interact with others?

### Listening for Self-Awareness

#### Cognitive

In what ways are they unaware of being swayed by the beliefs and priorities of others? How can they recognize better the particular ways that influence is exerted? How do they need to see the shaping influence that various layers of culture have on them—from social media, to mass media, to family, to specific vocational industry, etc.? What key relationships do they need to reconsider?

*Questions to Ask*

We respond to our troubles out of a certain perspective of the problem. That perspective is largely shaped by important relationships and key influences. You seem to believe [something] about [someone] in the context of your trouble. Where do you think that belief comes from?

- You seem to really care what [someone] thinks. What does he/she believe about this situation or about you?
- What kinds of things do you like to listen to? Watch? What are the basic beliefs those stories and songs imply about [something]? Do you think the hours you spend hearing these things influences you at all?
- How might you need to reconsider the way you relate to [someone]? How might you need to reconsider the influence [vocational voices, media voices, etc.] has on you?

**Affective**

What do their feelings indicate about what they are wanting from people? How are they not seeing the connection between their emotional responses and the values they have adopted from the culture? How might they feel differently if their values aligned more closely to God's?

*Questions to Ask*

Our feelings in relationship reveal desires that are active below the surface. We want things from people, and we are influenced by what they want from us. Why do you think you feel this particular emotion when you interact with [someone]? What are you wanting from them?

- Have you considered that part of your trouble is how deeply you're valuing [something], not because God says it's important, but because [someone] says it's important?
- If [someone] didn't value [something], do you think you would?
- We tend to mimic the desires of other people—what they value, we tend to value. What they are repulsed by, we are repulsed by. How would you say their *wants* shape your *wants*?
- How do the values of culture shape your emotional responses more than the values of God revealed in Scripture? How might you feel differently if your desires were different?

**Volitional**

In what ways are they unaware of being shaped by the priorities of others? How are they motivated by self-interest in their behaviors? How do they come across relationally in ways they're not aware of? What do their choices indicate about their relational commitments?

*Questions to Ask*

Our commitments and choices are strongly influenced by the company we keep. Do you think the choices you made in this situation are influenced at all by people around you? Or by the commitments that drive your culture?

- Have you ever considered how the priorities that shape your behavior might be more reflective of the priorities of those around you than they are of God's priorities?
- But, our choices also influence others. The commitments that motivate you are always making an argument to others about what they should be committed to. How do you use your influence on others?
- How do other people describe you as coming across? In a conflict, what do they say about you? Do you think there is any legitimacy to their concern?
- We are all in some way committed to our own benefit, but it often takes on a bad form that seeks that benefit apart from

God and at the detriment of others. How do you think your commitment to self-interest has done this?

## Helping Them Be Aware of Their Own Self-Perception

Self-perceptions are often the most tender issues a counselor can address, so humility and carefulness should characterize exploration of a person's opinion of self. People are generally not aware of their layers of identity. A counselor should not presume or make declarations, but seek to challenge people to consider what their responses to life indicate about what they think of themselves.

### Listening for Self-Awareness

#### Cognitive

What does the way they interpret their troubles indicate about what they believe about themselves? Do they understand themselves in light of biblical categories or is there some rival standard of judgment? If believers, how prominent is their identity in Christ in their self-conception?

*Questions to Ask*

All of us construct some perspective of ourselves, and the building material we use comes from many different sources. Some of it is high quality material (sources that agree with Scripture) and some of it is poor quality material (sources that disagree with Scripture). You seem to believe [something] about yourself. What material do you think goes into that construction?

- Why are you drawn to this material?
- How often do you consider what God thinks of you? Where would you go in Scripture to find evidence for how God thinks of you?

#### Affective

What do their feelings indicate they want to be true of themselves? How do those feelings reflect a biblical or a rival value system?

How does their "ideal me" compare to the priorities of their given identity?

*Questions to Ask*

The feelings we have about ourselves are bad guides, but great gauges—gauges to what value systems we're measuring ourselves by. So, a feeling about yourself reveals what you are wanting to be true of you. Have you ever wondered why you consistently feel [specific emotion] about yourself? What do you think you're wishing were different?

- Why do you think those specific differences would make life better?
- Do you really think those "ideal me" qualities would give the things they promise?
- Do you know anyone else who has those qualities? Do you think their life is really as ideal as you imagine it to be?
- How do those "ideal me" qualities square with what Scripture says about you? How do they overlap, and how do they rival the biblical value system of self?

**Volitional**

How does commitment to a particular constructed identity show itself in their words and behaviors? What do their choices indicate about their self-commitments? How would Godward commitments reshape these self-commitments?

*Questions to Ask*

All of us act out of a certain identity. In the situation we're discussing, what identity do you think was motivating you? Who are you trying to be?

- In other words, actions prove what we're dedicated to, particularly about ourselves. What do your choices show about your dedications?
- How might various forms of media shape your self-conception?

- Our pursuits reinforce and shape our self-conception. How do your particular pursuits do this? Consider, for instance, the media you take in—your music, your TV, etc.—what do they say you should see your ideal self? Also, consider the implicit ideals of self within the various pursuits of life—such as hobbies, social circles, vocation, etc.
- How do these commitments square with the commitments God says lead to lasting life? How do your commitments overlap or rival the commitments of God as revealed in Scripture?

## Helping Them Be Aware of Their Responses to the Triune God

Counselors try to make people more aware of their responses to all of life, and particularly how those responses relate to the way they respond to God. A counselor needs to make this connection explicit. Specifically, human hearts were designed to worship God with their dynamic functions: the way people dynamically respond to anything says something about how they are worshipping God. The way people relate to a visible world is directly connected to the way they relate to an invisible God. Counselors are constantly attempting to help counselees see what they need to perceive in themselves more clearly about their understanding of and disposition toward God.

### Listening for Self-Awareness

#### Cognitive

What does their understanding of the current trouble indicate about their beliefs about God? How does Scripture affirm or challenge those beliefs? What attributes of God or the gospel of Jesus Christ are not adequately present or active?

*Questions to Ask*

Your understanding of the present struggle you're in actually
has everything to do with your understanding of God. He is the
one who oversees the details of your life, so how you interpret those
details has to do with him. Earlier, you said [statement] about your
current struggles. What does this imply about God?

- What do you think God would say about himself in
  response? Are there aspects he would affirm, and others he
  would deny?
- Where can we look in Scripture to find out?
- How do you think the gospel—that is, the person and work
  of Jesus Christ—bring a fresh vision of who God is to you
  in this situation?

**Affective**

What do their feelings indicate they are wanting from God?
How do their feelings toward God fall short of those modeled in
Scripture? What rival value system are they measuring God by?

*Questions to Ask*

You seem to feel certain emotions (or no emotion) toward God.
What do you think your feelings are indicating your wanting from
God?

- How do those feelings toward God square with the full range
  of emotion toward God you see modeled in Scripture (from
  joy to sorrow, confidence to anxious longing)? How do your
  emotions line up with Scripture, and how do they not?
- What we want from God is informed by value systems we
  hold that we're not always aware of. And we tend to measure God by that value system. Our idea of his goodness,
  his wisdom, or his love are reflections of what we want from
  him. What rival value system might you be measuring God
  by?

- What might you be expecting from God before you are willing to call him good or loving? How does Scripture define his goodness and his love?

**Volitional**

What do their choices indicate about their commitment to God? How do these choices pattern themselves as pursuits? How do these pursuits square with Scripture's instruction?

*Questions to Ask*

Our choices over time form patterns—these patterns can be called pursuits. What do your pursuits in life generally indicate about your commitment to God? In other words, if God is supposed to be your supreme commitment, and therefore your supreme pursuit, what does an honest look at how you use your time indicate about your commitment to God?

- How do you understand your other pursuits as servants to, not rivals of, a pursuit of God? What's the difference?
- The best gauge to evaluate individual choices is how they display commitment to God. A key moment for you was when you [situation]; in response, you chose to [choice]. How did that display a commitment to God or fail to?

# CHAPTER 12

. . . .

# RELATE: LOOKING TO JESUS, THE AUTHOR AND FINISHER OF FAITH

*If faith is the sole condition of the Divine act of grace*
*which makes the beginning of the new life,*
*then it alone can be also the condition of every furthering*
*of that life. The ultimate aim of every exhortation*
*can only be to strengthen faith.*

— *Franklin Weidner*[1]

As people grow in self-awareness, they will inevitably see more clearly how far short they fall of perfection. They will see both their weakness and their sin, both of which will cause pain. That pain is one of the holiest experiences a person can have, not because the pain itself has value, but because pain provokes movement. And movement is necessary to the growth of a soul. But movement in and of itself can be dangerous, depending on the direction it takes. People can head inward, simply building up defensive walls made with bricks of self-justification, held together with the mortar of self-deceit. But if they move outward, they step into a light that exposes rather than conceals.

Why would anyone do such a thing? Because in the light is where grace is found. Jesus stands in the light, inviting people to come to him, to trust that the light is safe because he is there. Without light, people do not notice their imperfection. Jesus came to those who are willing to notice their imperfection, willing to step into the light to see just how critically they have failed to be what they were supposed to be.

In the previous two chapters, I outlined the first two tasks in a counseling methodology. Understanding a person's experience, then helping them to understand it themselves will only be helpful if they have somewhere to go with this greater awareness. Self-awareness for its own sake will not yield change. That experience has to be measured against an ideal. Every psychotherapy does this with its own ideal, a model of healthy functioning that serves to expose what is undesirable. Christian theology holds up an ideal that is not merely a conceptual construct, but a living person. Jesus is the perfection of humanity who came to restore the flawed and broken. One of the grandest titles given to Jesus in Scripture is "the author and finisher of our faith" (Heb. 12:2 NKJV). Faith is the means by which the heart's dynamic functions are restored to proper use. So that means Jesus is the one who starts and finishes the renovations needed in the human heart.

Counseling should attempt to be moving people toward faith—helping them, in all their experience of life, relate to Jesus, in all his experience of life. He is able to sympathize with human experience in every way, yet he perfected it by his perfect obedience to God (Heb. 4:15; 5:8–9). Every function of his heart was used for the exact purpose it was designed for: to worship God by loving him and his people. And Jesus sits on a throne called grace to give mercy and help whenever his people need it (Heb. 4:16). Faith is not just one possible avenue to healthy human function—it is the only way to participate in the completed humanity Jesus accomplished.

For this reason, the third task in this counseling methodology is to relate. The primary goal of counseling is to proclaim the Word of God into a person's experience in hope that the Spirit will produce faith in Christ, which renovates the dynamic functions of the heart. Faith, brought about through the Word, is the means by which the triune God relates to dynamic human beings, restoring them to be like him.

Properly relating to Christ is to trust the words he says. Methodologically, this means that counseling must involve careful interaction with God's Word. To do so, counselors must know Scripture well enough to relate the heart of Christ to people's experiences. Counselors need to know what God would say about the beliefs, values, and commitments of a person's heart. This requires a sound hermeneutic and a loving familiarity with the Word.

Counseling is in one sense a ministry of proclamation. I am not implying it is like a counselor preaching at a person. Rather, I mean that the Word of Christ is central to the interaction between counselor and counselee, whether that interaction is primarily characterized by listening with the compassion and categories of Scripture, by asking questions that explore various functions of a person's heart as described in Scripture, or by offering counsel that seeks to form biblical faith by describing some aspect of the gospel of Christ appropriate to the counselee's situation.

The primary purpose of Scripture is to elicit faith in the gospel of Jesus Christ. Counselors may have their Bible open the whole time and misuse it entirely. Every use of Scripture must drive at faith in Christ, as an expression of the faith-centered understanding of human response.[2] For instance, when facing a young man who keeps returning to pornography, a counselor may refer to a verse such as 2 Timothy 2:22, "Now flee youthful lusts and pursue righteousness, faith, love, and peace, with those who call on the Lord from a pure heart," apart from its theological context in the gospel. Biblical counselors may spend their time admonishing the young man to put off the old behavior and put on the new, give him methods to establish the discipline, and warn him against failure, all without explaining that the power to change is an effect of Jesus's life, death, and resurrection, and this good news is continuously received by the exercise of faith.

The need for faith makes the whole counseling process—and especially this third task—utterly dependent on God's action. Faith is something ultimately produced neither by the counselor nor the counselee.[3] Counselors must pray as if their biblical methodology were only complementary to the Holy Spirit's grounding work. Counselors ask for God to grant in their counselees' experience the benefits Christ already accomplished on their behalf. And so, counselors learn to be beggars, pleading with God on behalf of others.

This pleading makes counselors patient. Faith is imperfect in the present age. Counselors must base their expectations on the fact that change can take a long time. Faith will not be perfectly operative in every dynamic function of the heart as long as a person is still fighting their sinful nature. Biblical instruction is always given in the context of the present reality that sin is still present in the hearts of believers.[4] The apostle Paul longed for the resurrection from the dead as the only time he could close his grasp on perfection (Phil. 3:2–14). Counselees live in the same reality: moral corruption and physical brokenness will plague them until Jesus returns.

Counselors must maintain the tension between present and future realities. On the one hand, counselors acknowledge God's good instruction to be righteous in the dynamic functions of the heart. The promised, future perfection indeed invades the present age, and changes people now. Counselees, by faith, can function in significant measure according to the righteousness of God. On the other hand, people still live in a present age marked by futility. This means that the heart will never be perfectly unified to function in accordance with God's design prior to heaven. Because the heart will not be perfectly consistent with God's design, counselors must avoid prematurely concluding that counselees' faith is not genuine even in the face of serious problems with regard to their thinking, feeling, and choices. The progressive nature of sanctification, the growth of faith, in these areas requires patient direction that avoids quick dismissal.[5]

If a Spirit-dependent, realistic call for faith is the goal, what does that task looks like practically? The rich landscape of Scripture has many stories, poems, admonitions, parables, prayers, and descriptions that will direct counselors. The themes or insights presented in the following sections represent only a portion of Scripture's vast, rich material. What follows are a few, foundational truths as examples of relating the world of Scripture to the world people experience.

# 3. Relate: Looking to Jesus, the Author and Finisher of Faith

| | Cognition:<br>Thought and Belief | Affection:<br>Desire and Feeling | Volition:<br>Will and Choice |
|---|---|---|---|
| *Only faith in Christ gives the right outlook on circumstances (Phil. 4:4–13)* | | | |
| **Circumstance** | Circumstances of life occur by the meticulous sovereignty of God (Pss. 139:16, 75:6–7; Prov. 3:5, 20:24, 21:1), who is to be trusted (1 Pet. 1:6–10). Though he directs evil circumstances, he does not do evil, but hates it (Job 1:21–22; Luke 22:22). | Faith involves both directing emotional responses that arise in circumstance and submitting to God the desires that lead to those responses (Mark 14:34–36; Luke 12:50; 22:39–46). | Faith is demonstrated in action amidst circumstances (1 Pet. 1:6–7, 13–20). Though circumstances may not change, a believer can always act faithfully in them (1 Cor. 10:13). Give practical decisions to make. |
| *They can only love others when they receive Christ's love by faith (1 John 4:7–21)* | | | |
| **Others** | Faith helps them love others, which includes believing what is charitable and realistic. Help them see how faith frees them from both controlling and being controlled by others (Ps. 118:8; Luke 6:37–38; Rom. 12; 1 Cor. 13; Gal. 5:14–26). | Faith changes what they want out of relationships, and thus the emotions within. Also, they will measure others based on God's values and not their own self-centered ones (Ps. 56:10–11; Prov. 29:25; Heb. 13:4–6; 1 John 4:20). | Faith changes core relational commitments from self-serving to self-emptying. Also, personal commitment to God's people grows (Prov. 13:20; Heb. 10:24–25; 1 John 2:15–17; 3:11–18). |
| *Their given identity prioritizes their union with Christ by faith (Rom. 6:5–11)* | | | |
| **Self** | Faith reinforces what is most true of a person: their given identity as created, fallen, and especially redeemed. Identity in Christ must become their central consideration of self (Gal. 2:20; Phil. 3:3–16). | Right feelings about self come from right values about self. Faith helps them see the key values God considers important in their identity, thus expelling rival values (2 Cor. 1–10). | Their identity is chiefly as child of God. Thus, obedience is central to their role in the world. This commitment will show itself in long-term patterns of action that reinforce godly character (1 Pet. 1:14–18; 1 John 3:1–3). |
| *They can only love God by knowing Christ's love for them by faith (Eph. 3:14–21)* | | | |
| **Triune God** | They were designed to know God, which includes knowledge of him. Faith shows particular aspects of God's character and redemptive intention that build up (Jer. 9:23–24; Eph. 1:15–19; Col. 1:9–12; 2 Pet. 1:5–7). | They were designed to value God as he has revealed himself, and to express the full range of emotion to him. Faith allows them to value God as superior to other desires (Pss. 13, 16, 42–43; Lam. 3:1–26; Mark 14:32–36). | They were designed to obey God willingly, which means they submit their priorities to his. The heart was designed to benefit from God as supreme commitment (Luke 14:25–33; 1 John 5:1–5). |

## Relating Circumstances to Christ

Only faith in Christ gives the right outlook on circumstances. Paul wrote Philippians 4:13, "I can do all things through him who strengthens me," in context of finding contentment in "whatever situation I am." Such a statement is impossible apart from a vision of the world that starts with confidence in who Jesus is and the certainty of what he promises. So, the command "do not be anxious about anything" (Phil. 4:6) is a command to trust what God has chosen for them is better than counselees' own perception of what ought to be. Show them how faith in Christ would change the way they are perceiving their situation.

### Possibilities for Relating Experiences to Christ

#### Cognitive

They have understood the circumstances of their lives according to certain active beliefs. What beliefs can you affirm? What beliefs need to be challenged? Scripture that speaks of a meticulously sovereign God also speaks of him as wise, loving, and attentive. In terms of the evil things that have occurred to them, show them how God is mysteriously grand enough to both allow evil circumstances to occur and to hate what occurred, mourn over the loss, and work for their healing (Job 1:21–22; Luke 22:22).

*Questions to Ask*

Let's turn to [specific Scripture] and read it together. The author who wrote this did not know about [the specific circumstance] when he was penning these words. But do you think he had experienced some form of suffering? How is that suffering similar to and different from yours?

- Yet, despite his suffering, he still says [specific truth] about God. How can we explain that?
- Why do you think it is so difficult for you to trust that God is wise and good in the particular circumstance he has allowed in your life? What might you be assuming about the

way the world should work? How does that assumption line up with what we see in Scripture?

- God is mysterious in the best sense of the word—not that he is sneaky, but that he is too big for us to wrap our minds around. This means he can both allow evil to occur to us and hate that specific evil. The Bible has a view of God that allows people to be honest with him about how suffering brings doubts because God is patient with our limitations.

### Affective

Faith involves directing emotional responses that arise in certain circumstances and submitting to God the desires that fuel those responses. The emotional responses are the intuitive expression of the deeper desires. Show a person what a controlled emotional response would be to the circumstance, one that is the outflow of no longer being controlled by a specific desire, but instead by a deep valuing of who Christ is to them. Like Jesus before them, they can submit deeply held desires to God even in the midst of emotional turmoil (Mark 14:34–36).

*Questions to Ask*

Remember the two levels of how emotions work—the immediate emotional response in the circumstance, and the deeper desires that drive those responses. We are responsible for both, but in different ways.

- Let's first consider your [specific emotion] in the circumstance. What about that response was faithful? Is there something you would change? How would you express yourself in a way that avoided old patterns?
- Now, let's consider the [specific desire(s)] that have lead to [specific emotion]. These desires will only lose their control of you when a deeper value has taken control. That deeper value has to be the wisdom and goodness of God in choosing these particular circumstances for you.

- How do you need to repent of being controlled by these desires? Let me give you a picture of how to acknowledge the goodness of a particular desire, but hold it with an open hand before the Lord.

### Volitional

Faith is demonstrated in action amidst circumstances. Help them see how their choices have been from a perspective of life that has not adequately weighed the loving kingship of Jesus. Commitment to trust him will give strength to make the kinds of choices amidst circumstance that will lead to life. God promises the ability to act faithfully in any difficulty (1 Cor. 10:13; 1 Pet. 1:13). Give them a vision for what that might look like, even if circumstances do not change.

*Questions to Ask*

Your actions in response to circumstances show the true commitments of your heart. Where do your commitments align with God's? How can I support you in those? Where would you like to change your commitments? What if you were more deeply committed to trusting God's goodness in these circumstances? How might your [specific choices] be different?

- You will only be freed from enslavement to your own perspective of what your life ought to look like as your commitment to God's purposes grows. How do you need to repent of insisting that your own ideals are more worthy of your loyalty than God's ideals?
- Do you believe that Jesus Christ is able to both forgive and to strengthen your resolve to be like him, rather than to have what you want? What might be preventing you from believing that?

## Relating Their Relationships with Others to Christ

Counselees can only love others when they receive Christ's love by faith. Their ability to fulfill the law of love is granted only by faith in

Christ (Rom. 13:8; 1 John 4:7–21). Faith allows people to change the way they naturally act toward others: by either manipulating others for their own desires or avoiding others when they have no use for them. In stark contrast, love is a commitment to the eternal good of others at cost to self. Only by receiving such love from Jesus can people share this love with others.

### Possibilities for Relating Human Experience to Christ

#### Cognitive

Scripture calls believers to have a perspective of others that is both realistic about their sin and weakness (Rom. 3:10ff) and charitable about their worth as the image of God and capacity for redemption in Christ (1 Cor. 13). Help people see how their beliefs about certain people may err in one or both ways. Also, how should they reconsider the influence that certain relationships (or entire relational circles) have on them?

*Questions to Ask*

We've seen how you believe [particular belief] about [particular person]. Scripture tells us to love others, which involves having a view of them that is both realistic and charitable. How do you think your perspective of this person needs to be affirmed? How does your perspective need to be corrected?

- We've seen how your assumptions about life are heavily influenced by [specific voices, whether relationships, media, etc.] in a negative [or positive] way. How do you need to limit [or encourage] the power of that influence?
- God designed you to be influenced by others in good ways for the building of your soul. What are potential relationships that will build into an accurate perception of the world?

#### Affective

Faith in Christ changes what they want out of relationships, and thus the emotions they will feel in them. Instead of being motivated by self-centered desires for what others can do for them (e.g., "I want her to like me"), they are freed by a deeper desire for God's glory in the relationship (e.g., "I want her to be built up in the Lord"). This will change the emotional texture of the relationship—less fear and hurt, and more genuine grief as well as hope. Also, faith frees them from measuring others by old value systems—such as appearance, desirability as a mate, social influence, etc. Instead, they will begin to assess people according to what God says is valuable. This, in turn, will allow them to be more characterized by godly emotions toward others—less self-justifying disgust or anger, more sympathy and hope.

*Questions to Ask*

We've seen that you feel [specific emotion] consistently regarding [specific person], and we've been able to attach that feeling to [specific desire]. We know that feeling is conditioned by the way the other person treats you, but it is also your response. It is a response that is not random, but makes sense according to what you are desiring. What do you think God would say to you about that desire? How would he affirm it, and how would he challenge it? Where in Scripture could we go to find God's opinion on the matter?

- We have also seen that you tend to judge [specific person] based on a [certain value] that you think they ought to show. How does that value measure up to the values we see in Scripture? Does God share your opinion on what ought to be important in others?

**Volitional**

Commitments are shown in the way people treats others. Since faith in Christ will change people's relational commitments, it will also change the way they treat others. A commitment to the redemptive good of others means that choices are made from self-emptying, not self-serving commitments (1 John 3:16). Renewed commitment to Christ also makes a person committed to Christ's people. Fellowship becomes a vital means of imitation and encouragement (Prov. 13:20; Heb. 10:24–25).

*Questions to Ask*

Whether we realize it or not, we always have certain purposes in the way we treat others, and this shapes the way we treat them. We have seen that you want [specific desire] from [specific person]. How does that shape the way you treat them? What would God say about your actions? What would he say about the desires that shape those actions?

- We've also seen that the people who exert the most influence on your outlook on life are [specific people, media, etc.]. Knowing that we were designed to imitate the people we value most, would you say these influences help you toward godliness or away from it? How does your relationship with them need to change?

- What people has God placed in your life to show a deeper commitment to? Who are you uniquely positioned to serve? Dedication to Christ deepens dedication to them.

## Relating Their Self-Perception to Christ

Their given identity prioritizes their union with Christ by faith (Rom. 6:5–11). For Christians, their union with Christ is the most important truth about them. People are in a long process of submitting their constructed identity to their given identity. In other words, growing in maturity as a person is the day-by-day process of conforming my perspective of myself to God's perspective of me.

### Possibilities for Relating Human Experience to Christ

#### Cognitive

Faith reinforces what is most true of a person—that is, their given identity as created, fallen, redeemed, and newly created. The truths attached to each of these elements form the baseline of every belief they have about themselves. If a belief they have about themselves does not square with these, then it must be opposed, because it is a false construction. Faith makes these truths about their given identity more and more active in their constructed identity. In other words, their identity in Christ must become their central consideration of self (Gal. 2:20; Phil. 3:3–16).

Note for unbelievers: Their given identity includes their created value and fallen corruption. A counselor should not ignore either element when discussing their self-perception since they'll need to understand both in order to make sense of their experience in this world. The closer their self-conception comes to God's conception of them in these first two elements, the more prepared they will be to value the redemption freely offered in Christ as necessary to the restoration of their design.

*Questions to Ask*

We've seen that you tend to think [specific belief] about yourself, and that belief has been shaped by [specific source]. How do you think that belief fits into God's perspective of you, as laid out in Scripture?

- How does this belief square with [key aspect of created, fallen, redeemed, newly created]? Perhaps you believe these aspects of your given identity, but they are less active than this old belief. Believing the gospel means believing what God says about you more deeply than what you naturally believe about yourself.

- What voices are reinforcing these beliefs about myself, rivaling God's voice? What should you do with those voices?

**Affective**

The way we feel about ourselves is one of the strongest motivations we have. Right feelings about self come from right values about self; and right values are an expression of faith in Christ. In other words, people will only be able to measure themselves according to God's standards when they have submitted themselves by faith to him. What we wish were true of ourselves changes from an established pattern of value to God's values only as we more deeply believe what he says is true and good (2 Cor. 12:1–10). Faith helps people see the key values God considers most important to their identity—only this can expel rival values that capture them.

*Questions to Ask*

We've also seen that you feel [specific emotion] about yourself quite a bit, and that this emotion is because you really want [specific desire] to be true of you. You seem to spend so much energy wishing you could be that, you don't have much left over for what God says you ought to be longing for. What does God say in Scripture you should most want for yourself? Let's consider some passages together.

- You tend to measure yourself according to values shaped by [specific sources]. What they tend to want, you want for yourself. Faith means a significant shift in the values you measure yourself by. Why is God a better source for the values you should adopt for yourself?

- Only when you embrace God's perspective of you as wise, good, and true will you be able to expel those rival values. Being popular, pretty, successful, etc. are not values that can deliver on what they promise. Your heart was designed to desire to be like what you value most; when you want to be like God, your heart is working right.

**Volitional**

Regarding self, the core commitment of faith is to relate to God rightly from one's true identity. All other commitments make way for this one. This identity is captured with various metaphors in Scripture, a key one being as redeemed child—thus, believers see their primary commitment is joyfully to obey their Father and to reflect his character (1 Pet. 1:14–18; 1 John 3:1–3). This commitment will show itself in long-term patterns of action that reinforce godly character.

*Questions to Ask*

Your pursuits in life show you functioning out [specific commitments] that are a core part of how you see yourself. But this is not the most important thing about you, according to Scripture. God speaks to you primarily as his child—redeemed to be like him. In other words, you belong to God, not yourself. How do the pursuits of your life—the regular actions of your day—show your commitment as child of God? How do they fail to?

- Grace meets us when our actions fail to live up to what they ought to be. You did not make yourself a child of God by doing what is right, but by receiving Jesus' love for you. Believing his love for you is how obedience becomes a joyful reflection of who you are rather than a fearful or embittered attempt to become something you're not. Let me show you from Scripture.

- Godly character is a long journey of small obedience. Has that obedience fallen off the priority list? If it has, it's because we have lost sight of the benefits of obedience compared to the benefits we see in other things. Let's consider in Scripture the main benefit of obedience: the freedom and joy of being like the free and joyful God.

## Relating to the Triune God

Counselees can only love God by knowing Christ's love for them by faith (Eph. 3:14–21). Their hearts will work right as they receive the love of God through faith in Jesus Christ. Faith includes understanding God's world-changing truth, desiring the pleasure of being near God, submitting to the benevolent authority of their King. God designed their hearts to love him and to love others, but they can only do this by knowing God's love first, as John wrote, "We love because he first loved us" (1 John 4:19). This love is dynamically received and dynamically expressed from the heart.

### Possibilities for Relating Human Experience to Christ

#### Cognitive

Knowing God is the most important thing people were designed to do (Jer. 9:23–24). In fact, the knowledge of God brings life

(Eph. 1:15–19). Their understanding of God will have a number of deficiencies, from thinking of him as anything from permissive to unreasonable, from uncaring to hateful. Sometimes, their understanding will center on something true of God, but so narrowly focused that other vital elements are ignored (e.g., a focus on his holiness to the exclusion of his mercy, or on his kindness to the exclusion of his righteousness). The gospel of Jesus Christ reveals God most truly for who he is as well as his intentions toward people (Col. 1:9–14). Counselees will need to see how their view of God needs to grow to match the color and breadth of how the Bible describes him. What particular aspects of God's character or redemptive intention will build them up?

*Questions to Ask*

When you think of God, you tend to focus on [specific belief]. But Scripture's view of God is much broader than this, and also includes [pertinent biblical truths]. How should these truths reshape what you focus on when you think about God?

- The Bible speaks of the knowledge of God as more valuable than anything else on earth. Yet, the pattern of your pursuits does not seem to agree with this. We pursue what we perceive as valuable. In what specific ways would your priorities need to change if you were to agree that the knowledge of God is more valuable than the [specific commitments] that seems to motivate you?

- It is sometimes difficult to see the immediate benefit of being under the Word—whether privately or corporately. We like to sense the purpose of things as we do them. But the knowledge of God is more like long-term building material for the soul. What do you think I mean when I say that? Let's consider from Scripture why knowing God leads to a better life.

## Affective

People were designed to value God as he has revealed himself, and not some preferred version of him. The only way for desires to function properly is to value the Creator more than anything he created (Rom. 1:25). What their emotions are tied to is a direct gauge of their desires, desires designed to be inclined toward God first (Pss. 16:11; 73:25–26). As desires are ordered rightly in worship to God, emotions will follow their contours. This does not mean that a person desiring God will only experience positive emotion. No, godly desires lead to the full range of godly emotion: sorrow to joy, fear to hope, anger to happiness (Pss. 13; 42—43; Lam. 3:1–26; Mark 14:32–36). These emotions are godly when they are Godward—expressed to him in faith and reflective of his values.

*Questions to Ask*

As we have established, we all tend to create God after the image of what we want him to do for us. For you, it seems to be [specific desire], and you feel [specific feeling] toward him because he's not meeting those expectations. But you were designed to value God as he has revealed himself, not as you prefer him to be. Let's consider how Scripture would direct us to submit this desire to God, and not God to this desire.

- Knowing God and being received by him is seen in Scripture as the supreme value of human existence. What benefits does this [specific desire] promise you that it can't possibly deliver? What benefits does the gospel promise—and deliver—that are superior? Why is it hard to see the gospel's benefits as superior? Only the eyes of faith will see the superior value of eternal things.

- You were designed to express the full range of your emotions to God, and failing to do so means you are either going to a less reliable refuge elsewhere or you are trying to master your emotion on your own. But God designed you to speak to him about your emotions—whatever they may be—as a necessary step in submitting them to him. It is through such expressive prayer that God reshapes the desires that lead to those emotions.

**Volitional**

People were also designed to obey God willingly, in affectionate trust that he knows best. The volitional aspect of faith can be summarized as submission to him as the One who is worthy of a person's highest loyalties. This call to God as supreme loyalty is costly, since no other loyalty should rival it (Luke 14:25–33).

*Questions to Ask*

You were designed for obedience to be a joy, not a burden. The reason it is often a burden is because we have remaining commitments to what we think is best. For you, that seems to be [specific commitment], shown in the pattern of choices that make up the pursuits of your life.

- The call to follow Jesus is a call to die to your old loyalties. This is one of the great ironies of the Christian faith: the gospel costs you nothing and it costs you everything. What is the hardest thing to give up in order to follow Jesus as the supreme loyalty of your heart? Why?

- Do you believe that God is willing to give you the ability to commit to him, in full assurance of faith? Do you believe you can make choices that are different from the patterns you've established for years and years? Or, does this seem impossible to you? If it seems impossible to you, you just might be closer to understanding grace that you ever have been. God is always proving himself to be everything. And he welcomes us into that everything. Remember, the miracle of faith in Christ is that it gives our hearts the ability to do things they could never do on their own. Plenty of places in Scripture promise this. Let's look at one.

# CHAPTER 13

. . . .

# RENEW: CALLING PEOPLE
# TO NEW RESPONSES BY FAITH

Faith is not mere passive acceptance of the gospel;
rather, it reaches into the very soul
and transforms one's life.

— *Thomas Schreiner*[1]

Medical students do not spend hours in a lab with cadavers only to satisfy their curiosity. Football players do not miss evenings out with their friends to sit in the film room only to improve their knowledge of the game. Musicians do not labor over music theory worksheets in the practice room only to acquire information. What is gained in the lab is expressed in the operating room; what is gained in the film room shows up on the field; what is gained in the practice room is expressed in the concert hall. Likewise, what is gained in the counseling room is expressed in the living room, the bedroom, the office.

Heart change occurs as it is lived out, shaping and reinforcing new values and commitments. Counselors, thus, help people strategize about how to respond differently in their context. Counselors surely consider the dynamics of the heart, and those considerations must affect people's conduct in the real world. So while a counselor's instruction does not begin and end with behavior, it certainly addresses behavior with specific, practical instruction and accountability.[2]

Thus, the fourth task in counseling is to renew—calling people to new responses by faith. Scripture speaks of the believer imitating Christ by the power of the Spirit as a pattern of active participation.[3] This Spirit-enabled imitation of Christ occurs by faith in the dynamic functions of the heart. In other words, faith necessarily works to change the beliefs, desires, and commitments of a person, and these changes are expressed in new ways of living. The dynamic heart comes alive as faith expresses itself in action: not just individual actions, but the patterns of action–behavior, and the established behavior–character. The commitments of faith have always been "far more than intellectual affirmations; they are convictions that entail the radical reorientation of one's life."[4]

The specific, practical instruction that follows gives a limited example as to how counselors can call their counselees to renewal. But, as with the other tasks, they should make use of the full breadth of Scripture's riches, far beyond the specific truths mentioned here. These are representative, not exhaustive, examples.

One last note before diving in: this fourth task, Renew, will require what I call prep work to be done between counseling sessions. Prep work is just homework that you do not call homework. I call it prep work because of the language of 1 Peter 1:13–14 about preparing the mind for action. Prep work better captures what you are trying to help your counselees do—prepare their heart to respond faithfully in the moment.

## 4. Renew: Calling Them to New Responses by Faith

| | Cognition:<br>Thought and Belief | Affection:<br>Desire and Feeling | Volition:<br>Will and Choice |
|---|---|---|---|
| | *Active faith means steady action in flawed circumstances from a heart<br>that trusts God's wisdom over their own preferences (1 Thess. 5:18)* | | |
| **Circumstance** | Engage their minds with the full truth of how God relates to their circumstances, according to the full breadth of his character: his wisdom, his hatred of evil, etc. (Rom. 8:18–39; Ps. 56). | Help them cultivate eternal desires that supersede temporal ones, through active pursuit. Equip them to speak to emotional responses to circumstance in light of larger realities of God's promises (Matt. 6:19–34). | Guide them to avoid passivity by planning action in their situation (1 Pet. 1:13). AND SOMETIMES Work to change situation if led by God in prayer and counsel from Kingdom values. |
| | *Active faith means loving others instead of fearing or using them (Rom. 13:8–10)* | | |
| **Others** | 1) Help them adjust to false beliefs about others. Love means having a realistic view of others that believes the best (1 Cor. 13:7; Rom. 12:17–21).<br><br>2) Help them undermine untruthful influences on them. | 1) Assist them to repent of ruling desires that cause negative emotions against others (James 3:13—4:12).<br><br>2) Help them take steps to avoid being influenced by people's unbiblical values, which lead to poor emotional responses. | 1) Love is committed action for the good of others (1 John 3:18). Guide them to rearrange their life for this.<br><br>2) They must take care not to imitate what is unbiblical in others' behavior, but what is righteous (Rom. 12). |
| | *Active faith means dying to self and living to Christ (Gal. 2:20)* | | |
| **Self** | Equip them to continually expose standards of self that rival their identity in Christ, working to crucify them through meditation on Scripture, thankfulness, prayer, renewed mission, etc. (Phil. 3:12–21). | Equip them to act against feelings of self that do not align with God's values by reframing situations that enforce false value. Submit deeply held desires regarding self to God's greater values (Ps. 73; 2 Cor. 12:1–10). | Life is not about self, but others. Help them determine how they can serve others, and thus experience the satisfaction of doing what they were designed for (Phil. 2:3–8; Col. 3:12–17). |
| | *Active faith means seeking God more than anything in life (Heb. 11:6, 13–16)* | | |
| **Triune God** | 1) Without regular Scripture intake, true belief about God becomes inactive. Make a plan to use various means to focus on pertinent truths: church, study, etc.<br><br>2)Teach prayer as dynamic (Ps. 119). | Help them feed desire for God and starve out other desires by what they pursue. Guide them to use Scripture to seek what they love. Feelings for God are not a goal, but a benefit of seeking him (Ps. 16). | Our duty before God can be summed up as one simple action in two parts: trust and obey (Rom. 1:5; 16:26). Seeking God is a choice, one that needs to be made countless times a day. Give a plan to seek God (Matt. 7:7–11). |

## Renewal in Response to Circumstances

Active faith means steady action in flawed circumstances from a heart that trusts God's wisdom over their own preferences. The world-shaping instruction of Paul to believers is "Rejoice always, pray without ceasing, give thanks in all circumstances; for this is the will of God in Christ Jesus for you" (1 Thess. 5:17–18). If they truly believe that what God has chosen for them fits his purposes better than their own preferences of what their life ought to look like, then they will continue being faithful in the basics. Help counselees consider how God is calling them to uniquely display his character in the unique circumstances in which he has placed them. This call will include expressing the proper grief and joy in trial, the proper trust and obedience in the mundane, the proper acceptance of reality and effort to overcome it.

Only as counselees seek God in prayer and the Word will they discern how best to respond in complex circumstances. God designed our dependence on him to require this process, not to be an automatic event. Sometimes, displaying God's character means persevering through difficult circumstances. Sometimes displaying God's character in a situation means removing oneself from it. Sometimes circumstances are so powerfully influential, stewardship of the heart means changing them. In certain situations, such as with an abused wife or a suicidal missionary, God's will for these people is to seek safety and justice. Changing circumstances is not always possible; but when it is, discerning when to do it is complex, involving multiple factors to consider. Seek help from appropriate legal and medical experts when navigating such situations.

### Regular Actions to Take by Faith

#### Cognitive

Engage their minds regularly with the full truth of how God relates to their circumstances. His sovereignty is coupled with his other attributes. His wisdom means that he knows what is best better than they do. His faithfulness means he is never forgetful or unkind in circumstances. His goodness means he hates the evil that occurs to people, and grieves with them over it (Ps. 56; Rom. 8:18–39). Give them specific reading assignments in Scripture, and perhaps some helpful articles or books. Be realistic to their capacities and schedule. Go for regularity, not perfection. Frame the passage with helpful questions to guide their thinking as you are trying to give them insights that adjust their understanding of circumstances to conform to God's.

*Questions to Ask*

One of the necessary aspects of acting rightly in these circumstances is knowing how God is relating to you through them. We have talked about [attributes of God or insight from Scripture], but knowledge is only active when it is reinforced. How can we regularly engage your mind with truth? Where can we anchor [specific number] of unhurried times with God in your week?

- Remember, your reading is for conforming your perspective of these circumstances to God's. Here are some [specific questions] I want you to answer from this text about how the Lord will help build a foundation for responding faithfully in these circumstances.

- But you also need in the moment help for when [particular difficult situation] arises. Listening to the voice of God means paying closer attention to him than to what these circumstances seem to be telling you. When circumstances seem to say [specific false belief], then you will be ready to respond [specific biblical truth].

**Affective**

Help them cultivate eternal desires that supersede temporal ones, through active pursuit. This will require them to stop cultivating desire for certain circumstantial ideals that have captured their hearts (e.g., desire for wealthier lifestyle by the TV they watch, desire for a better husband by the music to which they listen). In addition, equip them to speak to their emotional responses to circumstance in light of larger realities of God's promises.

*Questions to Ask*

We've seen that you wish your circumstances were different in a number of ways, such as [specific desires]. We've also seen how Jesus will help you no longer be captured by those desires. The way he helps you is to help you give those small desires over to him in exchange for larger ones. This happens through cultivation: weeding what is harmful and watering what is helpful. Think of weeds in a vegetable garden. Weeds are not harmful because they are poisonous to the vegetables. They're harmful because they steal water and nutrients. This is how desire works.

- We've determined that the weeds are [specific desires]. Now, let's consider how those weeds get into your garden. What are the main avenues in your situation that stir up those desires [specific media, habits, places, people]? How can we pull those weeds—in other words, lessen the influence of these things on you?

- Desire cannot be turned on like a light switch. It takes proper arrangement to grow. Think of Scripture intake as not just helping you know the right things, but love the right things. Approach God asking him to meet you there in relationship. The Holy Spirit stands ready to answer yes to this request—but on his terms, and not your own. So do not be discouraged if you do not receive the feeling of nearness to God that you expect. God is up to better things.

- Paying closer attention to what God values helps you pay less attention to what you are wanting in this situation. So, when circumstances stir up [specific desire], then you will be ready to respond with [specific value of God].

**Volitional**

Guide them to avoid passivity by planning action in their situation (1 Pet. 1:13ff). The tendency will be to respond to their circumstances how they always have. Without a decisive plan, responding differently will be nearly impossible. With a preset plan, their determination will be much stronger. Give a vision for what a faithful response would look like, and a simple strategy to execute when the situation arises. Sometimes, help them make a plan to remove themselves from a situation when it becomes overwhelming in its negative influence over their heart responses.

*Questions to Ask*

Taking action requires having a plan. You have to determine beforehand the specific steps you will take in order to encourage change. Remember, you're not changing yourself. You are cooperating with Jesus's work on your behalf. This should motivate your efforts, because they are undergirded by a strength you cannot imagine.

- We've determined what pursuits occupy most of your time and effort, such as [specific pursuits]. Now, let's determine how these need to change practically in order for the highest pursuits to get priority. What are two small steps you could make to order things better?

- When [specific circumstance] happens to you, you have historically responded by [specific actions in the moment]. What different action would be in line with Jesus's work in you? Let's walk through the specifics of how you can respond differently when this happens again.


## Renewal in Relationships with Others

Active faith means loving others instead of fearing or using them (Rom. 13:8–10). Both are not responses that come from faith. When people fear others, they are more controlled by others than by the God who made them to serve him. When people use others, they are controlling others made to serve God, not them. Love, however, always involves action done for the good of another at cost to self

(1 John 3:18). Personally receiving Jesus's love will change the way a person interacts with others. This section on relationships with others is two-directional, and will therefore give instruction about the way a counselee influences and is influenced by others.

## Regular Actions to Take by Faith

### Cognitive

First, help them adjust false beliefs about others. Believing the best about others is an aspect of love (1 Cor. 13:7). This does not mean that a person must trust everything others tell them. In fact, if others have proven untrustworthy, it is not loving to trust what they say. Rather, believing the best means treating them with the charity of redemptive hope. At the same time, a person should believe what is realistic about the faults and sins of others in a fallen world. This will allow them to navigate relationships wisely, being ready to show mercy in the face of an honest understanding of their failures and limitations (Rom. 12:17–21). In terms of action, this means accepting God's testimony of reality as a more reliable source of knowledge than anyone else.

Second, help them undermine untruthful influences on them. This is a vital part of biblical instruction (2 Cor. 11:2–4). You will have to point out those significant voices in their lives that are reinforcing false ideas, then help them strategize how to undermine their influence. This does not mean you cause relational destruction in their lives—only that you help strengthen their understanding of truth so that they will not be swayed by beliefs or values that are unbiblical.

### Questions to Ask

First, about your beliefs about others. We've seen how you believe [particular belief] about [particular person] and that Jesus calls you to have a view of them that is both realistic and charitable. How should this new perspective affect the way you treat him, as applied to the specific dynamics of this relationship?

- When you are tempted to fixate on [particular belief] about [particular person], you'll need to redirect your thinking to [particular biblical truth]. This will be difficult at first, but don't give up. You're establishing new patterns of thought in this relationship.

Second, about others' influence on your thinking. We've seen how [particular significant voice] is not speaking truth to you. How can we undermine the influence of that voice?

- That voice has been telling you [specific belief], but God says [specific biblical truth]. Listening to the voice of God means paying closer attention to him, so I'm going to give you [number] of passages to meditate on as you rethink what this voice has been telling you for so long.

**Affective**

First, having identified the desires that rule their heart in relationship to others, help them know what repentance looks like. Give a positive vision for what emotions no longer shaped by these desires might look like in the particular relationship. Walk them through confession to others for sins committed against them when appropriate (James 3:12—4:12).

Second, having identified how other people's unbiblical value systems are influencing them, help them take steps to undermine this influence. Keep in mind all of the possible significant voices in their life, from family to media. Undermining influence is often not cutting off a relationship entirely (though sometimes it is), but considering these relationships unreliable gauges of what is valuable, and no longer seeking their input.

*Questions to Ask*

First, about the desires that drive you in relationships. We've seen that you feel [specific emotion] consistently regarding [specific person], and we've been able to attach that feeling to [specific desire]. We've also seen that Jesus calls you to no longer be ruled by that desire. But what does repentance look like?

- You can think of it as involving three actions on your part, with a possible fourth. First, identify the desire before the Lord in the moment. Say, "Lord, I am wanting [specific desire] from [specific person]." Second, ask the Lord for help in the moment, saying, "Lord, this desire is too strong for me alone, and it will make me act destructively in this relationship. Will you help me?" Third, claim the promised help of the gospel, saying, "Lord, you have promised to give me anything I ask in your will. Your will is that I love this person more than my desires. I will obey by grace." Fourth, in cases where you've sinned against the person outwardly, identify both the sin and the desire that led to it, and ask forgiveness.
- Second, about the influence of other people's values on you. We've seen that you are strongly influenced by [significant voice], and it makes you want [specific desire] in ungodly ways. We've also seen that Jesus frees you from these values ruling over you. What specific actions do you need to take to undermine their influence on you?

**Volitional**

First, guide them to rearrange their life to do good to others out of love, since love is committed action (1 John 3:18). Without intentional redirection, our pursuits will be self-seeking. But humans were designed to worship God by loving him first, and others second (Matt. 22:37–40). Challenge them to specific acts of love, beginning with the people they're most responsible for.

Second, as with beliefs and values, a person must take care not to imitate what is unbiblical in other people's behavior. People affirm those who act like them (Rom. 1:32), and so counselees need help seeing ways to remove themselves from behavioral influences that do not lead to godliness.

*Questions to Ask*

First, about your actions toward others. Love is a committed action for the good of others, and it's what God designed for you.

But you have to go out of your way to make room for this in your life. Commitments are proven in choices.

- What particular actions can you take to love [specific person]? Let's think carefully about how you are uniquely positioned to uplift them.
- In order to make room for these actions, what might need to go?

Second, about the influence of other people's behavior on you. We've also seen that [specific people] influence you to behave in ways not honoring to God. What decisive steps do you need to take out of loyalty to Jesus Christ?

How do you need to take a stand against behavior [specific people] think is normal? What will this stand cost you relationally? Are you willing to face those consequences?

## Renewal in Self-Perception

Active faith means dying to self and living to Christ. The apostle Paul said what is perhaps the best summary of Christian identity in Galatians 2:20, "I have been crucified with Christ. It is no longer I who live, but Christ who lives in me. And the life I now live in the flesh I live by faith in the Son of God, who loved me and gave himself for me." Christians, therefore, complete who they are by relying on the grace of Christ to imitate the life of Christ in his actions. Jesus's death for sinners did not just come at the end of his life. He lived dying the whole way.

### Regular Actions to Take by Faith

#### Cognitive

Equip them to continually expose standards of self that rival their identity in Christ, working to crucify them through meditation on Scripture, prayer, disciplined thankfulness, renewed mission, and more. People constantly fall back into operating from layers of identity that are not primary. Aspects of their identity—vocation, family role, nationality, socioeconomic situation, sports loyalties, etc.—will always vie for ultimate identity. But who they are in Christ should be most prominent in shaping their actions (Phil. 3:12–21). They will need help thinking through the specifics of what this looks like in their lives.

Note for unbelievers: Jesus Christ remains the fulfillment of humanity, regardless of whether an individual believes this or not. So the active behavioral strategies you propose should still be in line with how Christ would act. Life will work better for unbelievers the more closely their actions conform to Christ's. You need to be clear with them that, without faith, the best they can do is spotty, self-motivated mimicry, not genuine imitation of heart. God, in his common grace, often lends this kind of success to those who do not believe, but it is at best temporary. Yet, counselors pray this common grace would be preparatory for salvation.

*Questions to Ask*

You will need to continually expose assumptions about yourself that contradict what God says about you in his Word. We've seen that you tend to think [specific belief] about yourself, and that belief has been shaped by [specific source]. How can you lessen your exposure to that source? One way is to know your tendencies as you head to work, hang out with that group of friends, etc. Let's write these tendencies out.

- We've also seen that Christ frees you to instead believe [specific biblical insight]. Listening to the voice of God means paying closer attention to him than to the voice inside you telling you other truths. Let's come up with a plan to put a few verses to memory so that you can identify when you are believing [old belief] about yourself, and instead tell yourself [biblical belief] about yourself.

- Who in your life can you share these insights with, so that they can serve to reinforce what's true and undermine what is false in your self-perception?

**Affective**

Equip them to act against feelings of self that do not align with God's values. They will often experience feelings about themselves that show they're falling back into old value systems. They need to be given strategies to talk themselves through how to reframe the situations that enforce false values that will inevitably come. Like Asaph when he saw the prosperity of the wicked and his soul was embittered to the point of wondering why it was worth belonging to God, people will fall back to old value systems by which to measure themselves without recognizing it: Am I rich enough, successful enough, put-together enough? They will need to be equipped to recognize and resist such unbiblical self-evaluations.

*Questions to Ask*

You will continue to have feelings about yourself that seem to rise up out of nowhere. But remember, we've seen that you feel [specific emotion] about yourself quite a bit, and that this emotion is because you really want [specific desire] to be true of you. But we've also seen that this desire is far less valuable than [biblical desire] that God wants for you. When you begin to feel this way, you will need a strategy to submit your self-perception to God.

- Similar to desires in relationship, you can think of this as involving three actions on your part: (1) Identify the desire before the Lord in the moment: "Lord, I am wanting [specific desire] to be true of me."(2) Ask the Lord for help in the moment: "Lord, I am having a hard time accepting your goodness in how you've made me and what you've chosen for me. This desire is too strong for me alone, and it will make me act self-destructively. Will you help me?" (3) Claim the promised help of the gospel: "Lord, you have promised to give me anything I ask in your will. Your will is that I die to what I want to be in order to embrace what you want me to be. I will obey by grace."

## Volitional

Life is not about self, but others. Help them determine how they can serve others, and thus experience the satisfaction of doing what they were designed for. One of the core aspects of Christian identity is that it is not primarily about self, but about how personal agency is used for the good of others. Self-focus is often a quagmire that counseling falls into—partially because there is so much to explore—but working for the good of the self requires turning the self outwardly to benefit others. Long before a person feels like his problems with self are solved, he needs to be turned outwardly. It is only when accompanied by outward action that inward reflection works well. This is what they were designed for, and a vital part of their identity in Christ (Phil. 2:3–8; Col. 3:12–17).

*Questions to Ask*

We've seen that your pursuits in life show you functioning out of [specific commitments]. Part of sorting out these commitments is to simply take action about the commitments God wants you to have—namely, commitment to others because of your commitment to him.

- Part of you finding satisfaction in who God has made you to be is in finding the particular role of service he's called you to. Who has God put in your circle of responsibility? How do you need to serve them in ways you have not?
- Even before we feel like your problems are solved, you need to turn outwardly. Just considering the basic schedule you keep, what will need to go in order to make room for this service?

## Renewal in Relationship with the Triune God

Active faith means seeking God more than anything else in life. It means believing that he is the source and perfection of anything a person can desire. Every created good is simply derived from his goodness. Those who follow God are commended for this primarily: that they wanted him more than any earthly benefit. God was their homeland in a better country, a reward above anything here on earth (Heb. 11:6, 13–16). Such faith made them turn away from privileged positions in Egypt, the comfort and security of established homes, the good opinions of people in power, grand memorials to their name, even release from their own executions. Such faith changes the way a person acts in this green earth, and is profoundly pleasing to God.

### Regular Actions to Take by Faith

#### Cognitive

God's Word and God's presence are closely associated throughout Scripture. Without regular Scripture intake, accurate belief about God becomes inactive. It's not that people necessarily begin to believe false things about God (though inactivity leads to this), it's that those beliefs fade from functional use. The Word of God centers a person's perspective of everything (Ps. 119). Make a plan to use various means to focus on pertinent truths: church, fellowship, reading plan, meditation, studies, etc. Prayer is also a vital part of seeking the presence of God, for by it God shapes the beliefs, desires, and commitments of the heart to conform to his. People do not naturally know how to pray, and the counselor will often have to help them see it as a living trans-action (an exchange of dynamic activity). Just consider the Psalms (see particularly Psalms 13, 31, 51). When they feel discouraged about prayer, remind them that the Holy Spirit prays with them, and Jesus prays for them (Rom. 8:26–27; Heb. 7:25).

*Questions to Ask*

We have seen that when you think of God, you tend to focus on [specific belief]. But Scripture's view of God is much broader than this, and also includes [pertinent biblical truths]. Without regular Scripture intake, you will fall back into those old misbeliefs. Let's make a plan to use a few different avenues of keeping Scripture in front of you.

- What would you say is the biggest hindrance to reading your Bible privately? How can I help you around those difficulties?
- What ministries of the Word at church have you not taken full advantage of? What relationships with biblically-minded people could you strengthen?
- Prayer is the other vital part of believing what is true of God, but it may not always feel that important. Why do you think it's so hard for you to do? Could it be that you are thinking of it as static—that is, one-sided and unchanging? Let's consider in Scripture how prayer is a dynamic exchange with an unseen God. Then, we can come up with a realistic strategy for guarding time for this relationship.
- When you are discouraged in prayer, how might it help to consider the fact that the Holy Spirit prays with you? And not only that, Jesus Christ prays for you from his privileged seat next to the Father. How does this help you when you feel bad at praying?

**Affective**

Help them feed desire for God and starve out other desires by what they pursue. The weed-and-water principle applies here. Often, like weeds, the pursuits that occupy a person's life are not poisonous—they just steal water and nutrients from the vegetables. Pursuits show what values are deepest in a person's heart. Often the main rivals to God are simple things like comfort, ease, amusement, respect, affirmation, pleasure, avoidance of pain, control, security, happiness . . . as the person conceives of it. The little pursuits that promise these things crowd out a pursuit of God as he reveals himself to be, which is more valuable than all else (Ps. 16). Guide them to use Scripture as seeking what they love, not just doing what they're obliged to. Also, in terms of feelings toward God, these must not be the goal in seeking him, but rather a benefit of that pursuit. Often, people will seek God to feel close to him, which is a subtle difference from seeking him for his own sake.

*Questions to Ask*

We desire what we pursue, and we pursue what we desire. Faith expresses itself in desiring God more than any of his created benefits. The weed-and-water principle applies here. Like weeds, the [specific pursuits] that occupy your life aren't necessarily poisonous. They just steal energy from pursuing God, who insists that he's more valuable than these other things. Our goal in pursuing Scripture is not just to read the Bible, but to want to read the Bible. Because it is where you meet the God you were designed to love.

- When you hear the words "devotional life," what do you feel? Why do you think you feel that way? Let's rethink your devotional life not as a task to be accomplished, but an avenue to seek what you love. Are you willing to ask God to help you value him above those other things?

- We often gauge our relationship with God based on how close we feel to him. Why is this dangerous? It's true that feelings show immediate desires—you do not feel like reading the Bible because you'd rather be doing something else. But if you chose to read anyway, you show your deeper value is for God, not your immediate preferences. The more you do this, the more you cultivate desire for God.

## Volitional

Our duty before God can be summed up as one simple action in two parts: Trust and obey. People cannot trust without obedience accompanying it; and they certainly cannot obey unless trusting that God has already loved them in Christ Jesus, prior to their obedience. Both aspects are the marching orders of a Christian in how they relate to God. God demands that we seek him, and promises that we will find him if we do so (Ps. 27; Jer. 29:13; Matt. 7:7–11). Seeking God is a choice, one that needs to be made countless times a day. Help make a plan to do so.

*Questions to Ask*

The Bible talks about duty in a very different way than we tend to. In Scripture, duty and delight agree. Our duty before God is actually quite simple. It's one thing, in two parts: Trust and obey. You cannot do one without the other. Do you know why?

- God built us in such a way that we do not immediately, passively relate to him. We have to seek him. Seeking him is a choice, one that you need to make countless times a day. How have you had too passive a view of your relationship with God? What particular ways can we plan for you to seek him?

## Conclusion

As you have read this book, my hope is that you too have come to see that without a holistic understanding of people, our approach to those in need of help will be lopsided, focusing on just one aspect of human experience—perhaps simply trying to correct faulty thinking, to stir different emotions, or to correct wrong actions. Focusing on one of these aspects of human experience to the exclusion of the others does not do justice to God's design. But understanding people well is never enough. The key to change will always be a dynamic relationship of faith with our heavenly Father, his Son, Jesus Christ, and the Spirit who empowers God's people. The dynamic heart daily needs the love and redemptive help of the triune God.

May the Father in heaven, the great Shepherd of the sheep, and the ever-present Helper lead you as you bring words of life to those you seek to help. And may those words be life to you as well!

···

# ENDNOTES

## Introduction

1.  George Herbert, *The Complete English Works*, ed. Ann Pasternak Slater (New York: Alfred A. Knopf, 1995), 52.

## Chapter 1

1.  Andrew Tallon, *Head and Heart: Affection, Cognition, and Volition as Triune Consciousness* (New York: Fordham University Press, 1997), 1.

2.  Abraham Heschel, *The Prophets* (New York: Harper & Row Publishers, 1962), 2:40.

3.  Nouns used to describe the inner function include *dianoia* ("mind"), *kardia* ("heart"), *psuche* ("soul"), *koilia* (lit. "hollow place"), *nephros* ("kidneys"), *nous* ("understanding, mind"), *horme* ("impulse"), *pneuma* ("spirit"), *sarx* ("flesh"), *splankna* ("intestines"), *syneidesis* ("conscience"), *noema* ("thoughts"). These terms and more fall into a single semantic domain referred to in *Louw-Nida Greek Lexicon* as "psychological faculties," and many of them have Old Testament correlates. J. P. Louw and Eugene Albert Nida, *Greek-English Lexicon of the New Testament: Based on Semantic Domains* (New York: United Bible Societies, 1989), 8, 19.

4.  For a full defense of the overlapping semantic orbits of this, see Jeremy Pierre, "Trust in the Lord with All Your Heart: The Centrality of Faith in Christ to the Restoration of Human Functioning" (PhD diss., The Southern Baptist Theological Seminary, 2010).

Though there are no lexical similarities between *kardia* and the rest of these terms (none of them share a root), these terms are actually quite close in their semantic proximity; therefore, they must be considered alongside *kardia* in order to arrive at as robust an understanding as possible of the nature of the inner man. Semantic classes are more important in determining meaning than formal classes. The terms from this semantic domain that will be considered in this present study are *kardia, psuche, pneuma,* and *nous.* These terms are important to consider because they generally establish the same categories of internal function that *kardia* does, namely cognition, affection, and volition. The biblical authors attribute these three loci of function to each of these anthropological terms and in so doing validate these categories of function.

The versatility of the terms used for man's internal function is apparent throughout—especially *kardia*, the primary term used to describe specific functions that occur within people. *Kardia* is arguably the most comprehensive and the most important, since it is the term most closely associated with the center of a person and with faith. Other terms that overlap *kardia* semantically sometimes have a slightly distinct emphasis, but they all can refer to various facets of internal functioning. In the case of *psuche*, the emphasis can be on the comprehensive fact that a human being has essential life. In the case of *pneuma*, the emphasis can be that a person's life is given by God and occurs in relation to him. *Nous* and *dianoia* are the most internally specific of the semantically overlapping terms considered here, with particular emphasis on the cognitive and volitional functions. But these terms, though not simply interchangeable in every context, are often used in ways that could be interchangeable. They are also used in parallel fashion frequently, indicating that the biblical authors did not think of them as independent compartments of the inner man.

Even in the Old Testament, in general, *leb* is used as "the seat of man's feeling, thinking, and willing," a term that "means less an isolated function than the man with all his urges, in short, the person in its totality (Pss. 22:26[27]; 73:26; 84:2[3])." Theo Sorg, "Heart," in *The New International Dictionary of New Testament Theology*, ed. Colin Brown (Grand Rapids, MI: Zondervan, 1979), 2:181.

Eichrodt refers to *leb* as "a comprehensive term for the personality as a whole, its inner life, its character. It is the conscious and deliberate spiritual activity of the self-contained human ego." Walther Eichrodt, *Theology of the Old Testament*, trans. J. A. Baker (Philadelphia: The Westminster Press, 1967), 2:143.

5. Friedrich Baumgärtel and Johannes Behms, "*kardia*" in *Theological Dictionary of the New Testament*, trans. Geoffrey W. Bromiley,

ed. Gerhard Kittel (Grand Rapids, MI: Wm. B. Eerdmans Publishing Co., 1965), 3:609–10.

6. Tallon cites Schrag, *Head and Heart*, 4.

7. Some uses of *leb* posit the heart as the seat of rational function. The heart is where both wisdom and understanding dwell (1 Kings 3:12; 4:29). Internal dialogue occurs in the heart (Gen. 17:17; 24:45), as does reasoning (Deut. 15:9). The thoughts of man which can be viewed by God occur in the heart (Ps. 139:23; Jer. 4:14).

8. The term *leb* is often used in conjunction with other terms to describe the emotional state of an individual or a group of individuals. The heart experiences joy (Deut. 28:47), merriness (Judg. 19:9; 2 Sam. 13:28; Zech. 10:7; Job 29:13; Ps. 45:1), sorrow (Deut. 15:10; Neh. 2:2; Pss. 34:18; 38:10; 55:4; 73:21; Prov. 14:13; Lam. 1:20; Isa. 15:5; 65:14), anguish (Jer. 4:19), anxiety (1 Sam. 9:20; 25:25), sympathy (Hosea 11:8), and upset (Deut. 19:6). The heart is the internal mechanism in which human desire takes places as well (Pss. 20:4; 21:2; 35:25; 37:4; 40:8; Prov. 6:25; 13:12; Num. 15:39; 1 Sam. 23:20; 2 Sam. 3:21; 2 Chron. 15:15; Job 17:11; 31:7; Eccl. 2:10).

9. The term *leb* indicates the seat of volitional activity. It is the place where intentions are housed (1 Sam. 2:35; 1 Kings 8:17; Jer. 23:20; Isa. 10:7). The heart can intend to perform an action in the future (1 Chron. 22:19; Ezra 7:10; Dan. 1:8; Jer. 7:31). Impulses toward action also come from the heart (Exod. 36:2; Num. 16:28). Baumgärtel makes a helpful observation that the renewal of the heart is often defined as the will being inclined in the right direction (e.g., Isa. 57:17; Ps. 119:36). Also, the full commitment of the whole man is expressed with the phrase "with all of the heart" (Pss. 9:1; 86:12; 111:1; 119:2, 10, 34, 69, 145; Isa. 38:3; Jer. 3:10; 24:7).

10. Michael Horton, *The Christian Faith: A Systematic Theology for Pilgrims on the Way* (Grand Rapids, MI: Zondervan, 2011), 390.

11. John M. Frame, *The Doctrine of the Knowledge of God: A Theology of Lordship* (Phillipsburg, NJ: Presbyterian and Reformed Publishing Co., 1987), 329.

12. Antonio Damasio, *Descartes's Error: Emotion, Reason and the Human Brain* (New York: Random House, 2008), 191.

13. Damasio points out that these emotive tendencies are engrained in human neurobiology. How the spiritual responses of cognition, affection, and volitional correlate with physiological realities will be addressed later.

14. Matthew Elliot, *Faithful Feelings: Rethinking Emotion in the New Testament* (Grand Rapids, MI: Kregel, 2006), 31.

## Chapter 2

1. James K. A. Smith, *Desiring the Kingdom: Worship, Worldview, and Cultural Formation*, Cultural Liturgies (Grand Rapids, MI: Baker Academic, 2009), 1:60.

2. Kevin J. Vanhoozer, *The Drama of Doctrine: A Canonical-Linguistic Approach to Christian Theology* (Louisville, KY: Westminster John Knox Press, 2005), 2. Emphasis added.

3. Ibid., 378.

4. Jonathan Haidt, *The Righteous Mind: Why Good People Are Divided by Politics and Religion* (New York: Vintage Books, 2012), 53.

5. Nicholas Wolterstorff, *Reason within the Bounds of Religion*, 2nd ed. (Grand Rapids, MI: Eerdmans, 1988), 66–67.

6. Ibid., 68.

7. Richard Lints, *The Fabric of Theology: A Prolegomenon to Evangelical Theology* (Grand Rapids, MI: William B. Eerdmans Publishing Co., 1993), 18.

8. Wolterstorff leaves room for this direction when pointing out that control beliefs are actualized in the Christian life by trusting commitment that determines action in an individual Christian's life and situation. *Reason within the Bounds of Religion*, 73–75.

## Chapter 3

1. Quoted in Henri Blocher, *Original Sin: Illuminating the Riddle*, New Studies in Biblical Theology (Downers Grove, IL: InterVarsity Press, 1997), 83.

2. G. J. Botterweck, *"yāda"* in *Theological Dictionary of the Old Testament*, ed. G. Johannes Botterweck and Helmer Ringgren (Grand Rapids, MI: William B. Eerdmans Publishing Co., 1986), 5:465.

3. G. Wallis, *"chamadh"* in *Theological Dictionary of the Old Testament*, ed. G. Johannes Botterweck and Helmer Ringgren (Grand Rapids, MI: William B. Eerdmans Publishing Co., 1986), 4:456–57.

4. Victor P. Hamilton, *The Book of Genesis: Chapters 1–17*, The New International Commentary on the Old Testament (Grand Rapids, MI: William B. Eerdmans Publishing Co., 1990), 190.

5. John Calvin, *Calvin: Institutes of the Christian Religion,* trans. Ford Lewis Battles, ed. John T. McNeill (Louisville, KY: Westminster John Knox Press, 1960), 1:246.

6. Dietrich Bonhoeffer, *Creation and Fall Temptation: Two Biblical Studies* (New York: Touchstone, 1997), 74.

7. Calvin, *Institutes* (II.i.4), 245.

8. John Frame gives an excellent and complex treatment of how an unbeliever has knowledge of God. He acknowledges that unbelievers have a knowledge of God, but they "lack the obedience and friendship with God that is essential to 'knowledge' in the fullest biblical sense—the knowledge of the believer" (58). Yet, he also recognizes that this knowledge is more than propositional, since "at every moment, they are personally involved with God as an enemy." Frame recognizes the relational nature of knowledge as well as the fact that true knowledge involves volitional submission (obedience). This overlaps with my observations about the interrelatedness of knowledge and volition as well as the relational nature of belief. John M. Frame, *The Doctrine of the Knowledge of God* (Phillipsburg, NJ: P&R Publishing, 1987), 49–61.

9. Ibid.

10. Cornelius Plantinga, Jr., *Not the Way It's Supposed to Be: A Breviary of Sin* (Grand Rapids: William B. Eerdmans Publishing Co., 1995), 2–3.

11. G. K. Beale, *A New Testament Biblical Theology: The Unfolding of the Old Testament in the New* (Grand Rapids: Baker Academic, 2011), 360.

12. G. K. Beale, *We Become What We Worship: A Biblical Theology of Idolatry* (Downers Grove, IL: InterVarsity Academic, 2015), 21.

13. Ibid., 222, 224.

**Chapter 4**

1. George Herbert, *The Complete English Works*, ed. Ann Pasternak Slater (New York: Alfred A. Knopf, 1995), 60.

2. David Powlison, *Speaking the Truth in Love: Counsel in Community* (Greensboro, NC: New Growth Press, 2005), 61.

3. Mark Twain, "The Professional" in *Student's Book of College English: Rhetoric, Readings, Handbook*, eds. David Skwire, and Harvey S. Wiener, 10th ed. (New York: Pearson Longman, 2005), 238–39.

4. The Greek word for "overwhelmed with sorrow," *perilupos* is a rare word that means "burdened with grief" in the present context of "despair unto death": "Nothing in all the Bible compares to Jesus's agony and anguish at Gethsemane—neither the laments of the Psalms, nor the broken heart of Abraham as he prepared to sacrifice his son Isaac (Gen. 22:5), nor David's grief at the death of his son Absalom (2 Sam. 18:33). . . . Jesus is aware of facing something more than simply his own death. In [Mark] 10:45 he spoke of the purpose of the Son of Man 'to give his life a ransom for many.' That was the objective description of his purpose; now we hear the subjective experience of it. In Gethsemane Jesus must make the first payment of that ransom, to *will* to become the sin-bearer for humanity. Jesus stands before the final consequence of being the Servant of God. . . . Jesus necessarily experiences an abandonment and darkness of cosmic proportions." James R. Edwards, *The Gospel According to Mark,* The Pillar New Testament Commentary (Grand Rapids, MI: Eerdmans, 2002), 432–33.

5. In the Old Testament, the metaphor of a cup is associated with God's wrath (Ps. 11:6; Isa. 51:17; Jer. 25:15; Ezek. 23:33; Zech. 12:2).

6. "*If it is possible* precedes the substance of the prayer and makes clear that Jesus was not pressing for anything that was against the will of the Father. The question at issue was not whether Jesus should do the Father's will, but whether that necessarily included the way of the cross. The kind of death he faced was the kind of ordeal from which human nature naturally shrinks; thus we discern here the natural human desire to avoid it. But we discern also Jesus's firm determination that the Father's will be done. So he prays for the avoidance of the death he faced, but only if that accorded with the divine plan." Leon Morris, *The Gospel According to Matthew,* The Pillar New Testament Commentary (Grand Rapids, MI: W. B. Eerdmans, 1992), 668.

7. "In his identification with sinful men, he is the object of the holy wrath of God against sin, and in Gethsemane as the hour of the Passion approaches the full horror of that wrath is disclosed." C. E. B. Cranfield, *The Gospel According to Saint Mark: An Introduction and Commentary,* Cambridge Greek Testament Commentary (Cambridge: At the University Press, 1959), 433.

8. "Herein lies faith: the ability to request openly another destiny than the one God has chosen but ultimately submitting to God's will whatever this may involve." Robert H. Stein, *Mark,* Baker Evangelical

Commentary on the New Testament (Grand Rapids, MI: Baker Academic, 2008), 662.

9. "His attitude is exemplary. He makes known the desire of his heart to God, but his primary concern is to accomplish God's will." Darrell L. Bock, *Luke*, Baker Exegetical Commentary on the New Testament (Grand Rapids, MI: Baker Books, 1996), 1760.

10. Bock calls Jesus's final words a prayer of trust because it includes a familial address ("Father") followed by a statement of faith "into your hands I commit my spirit." Taken from Psalm 31:5, "Jesus's prayer of trust is thus an expression of submission to God's will, in which Jesus expresses faith that God will deliver him." Bock, *Luke*, 1862.

11. Lane, *Hebrews 9–13*, 412.

12. Thomas R. Schreiner, *New Testament Theology: Magnifying God in Christ* (Grand Rapids, MI: Baker Academic, 2008), 591.

13. The first two verses of the chapter function as an introduction, and it is "only with v 3 that the anaphoric use of *pistei* begins. This verse is itself a hinge passage, linking the introduction to the exemplary witnesses in vv 4–7 by setting forth faith as a principle of interpretation for all of the examples subsequently invoked." Lane, *Hebrews 9–13*, 321.

14. People of faith understanding earthly realities in light of heavenly ones is an underlying principle of the entire epistle as well as a pattern of redemptive history. Donald Guthrie, *The Epistle to the Hebrews: An Introduction and Commentary*, The Tyndale New Testament Commentaries (Grand Rapids: Eerdmans, 2002), 15:234.

15. "It is significant to note that the verb used of the patriarchs' desires, 'aspire to, strive for' (note 1 Tim 3:1; 6:10), which does not appear in the LXX, was a common classical term for an intense longing for spiritual or heavenly things. The imperfective aspect of the verb, expressed by the present tense, suggests a continual perspective that was eschatological and which pervaded their whole lives." Peter Thomas O'Brien, *The Letter to the Hebrews* (Grand Rapids, MI: William B. Eerdmans Pub. Co., 2010), 421.

16. "Faith conferred upon those events a reality so substantial that he did not hesitate to act as though they were already beginning to happen. He appears to have recognized that the word of God is performative; it sets in motion circumstances that will eventuate in the promised reality." Lane, *Hebrews 9–13*, 339.

17. The use of *helomenos* in Hebrews 11:25, "choosing rather to be mistreated with the people of God than to enjoy the fleeting pleasure

of sin" is one of personal choice of one option over another. The term is explicitly volitional in nature. Paul Ellingworth, *The Epistle to the Hebrews: A Commentary on the Greek Text* (Grand Rapids, MI: W. B. Eerdmans, 1993), 611.

18. "His faith consisted in an emphatic refusal of the present, visible rewards of status and privilege in the certain expectation of the as yet unseen, but enduring, reward bestowed by God, to which he could only look ahead." Lane, *Hebrews 9–13*, 373.

19. Schreiner, *Romans*, 67–68. Moo agrees: "Do we have to choose between theology (*God* acting) and anthropology (the *human being* who receives)—as some have stated the dilemma? Could we not take 'righteousness of God' here to include *both* God's activity of 'making right'—saving, vindicating—*and* the status of those who are so made right, in a relational sense that bridges the divine and the human?" Moo, *The Epistle to the Romans*, 74.

20. Although he prioritizes the cognitive over the other aspects of faith I am presenting in this study, one scholar, nevertheless, says insightfully, "I take belief to be the cognitive dimension of a religious attitude, in which human life is interpreted within a religious frame of reference, a central story line that says: 'God has something to do with it.' Unbelief, however, is in the same way a religious attitude. Unbelief means that human life is interpreted within a religious frame of reference, a central story line that says: 'God has nothing to do with it.'" Reinder Ruard Ganzevoort, "Crisis Experiences and the Development of Belief and Unbelief," in *Belief and Unbelief: Psychological Perspectives*, eds. Jozef Corveleyn and Dirk Hutsebaut (Amsterdam: Rodopi, 1994), 24.

Ganzevoort continues, "Both belief and unbelief are central story lines that express an interpretation of the facts of life and give an answer to the questions concerning the relationship between God and our lives." Ibid., 30.

21. Richard Lints, *The Fabric of Theology: A Prolegomenon to Evangelical Theology* (Grand Rapids, MI: William B. Eerdmans Publishing Co., 1993), 18.

22. Ibid., 120.

23. Alvin Plantinga, *Knowledge and Christian Belief* (Grand Rapids, MI: William B. Eerdmans Publishing Co., 2015), 63.

24. Jonathan Edwards, *The Sermons of Jonathan Edwards: A Reader* (New Haven, CT: Yale University Press, 1999), 21.

25. Luther's conception of the necessity of immutability is instructive here: people's will, determined by their nature, will act, and this action occurs within God's sovereign direction. Luther contrasts this with the necessity of compulsion: people are forced to act against their will by God's sovereign direction (the view of which Erasmus accuses him). While issues of God's sovereignty are pertinent to this discussion, the most helpful point to be made here is that out of people's nature (the new man by faith in Christ versus the old man by unbelief) determines their volitional activity. Martin Luther, *The Bondage of the Will*, trans. J. I. Packer and O. R. Johnston (Old Tappan, NJ: Revell, 1957), 102ff.

26. Udo Schnelle, *Theology of the New Testament* (Grand Rapids, MI: Baker Academic, 2009), 307.

27. Thomas R. Schreiner, *New Testament Theology: Magnifying God in Christ* (Grand Rapids, MI: Baker Academic, 2008), 531.

28. I. Howard Marshall, *New Testament Theology: Many Witnesses, One Gospel* (Downers Grove, IL: InterVarsity Press, 2004), 444.

## Chapter 5

1. Michael Horton, *The Christian Faith: A Systematic Theology for Pilgrims on the Way* (Grand Rapids, MI: Zondervan, 2011), 387.

2. Michael R. Emlet, "Understanding the Influences of the Human Heart," *Journal of Biblical Counseling* 20 (2002): 47–52.

3. Carefully thinking Christians may be hesitant to accept the psychosomatic unity of man on the legitimate grounds of not wanting to open the door inadvertently to monism or to the biological reductionism that looms so mightily today. Two scholars offer insightful distinctions in this regard. The first scholar, Gundry, asserts that the biblical view of man is a unity of parts rather than a monadic unity, and to illustrate this point, he uses the term "interpenetration" to describe how the soul interacts with the body and its members, "The soul *has* a body and the body *has* a soul and man as a whole *is* both, a psychophysical unity—but a unity, not a monad…not atomic indivisibility." Robert Horton Gundry, *Soma in Biblical Theology: With Emphasis on Pauline Anthropology* (Cambridge: Cambridge University Press, 1976), 121–22.

The second scholar, Cooper, renders this same concept differently by distinguishing between what he labels as "functional holism" and "ontological holism." Ontological holism, which "defines the very being of an entity and its constituents in terms of their systematic unity" and in which "no parts can survive the dissolution of the whole intact" implies that the soul cannot survive the body at death, an untenable proposition in light of Scripture. Functional holism, on the other hand, is a way of describing the "phenomenological, existential, and functional unity" of body and soul. John W. Cooper, *Body, Soul, and Life Everlasting: Biblical Anthropology and the Monism-Dualism Debate* (Grand Rapids, MI: William B. Eerdmans Publishing Co., 1989), 46–47.

4. Internet Gaming Disorder is not included in the main body of the *Diagnostic and Statistics Manual*, 5th ed., though it uses this label for a disorder being researched. American Psychiatric Association. See the summary released by the APA at http://www.psychiatry.org/psychiatrists/practice/dsm/dsm-5.

## Section 2

1. A. W. Tozer, *The Knowledge of the Holy* (New York: Harper Collins, 1961), 1.

## Chapter 6

1. George Herbert, *The Complete English Works*, ed. Ann Pasternak Slater (New York: Alfred A. Knopf, 1995), 167.

2. J. I. Packer, *Knowing God* (Downers Grove, IL: InterVarsity Press, 1973), 15.

3. Bruce Ware gives a helpful criterion for determining when biblical descriptions of God are intended to be understood anthropomorphically: "A given ascription to God may rightly be understood as anthropomorphic when Scripture clearly presents God as transcending the very human or finite features it elsewhere attributes to him." "An Evangelical Reformulation of the Doctrine of the Immutability of God" *Journal of the Evangelical Theological Society* (Dec. 1986), 442–43.

4. Heschel, *The Prophets*, 2:40.

5. Gerald Bray, *The Doctrine of God*, in Contours of Christian Theology, ed. Gerald Bray (Downers Grove, IL: InterVarsity Press, 1993), 64–66.

6. Matthew A. Elliott, *Faithful Feelings: Rethinking Emotion in the New Testament* (Grand Rapids, MI: Kregel Academic & Professional, 2006), 111.

7. Scholars point out that this fear of the Lord contains both rational content and emotive response. The fear of the Lord often correlates with his law, statutes, commands, and ordinances (Prov. 1:7–9; 9:10),

yet also refers to the heart's loving valuation of God (Prov. 16:6–8; 19:23; 23:17–18). See Bruce Waltke, *The Book of Proverbs* (Grand Rapids, MI: Eerdmans, 2004), 100–101.

8.  Bruce K. Waltke, *An Old Testament Theology* (Grand Rapids, MI: Zondervan, 2007), 892.

9.  Christian Smith and Melina Lundquist Denton, *Soul Searching: The Religious and Spiritual Lives of American Teenagers*, Reprint ed. (Oxford: Oxford University Press, 2009).

10. Timothy Ward, *Words of Life: Scripture as the Living and Active Word of God* (Downers Grove, IL: InterVarsity Press, 2009), 113. In light of this action, the sufficiency of Scripture can be defined in this way, "because of the ways in which God has chosen to relate himself to Scripture, Scripture is sufficient as the means by which God continues to present himself to us such that we can know him, repeating through Scripture the covenant promise he has brought to fulfillment in Jesus Christ."

11. Peter Jensen points out that the gospel (and its mission) is itself the very "pattern of revelation." He says that the gospel "teaches us what revelation is and what it achieves." Put differently, the intended outcome of the communicative act of God is displayed in the gospel's achievement of faith in Christ (Rom. 10:17). Peter Jensen, *The Revelation of God*, Contours of Christian Theology (Downers Grove, IL: InterVarsity Press, 2002), 37.

12. "To believe in the 'word of Jesus' does not mean to accept the sounds his mouth produces as he forms sentences. That is part of it, but the reader is aware that Jesus Christ *is* the Word. Acceptance of the word of Jesus is unconditional trust and commitment to all that his words and his deeds reveal, cost what it may." Merrill C. Tenney, *John: the Gospel of Belief: An Analytic Study of the Text* (Grand Rapids, MI: Eerdmans, 1948), 174.

## Chapter 7

1.  Richard Lints, *Identity and Idolatry: The Image of God and Its Inversion*, New Studies in Biblical Theology (Downers Grove, IL: Apollos Press, 2015), 160.

2.  Hendrikus Berkhof, *Christian Faith: An Introduction to the Study of the Faith*, trans. Sierd Woudstra (Grand Rapids, MI: William B. Eerdmans Publishing Company, 1979), 450.

3. John Calvin, *Institutes of the Christian Religion*, vol. 1, ed. John T. McNeill, trans. Ford Lewis Battles (Louisville: Westminster John Knox Press, 1960), 35–37.

4. This contrast could be made in many different ways: real identity versus perceived identity, the true self versus the fabricated self, maybe even self-reality versus self-perception. Kierkegaard is insightful on this point, even if one does not adopt his entire outlook. He forged the way for a Christian consideration of the self in relation with self, particularly in his understanding of despair as the failure to be one's true self.

5. G. C. Berkouwer, *Man: The Image of God* (Grand Rapids, MI: Wm. B. Eerdmans, 1962), 195.

6. Thomas R. Schreiner, *New Testament Theology: Magnifying God in Christ* (Grand Rapids, MI: Baker Books, 2008), 96.

7. G. K. Beale, *We Become What We Worship: A Biblical Theology of Idolatry*, 298.

8. This new identity is established as faith is granted to the heart. This new identity becomes operative in the dynamic functions of the soul. Herman Ridderbos explains, "This nature of the new life has become clear to us in particular from the significance of faith in it, as the way in which the new creation of God is effected and communicated in the reality of this earthly life, and is to be characterized as new obedience." Herman Ridderbos, *Paul: An Outline of His Theology*, trans. John Richard De Witt (Grand Rapids, MI: Wm. B. Eerdmans Publishing Co., 1975), 253.

9. Skee-Lo, "I Wish" in *I Wish* (Hollywood: Sunshine Records, 1995).

## Chapter 8

1. This quote is a popular paraphrase of the contents of "The Principle of Association," in Jim Rohn, *7 Strategies for Wealth and Happiness: Power Ideas from America's Foremost Business Philosopher* (New York: Three Rivers Press, 1996), 129–35.

2. Andrew Fuller, *The Complete Works of Rev. Andrew Fuller* (Philadelphia: American Baptist Publication Society, 1845), 1:87.

3. Bruce A. Ware, *Father, Son, and Holy Spirit: Relationships, Roles, and Relevance* (Wheaton, IL: Crossway Books, 2005), 132–38.

4. In Vanhoozer's theo-dramatic model of doing theology, he claims that to be human is to be a communicative agent who can enter

into dialogical relationships with God and others. People's response to and engagement with others is where personhood is expressed. Kevin J. Vanhoozer, *The Drama of Doctrine* (Louisville, KY: Westminster John Knox Press, 2005), 367–368.

    5.  G. K. Beale, *We Become What We Worship: A Biblical Theology of Idolatry* (Downers Grove, IL: InterVarsity Academic, 2015), 300.

## Chapter 9

    1.  Harrod and Funck, "Come Clean" in *Live* (Heated Brick Records, 1998). Lyrics by Brian Funck, drawn in part from the poetry of Lawrence Ferlinghetti, *Coney Island of the Mind* (New York: New Directions, 1968).

    2.  John Milton, *Paradise Lost,* ed. John Leonard (London: Penguin Books, 2000), 9.

    3.  Mica R. Endsley, "Toward a Theory of Situation Awareness in Dynamic Systems" *Human Factors* 37, no. 1 (1995): 32–64.

    4.  Nathaniel Philbrick, *Into the Heart of the Sea: The Tragedy of the Whaleship Essex* (New York: Penguin Books, 2000), loc 2531, Kindle.

## Chapter 10

    1.  Harper Lee, *To Kill a Mockingbird* (New York: Warner Books, 1960), 30.

## Chapter 11

    1.  Charles Dickens, *The Life and Adventures of Nicholas Nickleby* in The Works of Charles Dickens, vol. 5 (London: Chapman & Hall, 1901), 114.

## Chapter 12

    1.  Revere Franklin Weidner, *Biblical Theology of the New Testament* (New York: Revell, 1891), 2:161.

    2.  Consider Goldsworthy's helpful caution, "It cannot be stressed too much that to confuse the gospel with certain important things that go hand in hand with it is to invite theological, hermeneutical and spiritual confusion. Such ingredients of preaching and teaching that we might want to link with the gospel would include the need

for the gospel (sin and judgment), the means of receiving the benefits of the gospel (faith and repentance), the results or fruit of the gospel (regeneration, conversion, sanctification, glorification) and the results of rejecting it (wrath, judgment, hell). . . . When we confuse the fruit of the gospel in the Christian life for the gospel itself, hermeneutical confusion is introduced. The focus easily turns to the life of the believer and the experience of the Christian life. These can then become the norms by which Scripture is interpreted." Graeme Goldsworthy, *Gospel-Centered Hermeneutics: Foundations and Principles of Evangelical Biblical Interpretation* (Downers Grove, IL: IVP Academic, 2006), 59.

So, faith is not the central theme by which Scripture is interpreted; the gospel is. Rather, faith is the means by which the gospel—itself the interpretive center of Scripture—is received. It allows a person to interpret not only Scripture in light of the gospel, but also life.

3. God's initiative in providing salvation at large as well as applying it to the individual was not predicated upon anyone's faith. It was completely his own act, from beginning to end. This is certainly the Pauline understanding of it, "Here is the power of God's grace: that Christ did not die for the righteous, for the morally acceptable, for the noble of heart who are never anxious. Indeed Paul even sees in the crucifixion that Christ did not die for those who believe. Neither Christian faith nor faith of any sort is a presupposition to God's invading apocalypse of love in the crucifixion of the Messiah. On the contrary, the crucifixion is God's revelation of that gift of grace that, not assuming or presupposing faith, calls faith into existence." J. Louis Martyn, *Theological Issues in the Letters of Paul* (Nashville, TN: Abingdon Press, 1997), 288.

4. The writer of Hebrews, for instance, even in calling his readers to holy living, still must instruct them to "lay aside every weight, and sin which clings so closely" in order to run the race set before them (Heb. 12:1). The expression "the holding-tightly sin" is a clear indication of the writer's understanding of residual sin being operative in the hearts of believers.

James says that trials test one's faith to bring about steadfastness "that you may be perfect and complete, lacking in nothing" (James 1:4). This implies the attainability of perfection but for the fact that this statement is made in the context of explaining why trials are necessary and good for the Christian life: to produce completion. Yet, trials never leave the life of a Christian, as the overall thrust of the letter makes clear. James's main point is to make use of each trial to entrust oneself to God and grow in steadfast faith. Furthermore, James also acknowledges that "we all stumble in many ways" and says the only one who can claim perfection is he who "does not stumble in what he says" to demonstrate the importance of the tongue for moral purity (James 3:2). But the language he uses of how difficult the taming of the tongue is implies the impossibility of the task.

Peter as well instructs believers to "not be conformed to the passions of your former ignorance, but as he who called you is holy, you also be holy in all your conduct, since it is written, 'You shall be holy, for I am holy'" (1 Pet. 1:14–16). Yet he also knows the necessity of telling them to "put away all malice and all deceit and hypocrisy and envy and slander" (1 Pet. 2:1) and to "abstain from the passions of the flesh, which wage war against your soul" (1 Pet. 2:11). Peter understood that sin was still present, influencing the functions of the hearts of these believers.

5. The progressive nature of sanctification is further demonstrated in texts such as 1 Thessalonians 4:1, "Finally, then, brothers, we ask and urge you in the Lord Jesus, that as you received from us how you ought to live and to please God, just as you are doing, that you do so more and more." See also 1 Peter 2:2, "Long for the pure spiritual milk, that by it you may grow up to salvation."

## Chapter 13

1. Thomas R. Schreiner, *New Testament Theology: Magnifying God in Christ* (Grand Rapids: Baker Academic, 2008), 531.

2. One can infer from biblical counseling literature the general concern for faith's necessary involvement in human functioning as well as the importance of Scripture to faith's establishment in the human soul. For instance, in establishing that Scripture is the means by which people know Christ, the central relationship that brings about the restoration of humanity, Lane and Tripp assert that change is not merely cognitive (though it is cognitive) or behavioral (though it is behavioral), but occurs in a holistic way because it "begins in relationship to Jesus and is brought to completion within an ever-deepening union with him." Put differently, the restoration of human function is through relational faith. Timothy S. Lane and Paul David Tripp, *How People Change*, 2nd ed. (Greensboro, NC: New Growth Press, 2008), 47.

Also consider a central tenet of the givens of the human condition in David Powlison's "Affirmations and Denials," a document that serves for many in the field of biblical counseling as a statement of faith: "We *affirm* that the ideal for human functioning is faith working through love. Such love for God and neighbor is the standard against which to specifically understand what is wrong with people. It is the goal to which counseling must specifically aspire. We *deny* that any other standard or goal is true." That standard and goal of counseling is "faith working through love"; as established, love is the fulfillment of God's will for human function, and this only occurs by means of faith. David Powlison, *Speaking Truth in Love: Counsel in Community* (Greensboro, NC: New Growth Press, 2005), 171.

3. All of Scripture should be used to elicit faith that is active on the human receiver's part. Frame points out that this activity of faith and its manifestation in good works are the call of the breadth of the genres and epochs of Scripture: "(1) Scripture contains not only narrative, but also laws, proverbs, songs, letters, and apocalyptic, all of which have distinct purposes that preachers should bring out. (2) The intention of biblical writers in describing biblical characters is in part, indeed, to present them as positive or negative examples for human behavior (as Rom. 4:1–25; 1 Cor. 10:1–13; Heb. 11; Jas. 2:21–26; 5:17–18; 2 Pet. 2:4–10; Jude 8–13). (3) Scripture explicitly tells us to imitate Jesus (John 13:34–35) and Paul (1 Cor. 11:1; 2 Tim. 3:10–11), indeed to imitate God the Father (Matt. 5:44–48; 1 Pet. 1:15–16). And Paul tells Timothy also to be an example (1 Tim. 4:12). Imitation is an important means to the believer's sanctification. (4) The whole purpose of Scripture is application: to our belief (John 20:31) and our good works (2 Tim. 3:16–17)." John M. Frame, "Machen's Warrior Children," in *Alister E. McGrath and Evangelical Theology: A Dynamic Engagement*, ed. Sung Wook Chung (Grand Rapids: Baker Academic, 2003), 135–36.

4. Frank Thielman, *Theology of the New Testament: A Canonical and Synthetic Approach* (Grand Rapids: Zondervan, 2005), 698.